&Literacies Learners

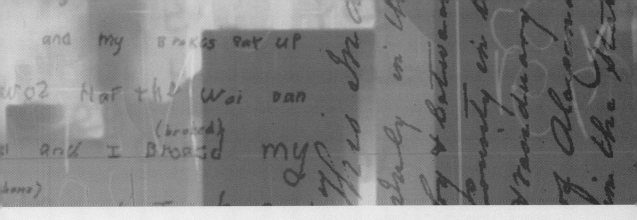

2nd EDITION

Literacies
&Learners

CURRENT PERSPECTIVES

EDITED BY

David **GREEN**
Rod **CAMPBELL**

Prentice
Hall

Pearson Education Australia
Unit 4, Level 2
14 Aquatic Drive
Frenchs Forest NSW 2086

www.pearsoned.com.au

Acquisitions Editor: Nicole Meehan
Senior Project Editor: Kathryn Fairfax
Editorial Coordinator: Jill Gillies
Copy Editor: Janice Keynton
Proofreader: Tom Flanagan
Cover and internal design by Antart Design
Typeset by Midland Typesetters, Maryborough, Vic.

Printed in Malaysia

1 2 3 4 5 07 06 05 04 03

National Library of Australia
Cataloguing-in-Publication Data

Literacies and learners: current perspectives.

2nd ed.
Bibliography.
ISBN 1 74009 832 3.

1. English language—Study and teaching (Early childhood).
2. English language—Study and teaching (Primary).
3. Literacy—Study and teaching (Primary). 4. Literacy—
Study and teaching (Early childhood). I. Campbell, Rod,
1945– . II. Green, David. 1944– .

372.6

An imprint of Pearson Education Australia

contents

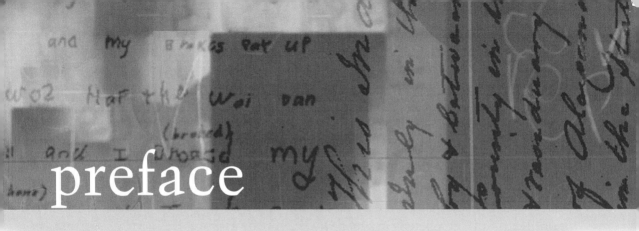

preface

THIS REVISED EDITION continues to question commonsense notions of language and language learning, and to explore the major theories and issues in the fields of language, language acquisition and language education. The book has been written principally for primary and early childhood teachers and for teachers in training. However, we believe that contemporary theories of learning language and literacy should be available to anyone who is interested. A more informed public debate on literacy issues can do much to improve literacy education.

Three major themes permeate this book:

- language is a social practice that takes place in Discourses

- we need to think of multiple literacies rather than literacy as a single entity

- a contemporary, democratic, media-saturated society demands that all its citizens be critically literate.

LANGUAGE AS SOCIAL PRACTICE IN DISCOURSES

Language never happens in a vacuum. Its forms and content arise from the interactions of people in social situations and reflect their roles and relationships. Consequently language is always surrounded by and affected by values, customs and rituals—the Discourse that Jim Gee has so ably described. Such Discourses operate also at an institutional level, and the language of these institutions must be seen in the context of the Discourse of particular institutions such as courtrooms, parliaments or classrooms. Having to perform in a courtroom for the first time would be intimidating for you. Apart from the difficulties that the legal jargon might present, such language is embedded in rituals, customs and ways of behaving which help to position you as an outsider. For some children, coming to school may be similarly problematic. Classrooms also have their own Discourses. A sensitive teacher can mediate the child's entry to these Discourses.

In Chapter 1, Green explores the first courtroom experience of a lawyer in the movie *My Cousin Vinny*, and the consequences of his failure to fully understand the institutional Discourse. In other chapters, Campbell and Baker explore the

Discourses inherent in adult/child interactions, and Cairney explores the differences between home and school Discourses.

MULTIPLE LITERACIES

In contemporary Western society, literacy has come to mean more than the middle class print literacy that pervades classrooms. A person may have difficulty with a print text but be competent in processing such texts as a web page with hypertext, a visual text on an advertising board, or a symbolic text on a circuit diagram. In addition, some people may be considered competent language users in a peer group situation in their neighbourhood or at their local bingo hall, but be considered incompetent at a tax office audit or in a classroom.

Healy picks up the notions of visual and technological literacies, as does Cairney in discussing the relationship between children's home and school Discourses. Both writers stress the need to be literate in multiple ways and for institutions such as schools to cater for and recognise these multiple literacies. This does not mean that we see print literacy as any less important. In fact, in the chapters on teaching reading and writing there is a heavy focus on print literacy. We do not focus only on children's print language development. We hope also to deepen your understandings of your own reading and writing practices in both print and other symbol systems.

Becoming a competent user of language is also an exercise in the development of a personal style of language use. Written language, by virtue of the need for its meaning to be maintained across time and space, makes use of different conventions from those of spoken language. In Chapter 5, Campbell and Ryles provide a model for considering the forms and functions of the grammars of written English, and provide examples of some of the social uses of language.

CRITICAL LITERACY

There are several dimensions to the notion of critical literacy. Firstly, critical literacy involves an attitude towards texts that tries to disrupt what might be a 'common-sense' interpretation of the text and challenges the ideology and power relations that the text takes for granted. When examining the story of Cinderella, a person with a critical perspective might ask questions about the roles played by the main protagonists, why they were described in the way they were, and whether to accept the assumption that Cinderella will live happily ever after simply because she married the prince.

Also, critical literacy is a way of looking at how the grammars of language are used in ideological ways, and how language can and is used as a powerful weapon in marginalising particular groups of people on the basis of class, race or gender. One important concept is the notion that language both reflects and creates our world. Campbell and Baker pick up this theme in terms of talk between adults and children.

Campbell and Ryles look at the role grammar plays in ideologically positioning readers; and in the final chapter, Green presents a snapshot of a primary classroom in which a major focus is to make all children critically literate.

This book has been designed for you to undertake your study of language and literacy as both a personal and social journey. By its very nature, using and understanding language is a lifelong activity, and is best learned in its use with other people—whether in front of you as speakers and listeners, or distanced from you by time and space. Many of the activities have been organised for you to share your perceptions with others so that your 'learning about language' journey becomes more effective and enjoyable as a cooperative activity. We wish you *bon voyage*.

Rod Campbell
David Green

about the authors

Rod Campbell is an education consultant in literacy and language education and curriculum to schools in Australia, Singapore and China. He has taught in primary, secondary and special schools, has worked as a school psychologist, and has been a lecturer in curriculum and language in early childhood and primary education. His doctoral thesis and other publications, as well as much of his consultancy activity, reflect his interest in teaching knowledge and application of English.

David Green is a former primary school teacher and principal, and for 27 years taught literacy education and children's literature at Queensland University of Technology in Brisbane. He is now an educational consultant to schools and a part-time lecturer at Griffith University and the McAuley Campus of the Australian Catholic University.

Carolyn Baker is Associate Professor in the Graduate School of Education at the University of Queensland. She has published widely on early literacy, on the sociology of age relations, and about many forms of institutional talk. Associate Professor Baker's books, chapters and articles are published internationally as well as nationally.

Trevor Cairney was Professor of Education and Pro Vice Chancellor of Research at the University of Western Sydney. He has written eight books and more than 160 articles and reports about many dimensions of literacy education. Professor Cairney has gained national and international prominence for his research into family literacy and into ways for improving home and school environments for literacy learning. Trevor has recently been appointed as Master of New College at the University of NSW.

Annah Healy is a senior lecturer in Primary Language and Literacy Curriculum Studies in the Faculty of Education at QUT in Brisbane. Her specific interests are in multiple literacies, particularly in how children learn about reading and texts across media. Annah recently coedited *Critical Literacies in the Primary Classroom*, 1998 (PETA Publication). She has recently completed her PhD study titled *Children reading in a post-typographic age: two case studies*.

Nicole King is a deputy principal at a primary school in Brisbane and has been a teacher in early childhood and special education for many years. She has published widely at the professional level, particularly in the fields of oral language development and education, speech and communication, and family counselling. Ms King is a co-writer of the *Magic Caterpillar Building Blocks to Literacy Programme* (2002).

Judith Rivalland is Associate Professor and Chair of the Primary and Early Childhood Studies Programs at Edith Cowan University in Perth. She has been involved in the development of many programs for language and literacy education in Australia, and was a consultant for the First Steps Project. Dr Rivalland has been an active member of a number of major research studies into literacy and education in Australian schools.

Graham Ryles is an education consultant in Melbourne and has many years experience as teacher, principal, educational psychologist, language education consultant and workplace trainer. He has published books on literacy assessment, and is coauthor with Rod Campbell of *Grammar in its Place* and the series of books for primary school classrooms, *Grammar in Context*.

Chapter 1

The nature of language: the culture of texts

David Green

> *If meaning is not rooted in the signs and texts themselves, or in what is 'in' people's heads, then education cannot be seen as the overt teaching of facts or skills. Education is always and everywhere the initiation of students as apprentices in various historically situated social practices so that they become 'insiders'*
>
> *— Gee 1992:290*

THIS CHAPTER WILL INTRODUCE the broad issues that are explored in the subsequent chapters. The aims are:

- to problematise our everyday/commonsense notions about language and texts
- to begin exploring the notion that both language and texts are forms of social practice
- to begin exploring the implications for schooling that flow from contemporary language theories.

INTRODUCTION

In the 1994 film *My Cousin Vinny*, Joe Pesci plays the role of an inexperienced but streetwise solicitor from New York. He travels to a small town in Alabama to defend his nephew who has been charged with murder. On his first day in the Alabama court, Vinny is immediately marked as an outsider by his dress (he wears a leather jacket), his dialect (Brooklyn), his choice of words (not 'lawyerly'), and because he clearly does not know the procedures of this particular courtroom. Here are some of the judge's comments to Vinny, delivered in an Alabama accent that Vinny often doesn't understand:

> *Don't talk to me sitting in that chair ... when you address this court, you will rise and speak to me in a clear, intelligible voice.*
>
> *Next time you come into my courtroom, you will look lawyerly. Comb your hair, wear a suit and tie, and that suit better be made out of some kind of cloth. You understand me?*
>
> *Now the next words out of your mouth are either going to be 'guilty' or 'not guilty'. I don't want to hear commentary, argument or opinion. If I hear anything other than 'guilty' or 'not guilty', you'll be in contempt. I don't even want to hear you clear your throat. I hope I've been clear. Now, how do your clients plead?*

Unfortunately, Vinny does not literally conform to the judge's request, is found to be in contempt of court, and is taken off to jail.

When I first saw this film, I was struck by the similarities between Vinny's situation and that experienced by many children in classrooms, especially if they are new to the classroom. We even have the class bully (the prosecutor) snigger at Vinny's discomfort. Then I asked myself this question about Vinny: Why does this otherwise intelligent man fail in this particular situation? He isn't stupid, he isn't illiterate, and he does know the law (he eventually wins the case).

It would be just as legitimate to ask that question about those children who are 'failing' literacy in the early years of school. Why are they failing? Is it because they are stupid, lazy or poor? Or could it be that the classroom itself is part of the problem? Could it be that the institution of the school creates failure for some children?

LANGUAGE AS A SOCIAL PRACTICE

To understand why Vinny doesn't fit into this courtroom (and perhaps why some children do not succeed in language classrooms), we need to think of language not as a set of cognitive skills that we either have or do not have, but as forms of behaviour that always take place in social and cultural contexts. James Gee calls these social contexts 'Discourses':

> *A Discourse is a socially accepted association among ways of using language, of thinking, feeling, believing, valuing, and of acting that can be used to identify oneself as a member of a socially meaningful group or 'social network' (Gee 1990:143).*

Gee discriminates between this definition of 'Discourse' and 'discourse' (without the capital letter). He uses 'discourse' to mean 'connected stretches of language that make sense'. Thus Gee sees discourses as part of Discourses. But the key point here is that Discourses determine how people view language, and more importantly, how they practice it. Stop and think for a moment of the different Discourses in which you take part (family, school, sporting and social clubs, work) and reflect on the different ways language is used in each of these Discourses. We should also keep in mind that each of these Discourses is inherently ideological and resistant to internal criticism. I will return to this matter of ideology later.

The point to be made here is this: Vinny was in a Discourse that actively constructed him as an 'outsider'. The other people in the courtroom (the prosecutor, the policeman) were able to snigger at Vinny because they were familiar with the rules of the game and were aware of Vinny's transgressions in a way that Vinny couldn't be.

The term 'insider' implies (a) a meta-awareness of the processes operating in the particular language situation, and (b) some level of empowerment for the language users/consumers who have that awareness. This clearly was not the case for Vinny. In the courtroom there were fixed codes of behaviour, including language behaviour, that were unfamiliar to him. Moreover, the ultimate authority for determining what constituted appropriate behaviour was in the hands of the insiders.

INSTITUTIONAL DISCOURSES

Vinny's courtroom problems demonstrate an institutional Discourse, and his experience is what frequently happens when someone is in an unfamiliar institution. I'm sure you can think of some other examples, such as a visit to the tax office or the first day at a new job. We need to remind ourselves constantly that schools, too, are institutions with particular social practices, including language practices, and that in every classroom you are likely to find at least one Vinny struggling to come to terms with the particular Discourses of that particular institution.

Some children who are familiar with the social practices of the school, children from social backgrounds that practice literacy in similar ways, find the transition from home to school a comfortable experience. At the same time the school recognises, approves and rewards them. Other children, however, bring to school their own language practices that do not receive this recognition even though such practices have worked very well in their home communities. These children are not illiterate. They simply use their literacy in ways different from the ways valued by the school. Luke puts the point even more strongly:

> *Schools and teachers systematically tend to value and valorise those kinds of cultural capital/linguistic competence which fit the values of dominant classes and cultures, and in effect 'punish' children for not having* a priori *what schools are charged with delivering, that is, competence with school-style texts and literacy events (Luke in Unsworth 1993:32).*

This point is well illustrated in the scene from *My Cousin Vinny*. Note that the things the Judge finds offensive in Vinny, the things he 'fails' him on (vocabulary, dress, lifestyle, ignorance of protocol), are things he could only have had by being an 'insider', a member of the club. So Vinny's real crime is something he can't help because he is an outsider.

THE HOME–SCHOOL CONNECTION

James Gee (1990) and Sarah Michaels (1981) compare the story-telling styles of two young girls. One, a five year old, white, middle class girl, understands conventional story structure and syntax and is seen as a gifted child by her teachers. The second child is a year two African-American girl who tells highly original 'tall' tales reflecting both the story-telling culture from which she comes and some of its social customs:

> *... today's my grandmother's birthday an a lot o'people's makin' a cake again but my grandmother is goin t'get her own cake at her bakery an she's gonna come out with a cake that we didn't make cause she likes chocolate cream. An' I went t'the bakery with her an' my grandmother ate cup cakes an' an' she finally got sick on today an' she was growling like a dog cause she ate so many cakes. An' I finally told her that it was it was Friday the thirteenth, bad luck day.*

This story, however, was not seen to be appropriate for the morning talk session where factual recounting was valued. The child was chastised and eventually sent to the school psychologist for telling lies.

The difficulty here, of course, is that more than the child's story is being rejected. Her family, and her way of life, is being deemed unacceptable. Faced with such a conflict between school and home, a logical response from the child is to reject the social/language practices of the school.

In other landmark studies, Heath (USA) and Wells (UK) also found significant differences in some homes between the way language was used in those homes and the way it was used at school. Heath (1983) found great differences between three different communities in the way each community oriented its children towards written language and how to use it. Only one of these communities used written texts in ways that were similar to ways that schools use texts. The children from this community were subsequently found to be more successful at school than children from the other communities.

Wells (1985) also found that some families used oral language in a way that was compatible with classroom talk, especially in the manner of asking questions. Again, the children from these homes generally handled the transition to school more easily than children from other kinds of homes.

Earlier, Bernstein (1960) made a distinction between 'elaborated' and 'restricted' codes in language. Restricted codes are uses of language specific to a particular context and understandable only to people familiar with that context. An example of a restricted code would be: 'He scored outside Greasy's.' In elaborated codes, the speaker/writer takes less for granted: 'John Smith was able to buy heroin outside the hamburger shop on Lutwyche Road.'

Bernstein claimed that middle class children had access to both codes whereas working class children mostly had access only to restricted codes. This is significant when seen alongside Bernstein's claim that schools deal mainly in elaborated codes. Bernstein later denied the suggestion that his studies had shown working class children lacked either linguistic resources or abstract reasoning. What his work did show, however, was that language practices developed in the social context of the home and community have the potential to either complement or conflict with the language practices of schools, thus either advantaging or disadvantaging particular groups of children.

The contrast between home and school literacies is much more complex than the simple proposition that children who are read to at home are advantaged. One has to ask: Read to in what ways? Luke (in Unsworth 1993: 29) cites the example of children who have learnt from their community that texts such as Bible stories are literal and are to be accepted as factual. Any doubt as to meaning is resolved by the authority of parents and teachers. These children often have trouble in school when imaginative/figurative responses to texts are required such as when they are asked to put themselves in the position of a character and consider how else that character might have behaved; or when children are asked to interpret an author's use of metaphor.

TEXTS: WHERE IS THE MEANING?

A second important aspect of critical social theory concerns the nature of texts. This is sometimes referred to as the discourse/text analysis aspect of critical social theory. This focuses on texts themselves rather than the Discourses, and asks less about *what* texts mean and more about *how* they mean. Fairclough (1989), Luke (1988) and Gee (1990) have demonstrated the ways that social power operates through texts, positioning readers, marginalising minority groups, and imperialistically promoting particular world views. Critical social literacy practices set out to foreground and contest these values. Consider the following text:

> Out in the yard, Mary played quietly with her dolls as Tom and Danny inspected Tom's new ball. Suddenly, Tom threw the ball as hard as he could at his younger sister. He was amazed

at how easily she snatched the ball from the air and threw it straight back at him. He was even more surprised when it hit him flush on the nose.

Their mother watched, unnoticed, from the upstairs window.

This text, like all texts, contains gaps: the age of the children, the type of ball, why the ball was thrown, the nature of the sister's skill, whether the brother was hurt, the character of the mother. These gaps are filled by the reader according to prior experiences, previous readings, reading strategies etc. How did you fill the gaps? What images did you construct? These will almost certainly be different from the images other people constructed.

We might also consider the stereotypical roles assigned to the children and the assumption that girls ought not to have advanced ball skills. And we need to consider the lexical (choice of words) and grammatical (sentence patterns) options taken up by the author.

So, reading or listening is much more than simply extracting the meaning from the text. Making meaning is complicated both by factors within the text and by what the reader brings to the text. And this meaning-making is complicated even further by the Discourse in which the reading takes place. Under what circumstances is the reader reading the text? Is the text part of a novel she is reading for pleasure? Is she a film producer reviewing a script? Is the text being read in a classroom prior to a comprehension test? Is it being read orally in front of the class? Each of these situations will affect the reading that is made of the text.

POST-STRUCTURALISM

Texts are seen in similar ways in post-structuralist and critical social theories. But post-structuralists claim there can be no definitive meaning of a text. Like critical theorists, they claim meanings are constructed in the act of reading and listening, and therefore will vary according to who is reading and listening, when and where they are reading and listening, and for what purposes. Any text contains the possibility of multiple meanings, and these meanings will vary according to context: social, cultural, historical and discursive.

Post-structural theorists criticise critical theorists who believe we can strip away the false ideology of texts and get at the 'true meaning' of the text (Morgan 1997:10–11). For post-structuralists, there is *no* ultimate truth. A post-structuralist, therefore, would interrogate the Tom and Mary text in the following ways:

- What are the possible readings of this text?

- How are these readings being promoted?

- Whose world view are we being asked to accept?

- Whose views are being marginalised?

- What is being assumed/naturalised by this text?

That final question will be explored under 'ideology' later in this chapter and again in later chapters. But the point can be made here that many texts take, as a given, certain ideological factors such as gender roles. It is assumed by the text that these are just the way things are in the world. The text positions the reader to see the world of the text in a particular way, creating a subjectivity, a way of looking at the world of the text that seems natural. A post-structuralist reader would challenge this 'naturalness', as would critical theorists.

Texts might also assume or naturalise a range of binary oppositions or dualisms: good/bad, man/woman, beautiful/ugly. These are assumptions that need to be challenged in terms of both their 'reality'—we might choose to see a characteristic such as beauty, morality or gender as a continuum rather than a mutually exclusive duality—and the consequences for the item in each duality that is denigrated by its comparison with a supposed superior.

There are obvious pedagogical consequences of poststructuralist and critical social theories. If meaning is neither in the text nor in the reader's head, then education cannot be seen as simply the teaching of facts or skills:

> *Education is always and everywhere the initiation of students as apprentices in various historically situated social practices so that they become 'insiders' (Gee 1992:290–1).*

In another place, Gee has called this kind of learning 'acquisition' or 'acculturation' (Gee 1987). His thoughts on this are important to modern language pedagogy and need to be explored a little further here.

> *Acquisition is a process of acquiring something subconsciously by exposure to models and a process of trial and error, without a process of formal teaching. It happens in natural settings which are meaningful and functional in the sense that the acquirers know that they need to acquire something in order to function and they in fact want to so function.*

> *Learning is a process that involves conscious knowledge gained through teaching … involves explanation and analysis … It inherently involves attaining, along with the matter being taught, some degree of meta-knowledge about the matter (Gee 1987:5).*

In looking at learning to read as 'acquisition' rather than 'learning', Gee equates learning to read with learning a Discourse, that is, a *use* for reading. Learning to read is therefore a secondary Discourse as opposed to a primary Discourse such as the initial learning of oral language in the home.

We need to challenge the 'naturalisation' of readings, to challenge the world view the text asks us to take. And we need to go further, to explore *how* the text is asking us to accept this world view. Such explorations will undermine the manipulation of readers by authorities, experts and teachers:

> *Anything that deflates the spurious authority of the text so that it becomes the object of engaging play is preferable to those silent, reverent encounters at the high altar of literary religion (Corcoran & Evans (eds) 1987:66).*

In concrete terms, teachers would be involved in the following:

- broadening the range of texts explored in the classroom to include what the children are reading outside school: television, advertising, junk mail, magazines, newspapers, romance novels, etc.

- exploring these texts in terms of the questions listed above (under this heading, 'Post-structuralism')

- creating an 'open' classroom in the sense that the Discourse permits, encourages and rewards verbal risk-taking.

Each of these factors will be explored more fully in later chapters of this book. But it needs to be said here, by way of example, that there is no place in the type of classroom we are describing for practices that limit the interrogation of texts to 'comprehension' exercises in which the reader must guess the teacher's interpretation of the text. The classroom context must support the acquisition of multiple Discourses while simultaneously providing the mechanisms for learning textual knowledge. The final section of this chapter looks more closely at a major theme in critical social approaches to language: that texts and Discourses are necessarily ideological.

TEXTUAL AND DISCURSIVE IDEOLOGY

I would define ideology as: 'Those values/beliefs/world views that, often unnoticed, underpin texts, social interactions or institutional rituals in the interests of a particular social group'. In arriving at this definition I have made a number of assumptions:

- Ideology operates wherever social interaction occurs but, of particular interest, it is to be found embedded in the rituals of social institutions such as schools, churches, the law and the media. These are what Althusser called 'ideological apparatuses', the cultural sites where ideologies are transmitted and internalised (Luke 1992:5).

- Because texts are embedded in social contexts and presented in social Discourses, texts are also necessarily ideological.

- In texts and institutional sites, the preferred social behaviour is often made to appear natural and inevitable (Fairclough 1989:2) or a matter of commonsense (McLaren & Lankshear 1993:404). In children's literature, when a group of girls and boys is isolated and in danger, it may seem natural that one of the boys assumes leadership of the group, shows initiative, is the bravest of the group. In a mixed race group, it may seem natural, and a sign of caring, for the European children to initiate an African child into the right way to behave. However, as James Gee points out, such cultural imperialism operates for the benefit and promotion of the dominant culture (Gee 1990:104).

- Ideologies are, by definition, contestable. An ideology represents *one* particular world view out of numerous possible world views, none of which can have an absolute claim to be the 'right' one. Moreover these ideologies are embedded in Discourse practices which both shape and are shaped by the individuals within those practices (Luke 1991 [unpublished paper]:7).

Therefore, in our classrooms, both the texts children use and the classroom practices are ideological. The stereotyping of girls as passive/subservient in a piece of literature is ideological; the streaming of children into ability groups is ideological; as is the use of standardised tests, based on white, middle class norms, in order to create those streams. You might like to reflect on how and why these examples are ideological.

The point I make here is that in looking at how ideological meanings are constructed in language classrooms, we must look not only at texts and readers, but also at the messages children receive in the classroom as to the purpose of language activities. The importance of this is well put by Freebody et al.:

> ... in literacy events in the classroom—structured interactions around and about texts— students learn a selective tradition of how to do things with those texts. Displays of these techniques in turn come to count as reading. At the same time, other ways of handling text, other kinds of semantic and pragmatic potentials and possibilities, are excluded (Freebody et al. 1991:436).

Snapshot 1.1

A grade 5 classroom in suburban Brisbane. The children are currently interested in legendary monsters such as Yeti, Bigfoot, the Yowie and the Loch Ness Monster as they work on a unit called 'Big and Beastie'. In the classroom they have comics, magazines, newspaper reports and a variety of print texts both factual and narrative, all of which deal with supposed sightings of the various beasts.

For this particular session, the children are asked to compare two newspaper stories each of which reports on the same Yowie sighting (the two stories are at the end of this chapter). There are four children who need assistance with the reading of these stories—two struggling readers and two children from non-English-speaking backgrounds. These children are assisted by a tape

recording of the two newspaper stories presented as radio news items. They use the listening post and as they listen to the stories they run their fingers under the print. They are then able to take part in group discussions of the text with other children.

The children are asked to note the differences between the two texts. They discover 17 differences. The teacher consistently refers to these differences as choices made by the writer. Her purpose here is to foreground the author and present the stories as constructions rather than simply snapshots of the way the world really is. Some of the differences noted by the children are: the different headlines; the use of a title (Dr Jones) in one story; the consistent use of terms like 'supposed' and 'reported' in one paper while the other reported the event as if it had happened; in one story the person sighting the creature is an eminent scientist. Turn to the texts and see if you can find the other differences.

The children are then asked to consider the significance of the choices made by these writers. They are able to explain that the choices make the sighting seem more credible in one reading than in the other. They are then told of the 'sighting' of a Yowie in the school grounds by their teacher. They are given the chance to interview the teacher and are asked to write this up as either a credible or non-credible event. The four children who had used the listening post do this writing task as a joint construction with the teacher aide.

You should note how this snapshot differs from what might have happened in a more traditional classroom. Note the range of texts employed, the catering for diverse learners and the critical exploration of the texts. And notice also how the sequence began with whole texts, moved to an examination of the parts of the text and concluded with a return to whole texts. This model is referred to as a 'Whole–Part–Whole' model and has been accepted by many teachers and school systems because it supports the notion that we acquire language when we use language to do something meaningful. In other words the 'Whole–Part–Whole' model maintains a focus on the 'meaning-making' nature of reading (see later chapters in this book; also see Healy 2000).

So, what has all this to do with Vinny's problems in that Alabama courtroom? In this chapter I have problematised the notion that language consists of a set of discrete skills that you either have or do not have, that are either right or wrong, and that the role of schools is to teach you the 'right' ones. Rather, I wanted to present the notion that language is a form of behaviour, a series of cultural and social practices that should be seen as appropriate (or not appropriate) for a given context.

IMPLICATIONS FOR TEACHERS

Each of these implications will only be introduced briefly here, but they will concern us more fully throughout this book.

Language teaching is political

Accepting the notion that language learning is 'cultural' rather than 'natural' shifts language away from the realm of personal development. Instead, language learning becomes 'cultural capital' (Bourdieu & Passeron 1977)—particular, culturally determined ways of doing things; not the only ways, but the ways that happened to be valued by dominant groups in the society. Thus, any differences in school achievement are not simply due to 'natural ability'. Rather, differences in achievement result from abilities gained from *insider* experiences that support some groups and place others at a disadvantage.

This socio-political aspect of language was central to the work of Paolo Freire (Freire & Macedo 1987). Freire claimed traditional literacy practices involve an imposition of texts and readings by the dominant culture, leading to the alienation and disempowerment of many people. Other writers, including Luke (1988), Lankshear (1994) and Gilbert (1993), would want to tie literacy to such a socio-cultural critique to study the individual's place within society and the forces controlling that place.

Literacy is not a unitary skill

There are multiple ways of being literate. People can be 'street' literate or literate in the ways of a bikie gang. They can be literate technologically, electronically or mechanically. They can be print literate, media literate or computer literate. And they can be classroom literate, although even this last term is problematic because there are various types of classrooms and therefore various ways of being classroom literate. But note that each of these literacies involves being an insider to a particular Discourse.

Classrooms contain diverse learners

In any classroom there are children from differing language and cultural backgrounds; children with differing learning styles; children with learning disorders; children with visual and auditory disabilities; children who are gifted and talented in a variety of different ways; and children with a range of behaviour problems.

These categories are not discrete and a child might occupy a number of them. The challenge for the teacher is to include each of these children as an insider to the classroom Discourses. The New London Group signalled that this changed attitude to diversity in schools was a key concept:

To be relevant, learning processes need to recruit, rather than attempt to ignore and erase, the different subjectivities—interests, intentions, commitments, and purposes—students bring to learning. Curriculum now needs to mesh with different subjectivities, and with their attendant languages, discourses, and registers, and use these as a resource for learning (New London Group 1996:72).

Classroom resources and classroom Discourses are interrelated

The textual resources in the contemporary classroom must reflect the notions stated above. Therefore, all such resources must be:

- relevant to the diverse range of learners in the class. For example, not all children relate to the white, middle class, suburban families who inhabit many of the traditional, primer style early reading books

- represented in a wide variety of forms, both factual and fictional, in a wide range of culturally relevant topics and issues. As well as quality print texts, there should be digital texts, multi-media texts and community texts such as junk mail, pamphlets, posters, newspapers, magazines and comics

- reproduced, reflected upon, researched and used in critically literate ways. The texts should be seen as sociocultural artefacts and critiqued in terms of choices made by the authors and in terms of the view of the world that these choices assume.

Activities

Discourses

Reflect back on the last 24 hours in your life. List the various language Discourses you have experienced. Consider the uses of language in each Discourse and reflect on the cultural and social contexts of the Discourse.

Texts

Marnie O'Neill (1990:93) considers it essential that children gain the following understanding of texts:

- A text is a *construction*, not a *reflection* of reality that is 'true'.

- Texts have constructed in them assumptions about, for example, race, gender or class, which a reader might challenge rather than accept.

- Gaps or silences in a text might be treated as problematic; filling them in different ways produces different readings.

- The ways in which readers fill gaps may not be idiosyncratic but arise from cultural or social values.

- While texts may offer the reader a particular position from which to read, the reader does not necessarily have to accept that position.

- Texts are sites for conflicting or competing meanings rather than consensual responses.

- Resistant or culturally critical readings offer more opportunity for equity of participation.

Consider what is meant by each of these points. See if you can relate each of O'Neill's points to a text you have read recently.

Annotated bibliography

Friere, P & Macedo, D 1987 *Literacy: reading the word and the world*. Bergin & Garvey, Boston, Mass.
A ground-breaking text that builds on Friere's earlier work, *Pedagogy of the oppressed*, to explore the links between illiteracy, poverty and powerlessness in a Latin American context. The authors highlight the important link between home/community literacies and institutional literacies such as school literacies.

Gee, J 1990 *Social linguistics and literacies: ideology in Discourses*. Falmer Press, London.
In keeping with Heath and Freire, Gee explains the social dimensions of education and literacy and emphasises the point that education is always ideological. His key concepts include the notion of multiple literacies, the distinction between 'discourse' and 'Discourse', and the distinction between 'acquisition' and 'learning'.

Gilbert, P 1993 *Gender stories and the language classroom*. Deakin University Press, Geelong, Victoria.
Focuses on children's story writing from a feminist, post-structuralist perspective and sees differences in both the gendered ideologies they contain and the way they are written.

Heath, SB 1986 'What no bedtime story means: narrative skills at home and school', in Schieffelin, B & Ochs, E (eds) *Language socialisation across cultures*. Cambridge University Press, NY, 97–124.
A shorter version of the study reported in her 1983 book (*Ways with Words*) in which she studies the different ways language is used in three American communities and the consequences these differences have for the children when they start school.

Lankshear, C 1994 *Critical literacy*. Australian Curriculum Studies Association, Canberra.
A clear, concise outline and rationale of critical social theory.

Luke, A 1993 *The social construction of literacy in the primary school*. Macmillan, Sydney.
Another clear and concise rationale of critical social theory, but in the specific context of Australian primary school education. Also makes useful analyses of other major theorists such as Heath and Gee.

References

Bernstein, B (1960) 'Language and Social Class'. *British Journal of Sociology*, 11:261–76.

Bourdieu, P & Passeron, J-C 1977 *Reproduction in education, society and culture*. Trans. R Nice. Sage, London.

Corcoran, B & Evans, E (eds) 1987 *Readers, texts, teachers*. Open University Press, Philadelphia.

Fairclough, N 1989 *Language and power*. Longman, London.

Freebody, P, Luke, A & Gilbert, P 1991 'Reading positions and practices in the classroom'. *Curriculum Inquiry* 21:4, 435–57.

Friere, P & Macedo, D 1987 *Literacy: Reading the Word and the World*. Bergin & Garvey, Sth. Hadley, Mass.

Gee, J 1987 *What is Literacy?* Conference Paper, Harvard Graduate School of Education.

Gee, J 1990 *Social linguistics and literacies: ideology in Discourses*. Falmer, London.

Gee, J 1992 'Literacies: tuning in to forms of life'. In F Christie (ed.) *The Politics of Literacy. A special edition of Education Australia*, Nov. 1992.

Gilbert, P 1993 *Gender stories and the language classroom*. Deakin University Press, Geelong, Victoria.

Healy, A 2000 *Teaching Reading and Writing in a Multiliteracies Context: Classroom Practice*. Post Pressed, Queensland.

Heath, SB 1983 *Ways with words: language, life, and work in communities and classrooms*. Cambridge University Press, NY.

Lankshear, C 1994 *Critical literacy*. Australian Curriculum Studies Association, Canberra.

Luke, A 1988 *Literacy, textbooks and ideology*. Farmer Press, UK.

Luke, A 1991 Unpublished paper.

Luke, A 1992 'The micropolitics of classroom narrative'. In B Green (ed.) *The insistence of the letter: literacy studies and curriculum theorising*. University of Pittsburgh Press, Pittsburgh.

McLaren, P & Lankshear, C (eds) 1993 *Critical literacy: politics, praxis, and the post-modern*. New York State University Press, Albany.

Michaels, S 1981 'Sharing time: children's narrative styles and differential access to literacy'. *Language in society*, 10:423–42.

Morgan, W 1997 *Critical literacy in the classroom*. Routledge, London.

New London Group 1996 'A pedagogy of multiliteracies: Designing social futures'. *Harvard Educational Review* 66(1), 60–92.

O'Neill, M 1990 'Molesting the text: promoting resistant readings'. In M Hayhoe & S Parker (eds) *Reading and response*. Open University Press, London.

Unsworth, L (ed.) 1993 *Literacy learning and teaching: language as social practice in the primary school*. Macmillan, Melbourne.

Wells, G 1985 Language, learning and education. NFER-Nelson, London.

APPENDIX 1: THE YOWIE SIGHTINGS

SCIENTIST SEES YOWIE

The whole world is talking about the town of Kingaroy after a Yowie was seen there yesterday.

The sighting was made by the famous scientist, Dr Thomas Jones of Queensland University. Dr Jones was on a camping holiday near Kingaroy when he made the sighting. He was following some very large footprints through the forest when he heard loud noises. He crept closer and in a clearing he saw the Yowie.

The creature was about 3 metres tall and was covered with dark hair like a gorilla. It had a human-like face, but its mouth was very big and it had long sharp teeth. It growled at Dr Jones and ran off into the forest.

Dr Jones took several photographs of the creature as it fled, but unfortunately the light was poor and the photographs are not very clear.

There have been several sightings of this creature in the last few years. Sheep have disappeared in the night and forest rangers often come across partly eaten bodies of kangaroos and other forest animals.

Dr Jones showed reporters a plaster cast of the Yowie's footprint and said he now planned to lead a full expedition into the forest to find the Yowie. This newspaper has given Dr Jones $10 000 towards the cost of the search and will send a video cameraman on the trip.

Dr Jones is regarded as the world's leading expert on strange creatures and has written several books on this topic.

ANOTHER YOWIE 'SIGHTING'

As another tourist season begins, the town of Kingaroy in Queensland has put itself on the map again with another reported sighting of a Yowie.

The sighting was reported by local writer and head of the Kingaroy Tourist Board, Tom Jones. Mr Jones was on a camping holiday near Kingaroy when he claims he saw the Yowie. He says he was following some very large footprints when he heard loud noises. He says he crept closer and in a clearing saw the Yowie.

Mr Jones told reporters the creature was about 3 metres tall and was covered with dark hair like a gorilla. He also said it had a human-like face with a large mouth and long, sharp teeth. Mr Jones said he threw an empty beer bottle at the monster and it ran off into the forest.

Mr Jones also said he tried to take photographs but he forgot to take the lens cap off his camera and none of the photos came out.

Many people in this small town say they have seen Yowies. None of these 'sightings' have ever been verified. Some farmers have reported missing sheep and local rangers have found half eaten kangaroos. But dingoes are known to roam in this area and they frequently attack other animals.

Mr Jones showed a large plaster cast of what he said was the Yowie's foot. He said he was hoping that local shops would give him some money so that he could make a proper search for the Yowie. The local newspaper has already given Mr Jones $10 000 towards the venture.

Mr Jones' book on the Yowie will be released in the shops tomorrow.

Chapter 2

The home–school connection in literacy and language development

Trevor Cairney

> *It would appear that at times teachers adopt very narrow definitions of parent involvement in schooling, which seek primarily to determine what parents or communities can do for teachers, or how schools can make parents 'better' at their role in the home, rather than how schools and parents can develop close relationships of mutual support and trust.*
>
> *— Cairney & Munsie 1995a: 5*

THIS CHAPTER WILL INTRODUCE readers to key issues concerning the importance of strong and open partnerships between home and school. It aims to:

- explore the diverse literacy practices of home and school
- describe the development of home–school initiatives in literacy
- outline how schools can build more effective partnerships with their communities.

INTRODUCTION

Snapshot 2.1

The Ahmed family lived in Sydney's inner city area. This Arabic family had been participating in a national evaluation of family literacy initiatives (Cairney, Ruge, Buchanan, Lowe & Munsie 1995). The two parents were actively involved in their children's lives, and their education was no exception. As parents they placed great importance on the Arabic language and languages other than English in general, and they provided a rich language environment for their children in the home and community. The following extract from the family's case study provides an insight into the nature of the parents' involvement in their children's education:

At home, the Ahmed children speak Arabic to both their parents and their siblings. Mr Ahmed often reads to the children in Arabic, but the children have only English books. They are all learning to read and write Arabic through attendance at Arabic school three times per week. Each of the children has attended Arabic lessons from a young age. Hannah, at five years of age, has not yet begun kindergarten but has already been attending Arabic lessons for almost a year. The two oldest children, a girl and a boy, currently attend single sex high schools. Mr Ahmed says that, for him, provision of an Arabic language program was an important consideration in deciding where to send the children to school. 'These days you need more than one language. ... I would like them to speak our own language, Arabic, so that for any job in the future, they've got two languages.' For Mrs Ahmed, however, it is far more important that they attend single sex schools where they will not be distracted by 'boyfriends and girlfriends', especially 'when they are in their early teens'. The children complete most of their school homework in isolation within their rooms, and their parents play a minimal part. Mr Ahmed indicates that he is less involved in his children's school work these days and comments, 'I used to help them before, but now they can do it by themselves'. When his son Joe was asked what he did if he encountered difficulty with his homework, he replied, 'Ask my brother or sister ... mostly it's maths; they show me how to get the answer and how to write it on the page'. In this very supportive home, much of the help with school literacy comes from siblings, not from parents.

The Ahmed children were living within at least two distinct cultures each day, and were negotiating multiple literacies in two languages. As well, they assumed many roles as students and family members. For example, at home they assumed informal roles as supporters of each other's school learning. They had different literacy needs to their parents and engaged in different literacy practices. There was also variation with age in the specific literacy practices of the children. The children shared many interests with each other and with children at school, but less with their parents who actively discouraged some practices that their friends (and perhaps even the teacher) valued. For example, the Ahmed children liked to watch television, but their father closely monitored their viewing habits, limiting both the time they spent and the programs they watched. He said he liked to watch programs with the children so that they could discuss it afterwards, usually the next day. At times, the children complained about not being allowed to watch television beyond 7.30 in the evening, insisting that they would still be able to 'get up early' next day, but Mr Ahmed argued that '... if you're thinking about what you watched last night when you are in school, then you're not thinking about school'.

CATERING FOR THE DIVERSE NEEDS OF LITERACY LEARNERS

The above introduction provides an insight into the diversity of this family's literacy practices in and outside school, as well as an indication of the complexity of the roles that teachers and parents play as supporters of language and literacy learners. One of the great challenges for schools in today's diverse society is to understand how to cater for the needs of all students within traditional school structures. One of the imperatives for teachers in many Australian schools in the last two decades has been the need to acknowledge and build on the language and cultural diversity of the students who enter schools each day. Students' acquisition of English literacy has been one of the major priorities for teachers within such schools. But the achievements of schools have been mixed, with differing levels of success in meeting the diverse needs of all learners. This chapter attempts to discuss key issues associated with the relationship between home and school while at the same time examining how schools might work more effectively to support positive partnerships with students' families. I will also argue that a thorough understanding of the differences between the literacy practices of home and school is vital to ensuring that all students are given the best chance to succeed at school, particularly for children from families for whom English is not the first language.

Two major theories have been suggested as explanations for persistent failure by schools and systems to ensure high levels of academic success for students from minority backgrounds. The first is the theory of *cultural discontinuity*, while the second can be termed the theory of *structural inequality* (Au 1993). Each of these theories has contributed to different approaches to the study of the causes of educational disadvantage of minority students.

The theory of cultural discontinuity, or cultural difference, suggests that cultural mismatches between teachers and students may result in difficulties in communication and interaction in the classroom (Erickson 1993). These differences, or mismatches, work against the literacy learning of students whose home culture does not reflect that of the school. Studies that adopt a cultural discontinuity perspective tend to focus less on broad issues of social and economic power, and more on the day-to-day patterning of specific activities (e.g. Delgado-Gaitan 1992; Heath 1983; Deyhle & LeCompte 1994; Malin 1994; Mulhern 1995). Au (1995:90) points out that a key assumption of cultural difference analyses 'is that there are systematic, identifiable differences in cultural values, knowledge and practices, and that these differences are related to students' chances for school success'.

The theory of structural inequality looks beyond mismatches between the culture of the home and the school. It suggests that the lack of educational success of students from minority backgrounds reflects structural inequalities in the broader social, political and economic spheres (Au 1993; Ogbu 1993). This theory takes into account the power relationships between groups, and argues that schools function to maintain the status quo. Critical analyses of social and cultural differences and the impact of these on school success tend to adopt a 'structural inequality' perspective (e.g. Ogbu 1992, 1993; Luke 1993; May 1995). This perspective attributes educational disadvantage to 'oppressive social structures that create vast inequalities in power and opportunity favouring the dominant group' (Au 1995:87). As Luke (1995:16) argues, schools 'naturalise particular interactional patterns and textual practices in ways that systematically exclude those students from economically marginal and culturally different backgrounds'.

However, like Au (1993), I want to argue in this chapter that neither the cultural discontinuity theory nor the structural inequality theory can adequately explain the continuing educational disadvantage of students from minority backgrounds. Both theories need to be considered in any attempt to improve students' chances of educational success.

These issues were explored in a major national children's literacy project conducted with my collaborator Jenny Ruge (Cairney & Ruge 1997). The purpose of the project was to explore differences in the language and literacy practices of schools, families and communities. In particular, it examined matches and mismatches between the discourse practices of home and school and the impact that such differences have on students' school success. The study involved detailed analysis of family, community and school contexts, and focused on families from a wide range of cultural and linguistic backgrounds. The research attempted to draw on both theories discussed above by combining elements of a cultural difference analysis with elements of a critical analysis. That is, while it focused on classroom level interactions and individual students at home and at school, it sought to understand these within the context of cultural and/or linguistic differences as well as broader issues of power relations in society.

The research was framed theoretically within a sociocultural view of literacy. Within this framework, literacy is not viewed as a single unitary skill. Rather, it is viewed as a social practice that has many specific manifestations (Gee 1990; Luke 1993; Welch & Freebody 1993; Cairney 1995a). Important to the study were perspectives on literacy which suggest that there are many forms of literacy, each with specific purposes and contexts in which they are used (Cook-Gumperz 1986; Moll et al. 1992; Barton 1994; Cairney 1995a). This view of literacy as 'social accomplishment of a group' (Bloome 1986; Cairney 1987; Cairney & Langbien 1989; Baker & Luke 1991; Santa Barbara Classroom Discourse Group 1992) suggests that teachers, students and parents construct their own models and definitions of literacy and sanction particular understandings, norms, expectations, and roles that define what it means to be literate. Literacy is viewed as a practice that cannot be separated from the people who use it. Literacy is also situated in sociocultural contexts defined by members of a group through their actions with, through and about language. Such a perspective involves 'a shift away from a view of individual learners to a view of learning as participation in a community of practice' (Moll 1993:2). The emphasis is thus, not how individual children learn, but instead why and how people learn through their participation in the practices that define specific groups and communities, how communities organise their resources, and how participation in the culture shapes identity.

In more recent work (Cairney 2002; Cairney & Ashton in press), we observed that the sociolinguistic diversity of literacy support that adults offer, makes it difficult (indeed unwise) to make simplistic statements concerning differences across literacy contexts, or even repeated occurrences of the same type of literacy event within a single context. We found that even when families appear to use similar forms of support, there are often subtle differences in the language strategies being used that may lead to different outcomes. These differences reflect sociolinguistic variations that teachers need to understand if they are to respond to the linguistic diversity present within classrooms to ensure equitable learning outcomes.

HOME–SCHOOL CONNECTIONS AND LITERACY SUCCESS

Literacy has long been seen as important as a means to empower people. In developing countries, campaigns for universal literacy are central to reform and in developed countries literacy is seen as an essential need for people to function as community members. While the need for literacy may have been overemphasised (see Graff 1991 for a full discussion of this argument), it is nevertheless important. However, it is not simply the acquisition of specific forms of literacy that is important. Some research seems to assume that literacy is little more than the '… ability to decode and construct symbols in order to write …' (Delgado-Gaitan 1990:41). But as the work of Freire (1970) has shown, literacy is also a social and political practice that cannot be separated from one's daily existence. Furthermore, one cannot simply redress social injustice, as evidenced in differential school achievement, by providing access to programs or even specific practices such as forms of literacy. Connell (1993; 1995) argues that justice cannot be achieved simply by providing ruling-class practices (such as specific forms of literacy) to the working class and expect this to ensure social justice. Education, he suggests, operates through relationships that cannot be neutralised to allow equal access and distribution.

Delgado-Gaitan (1990) suggests that it is by coming to understand one's conditions and collectively working toward changing them that people are empowered. While pre-schools, childcare centres and schools cannot change directly what children bring with them (nor would we necessarily want to), the staff in these settings can examine the discourse communities they create, and reflect on the role that these have in contributing to individual success or failure. Furthermore, schools can consider whether changes in the nature of classroom discourse will make a difference for some children. As well, teachers can attempt to search for ways to make the discourse patterns of schooling more transparent to families, and subsequently open up access to forms of cultural capital that have traditionally advantaged some in schools, such as specific literacy practices and resources.

Interestingly, research evidence suggests that there is far less literacy diversity within and between schools than one would expect, given the varied communities they serve (Cairney, Lowe & Sproats 1995; Freebody, Ludwig & Gunn 1995). In fact, a number of recent studies have shown that the literacy practices of the community and home are more diverse than that of school (Cairney & Ruge 1997). This finding is even more significant when viewed alongside other research that has suggested that the difference between the language and literacy of school and that of home/community is a significant factor in the achievement or non-achievement of students at school (e.g. Heath 1983; Scribner & Cole 1981).

As argued elsewhere (e.g. Cairney 1994; Cairney 1995b; Cairney & Munsie 1995a; 1995b), the match and mismatch in language and literacy between home/community and school, is of vital importance in addressing the specific needs of all students, in particular, those who experience difficulties with literacy and schooling. While the home has long been seen as a significant factor in children's school success, it appears that differences in school literacy achievement are not due simply to differences in the volume of pre-school or home literacy experiences. Indeed, many researchers have shown that virtually all children in highly literate countries such as the USA have extensive experiences with written language (Heath 1983; Harste et al. 1984; Teale 1986). Rather, differences in school literacy achievement seem to have more to do with student success and failure at dealing with the literacy practices of schooling rather than deficits in experiences or skills.

But there is obviously a difference between acknowledging a community's diversity and knowing how, as a teacher, to deal with it. Certainly the solution is not to seek to have families conform to school expectations of what it is to be literate, but some family literacy programs give the impression that this is exactly what they are seeking to do. (The term 'family literacy' is applied here in a general sense to refer to school and community based programs that attempt to support parents as they help their children with school literacy practices.) In truth, the initiators of any family literacy initiative immediately put themselves in a position of unequal power and hence begin to shape the agenda (no doubt unwittingly) to reflect their personal beliefs and expectations. Since schools have typically been responsible for initiating family and intergenerational initiatives (which seek to influence the literacy of one generation by offering help in literacy to another generation, typically by offering adult literacy programs in poor communities in the hope that this will lead to higher literacy standards of children as well), it is not surprising that many such initiatives have been dominated by concerns with school literacy.

We need more collaborative initiatives which seek to develop partnerships between families and other institutions (typically pre-schools or schools) that offer educational support and aim to increase awareness by each party of the other's literacy practices and needs (Delgado-Gaitan 1992). Family and intergenerational initiatives often aim to enable specific students to cope more effectively with school, but are based on the assumption that this requires changes, adjustments and learning on the part of families, teachers and school administrators. As well, the content and nature of the initiatives devised are developed collaboratively, and reflect the needs of all parties. In contrast, deficit driven initiatives are typically tightly structured programs devised for other people and involve little choice in what is done within the program.

One way in which these basic cultural influences can be minimised is by involving parents more closely in school education. The purpose in breaking down the barriers between home and school is not to coerce, or even persuade, parents to take on the literacy definitions held by teachers. Rather, it is to enable both teachers and parents to understand the way each defines, values and uses literacy as part of cultural practices. Schooling can then be adjusted to meet the needs of families. Parents can also be given the opportunity to observe and understand the definitions of literacy that schools support, and that ultimately empower individuals to take their place in society.

Parents are not simply a minor part of the educational process, some variable to be considered and addressed. There seem to be many misconceptions of the parent's role in schooling (Cairney & Munsie 1995a). Some see parents as 'keepers' who ensure that children are well fed, loved, and groomed and sent to school to be adequately 'trained' each day. Others see parents as home based 'warders' ensuring that standards of behaviour are conformed to, good habits set, and school-related tasks completed. Another view seems to be that parents are meant to be compliant 'apprentices' working with children at school (as helpers), and at home on a range of simple but effective training tasks.

All of these views have several things in common. First, they assume that parents have only a limited responsibility in relation to their children as learners. Second, they assume that the school is the site of the 'main game.' Third, they offer parents only a token role in children's education (Cairney & Munsie 1995a).

In contrast to such views, there is an alternative, which sees learning as a social process and the home as both the beginning of and the foundation for learning. In this alternative view, parent participation and partnership are essential.

MOVING TOWARDS PARTNERSHIPS BETWEEN HOME AND SCHOOL

Many of the earliest attempts to recognise the relationship between home factors and school success were little more than parent education programs. Some of the most significant early initiatives in this area occurred in the United Kingdom. Two influential projects were the Belfield Reading Project (Hannon & Jackson 1987) and the Haringey Project (Tizard et al. 1982). These initiatives involved varied activities including home visitation, the provision of take home books, and instruction on how to read with and to children (see Hannon 1995 for more details).

Many of the early programs in the United Kingdom, the USA and Australia focused on the need to offer parents a limited range of reading strategies to use with their children. One of the most commonly used was the Paired Reading technique. This simple technique was first designed by Morgan (1976), was refined by Topping & Wolfendale (1985), and later appeared in other forms, for example the New Zealand strategy of Pause, Prompt and Praise (McNaughton et al. 1981). Essentially, it involves an older reader (often a parent) sitting next to the child to read along with them. At first the parent and child read together. Later the child takes over the reading by signalling to the adult and continuing reading alone until a mistake is made, at which time the adult begins reading along with the child again (see Cairney & Munsie 1995a for further details). This strategy became a core part of many early programs in the United Kingdom, Australia and New Zealand.

While some of these early programs showed encouraging outcomes, there was a degree of inconsistency (see Hannon 1995). For example, the Haringey Reading Project found that some of the children whose parents were involved in their program made significant gains in reading achievement (irrespective of reading ability), while others made little (Tizard et al. 1982).

In the United States a number of major initiatives were also developed in the 1980s and early 1990s. These have typically involved the design of programs that aimed to involve parents more fully in their children's literacy learning. Notable programs included the Kenan Model (Darling & Hayes 1990), 'Parents as Partners' (Edwards 1990), the Missouri 'Parents as Teachers' project (Winter & Rouse 1990), and more recently, 'Project EASE' (Jordan et al. 2000).

However, while considerable effort and money has been put into these programs, Nickse (1993) points out that evidence concerning their effectiveness is modest. Similarly, in a review of 261 family and community literacy initiatives in Australia, Cairney, Ruge, Buchanan, Lowe and Munsie (1995) found that: there has been little evaluation of the effectiveness of family and community literacy initiatives; the majority of programs were initiated by schools; and initiatives varied greatly in terms of content but offered little recognition of the richness of literacy practices within the wider community.

In more recent times, home–school literacy initiatives have been designed increasingly to develop a sense of partnership with parents and communities. In each case, an attempt has been made to recognise the significant cultural differences between communities, and to adapt programs accordingly. For example, 'Project FLAME' (Shanahan & Rodriguez-Brown 1993) was designed for Mexican-American and Puerto Rican families, and involves components such as 'parents as teachers', adult learning, summer institutes and community experiences. An interesting feature of the program is its ability to adapt to the specific cultural and educational characteristics of the families.

Programs like this, including the Brisbane Intergenerational Literacy Project and the Hubei Intergenerational Literacy Project (Campbell & Chen 1995) have increasingly begun to recognise that relationships between home and school achievement are complex, and hence require initiatives that do more than simply offer parents information.

In Australia, a similar pattern of development has occurred with early initiatives in the 1980s focusing primarily on the provision of fairly limited strategies for parents to apply at home, and specific programs designed to involve parents in the home tutoring of their children who were experiencing literacy problems. However, there have been a number of recent attempts to involve parents more fully in their children's literacy and learning through integrated programs that seek to involve parents, children and teachers. One example was 'Making A Difference' (Furniss 1991). This was an intensive program that required teachers to work with Year 7 students who were experiencing difficulties with literacy. Parents and community volunteers were trained by a 'Making A Difference' teacher to work with the students. Contained within the program was a volunteer Tutor manual, which prepared parents and community volunteers to work with students.

Other programs like 'Talk to a Literacy Learner' (TTALL) and 'Effective Partners in Secondary Literacy Learning' (EPISLL) (Cairney & Munsie 1992; 1993a; 1993b) have been designed to focus on parents but with the aim of involving teachers, students and their parents in a partnership that would help students cope more effectively with the literacy demands of schooling. The TTALL program was designed to involve parents more closely in the literacy development of their pre-school and primary school children. It attempts to achieve this through an eight-week series of 16 two-hour interactive workshops, each of which is integrated with observation of literacy learners, classroom visits, practice of strategies, and a variety of hometasks. The EPISLL program was an outgrowth of the TTALL program. It is designed for parents of secondary aged children, and was developed at the request of parents. Parents were involved at every stage of the development and implementation of this project. It consists of 11 two-hour sessions that cover topics as diverse as reading and writing across the curriculum, learning, study, coping with teenagers, research work, using computers, and accessing resources. Both these programs have been evaluated and have been shown to have positive outcomes for parents, students, teachers and schools (Cairney 1995c; Cairney & Munsie 1993a; 1995c).

A more recent extension to these programs, the 'Parent Partnership Program' (or PPP) (Cairney & Munsie 1995c), has been designed as a vehicle to enable parents who had completed the 'Talk to a Literacy Learner' (TTALL) program to share their insights and experiences with other parents. The PP Program was developed in response to requests from parents who had finished the TTALL program and who wanted to continue to explore their roles in children's literacy learning. The 'Parent Partnership Program' involves parents as tutors visiting other parents in their homes to talk to them about their experiences in the TTALL program, to offer them simple resources, and to demonstrate several specific strategies they can use to support their children. Participants choose four topics from a set designed for parents whose children are aged from birth to 12 years.

What is common to all these more recent initiatives around the world is the effort that is being made to respond to community language and culture and to develop genuine partnerships with community members, not simply seek to impose school literacy practices.

What should be evident from the more recent innovative attempts to develop family literacy initiatives is that parents are viewed as equal partners, and that there is an effort to develop a reciprocal relationship between home and school. But as I have already argued, these programs must not simply be 'tokenistic' attempts to involve parents in school practices. As Harry (1992) argues, parent initiatives must forge collaborative relationships that create mutual understanding between parents and teachers. Such a 'posture of reciprocity' is associated with a shift from the school to parents and the community.

In essence, what some of these educators are arguing for is not the transmission of knowledge from schools to parents and their children, but rather a process of reaching mutual consensus between the partners. This process of reaching shared understanding is what Vygotsky (1978) called 'intersubjectivity'. It involves a shared focus of attention and mutual understanding of any joint activity. This process requires reaching agreement on the selection of activities, the purpose of the program, and strategies for achieving them. Programs that are imposed by teachers on communities 'for their own good' obviously fail to meet the conditions necessary for intersubjectivity to occur. Such programs frequently end with no appreciable impact on teachers and the school, and little long-term benefit for parents and their children.

However, whilst accepting the difficulties that surround some (if not all) of the programs in Family Literacy, these initiatives have flourished because parents, teachers and educators recognise that they offer access to specific literacy practices that help students and parents cope with school literacy and learning.

Obviously, involving parents more closely in school education has the potential to develop new understanding by each party of the other's specific cultural practices, and lead to the type of 'reciprocity' that Harry (1992) argues is needed. Teachers and parents do need to understand the way each defines, values and uses literacy as part of cultural practices. Such mutual understanding offers the potential for schooling to be adjusted to meet the needs of families. As well, it offers parents the opportunity to observe and understand the literacy of schooling, a literacy that ultimately empowers individuals to take their place in society.

At the level of program initiatives, we need to continue to explore the use of the many programs that are in existence and to develop other initiatives that open up greater possibilities for the development of effective partnerships between schools and communities. These partnerships are characterised by:

Morgan, RTT 1976 ' "Paired Reading" Tuition: A preliminary Report on a Technique for Cases of Reading Deficit'. *Child Care, Health and Development*, 2, 13–28.

Mulhern, M 1995 *A Mexican–American child's home life and literacy learning from Kindergarten through second grade*. Paper presented at the American Educational Research Association Annual Meeting, San Francisco, April.

Nickse, R 1993 'A typology of family and intergenerational literacy programmes: Implications for evaluation'. *Viewpoints*, 15, 34–40.

Ogbu, J 1992 'Adaptation to minority status and impact on school success'. *Theory Into Practice*, 21, 4, 287–295.

Ogbu, J 1993 'Frameworks—Variability in minority school performance: A problem in search of an explanation'. In E Jacob & C Jordan (eds) *Minority education: Anthropological perspectives*. Ablex, Norwood, NJ.

Santa Barbara Classroom Discourse Group 1992 'Constructing literacy in classrooms: Literate action as social accomplishment'. In H Marshall (ed.), *Redefining Student Learning: Roots of Educational Change*. Ablex, Norwood, NJ.

Scribner, S & Cole, M 1981 *The psychology of literacy*. Harvard University Press, Cambridge, Mass.

Shanahan, T & Rodriguez-Brown, F 1993 *The theory and structure of a family literacy program for the Latino community*. Paper presented at the American Educational Research Association Conference, Atlanta (USA), 12–16 April.

Teale, WH 1986 'Home background and young children's literacy development'. In W Teale & E Sulzby (eds), *Emergent Literacy* 173–206. Ablex, Norwood, NJ.

Tizard, J, Schofield, W & Hewison, J 1982 'Collaboration between teachers and parents in assisting children's reading'. *British Journal of Educational Psychology*, 52, 1–15.

Topping, K & Wolfendale, S (eds) 1985 *Parental Involvement in Children's Reading*. Croom Helm, Beckenham (UK).

Vygotsky, L 1978 *Mind and society: The development of higher mental processes*. Harvard University Press, Cambridge, Mass.

Welch, AR & Freebody, P 1993 'Introduction: Explanations of the current international "Literacy Crises"'. In P Freebody & A Welch (eds) *Knowledge, culture & power: international perspectives on literacy as policy and practice*. Falmer Press, London.

Winter, M & Rouse, J 1990 'Fostering intergenerational literacy: The Missouri Parents as Teachers program'. *The Reading Teacher*, 43, 382–386.

Chapter 3

Children learning language

Rod Campbell and Carolyn Baker

Childhood is to be understood as a social construct ... it makes reference to a social status delineated by boundaries that vary through time and from society to society (and) which are incorporated within the social structure and thus manifested through and formative of certain typical forms of conduct. Childhood then always relates to a particular cultural setting

— *Jenks 1996:7*

A human language is a system of remarkable complexity. To come to know a human language would be an extraordinary intellectual achievement for a creature not specifically designed to accomplish this task. A normal child acquires this knowledge on relatively slight exposure and without specific training

— *Chomsky 1975:4*

INTRODUCTION

Children in most contemporary societies clearly have a special place afforded them, and this special place is supported by ideas of the formative character of the early years of life, the preciousness of childhood, and the responsibility of adults for particular forms of care. Children are for the most part protected from adult life, particularly the difficult and dangerous aspects of adult life. Children are provided for by schools, the law, the media, and by the entertainment and toy industries as a special category of person, citizen and consumer. While this may appear as 'natural' when observed from within our current affluent culture, as Jenks and a number of other sociologists and historians have shown, childhood is best understood as a social construct that rests on ideas and institutions particular to specific times and places (Jenks 1982 & 1996; Jackson 1982; James & Prout 1990; Waksler 1991; Corsaro 1997). This shift of perspective leads to interests in how childhood is constructed through ideas and institutions, and through children's interactions with adults.

In all societies, children learn to communicate because language functions for personal and social reasons. The constant and necessary interactions with adults and other children reinforce the development of language. However, a corollary outcome from the interactions is learning one's place in family relationships and in society.

The aims of this chapter are to:

- analyse the social positioning of childhood, and to study the organisation of that position through talk and interactions with adults

- discuss ways in which children become language learners and users in the various institutional contexts that are part of their everyday lives

- introduce contemporary theories of initial language and literacy acquisition

- consider the implications of these linguistic, psychological and sociological constructs for teaching and learning practices in modern classrooms and early childhood settings.

CHILDHOOD, CULTURE AND LANGUAGE

Children learn to talk in many ways but they only learn their language, and its functions for them as members of a society, in interactions with other adults and children in their families and communities. In the communications-driven society of the millennium changeover, children are also exposed to information and entertainment from many other sources.

Children learn about language in many ways, and each of these ways is determined by the nature of the relationships between the child and the particular cultural agent with whom the child interacts. Modern communication systems such as television and radio are essentially one-way, so children will interact with the language displayed by these forms of communication in ways that are qualitatively different from the ways they will interact with adults, older children or age peers.

Contributing greatly to children's development of language is the theory that a society and its members maintain regarding the young developing child. Jenks (1996:4) notes that one of the dominant theories in many modern societies and cultures is the kind of implicit or tacit theory that adults hold about children and their development. Jenks (1996:5) believes that our commonly-held traditions about children as members of a series of institutions such as families, childcare centres and schools cements a view of childhood as a uniform entity. There are many rituals associated with childhood and being a child, and by virtue of their widespread application, these rituals and the understandings arising from them are established and unquestioned.

Young children are raised in a variety of family and childcare arrangements where relatively few of the adults are trained for their roles as caregivers. By the age of five, children attend schools and pre-schools, where they are attended to by teachers trained for the purposes of teaching them. In all these institutional arrangements established and operated by adults for children, there is an underlying assumption that children are imperfect adults, needing the direction and guidance of adults. Jackson (1982:1) views the status of children in modern Western-style societies as a special category of people with their own needs, set apart by the institutional and cultural structures developed to care for them. Another long-maintained metaphor is to regard children as vessels to be moulded in their development towards ideal maturity. The notion is not a new one, and can be found in Plato (*The Republic*, p. 58). In relation to the roles established for children attending schools, Donald (1993:38) points out the fascinating paradox of individual freedom being achieved through submission to pedagogic norms.

Play is one of the important processes by which children learn for themselves about their world and their place in it. Play allows children to implement systems for obtaining mastery of actions, and for testing new ideas and words and expressions. Yet even play can become part of the community taken-for-granted experience of childhood institutions and processes. There is a 'continuous lived social practice of being a child' that supports a community attitude of complacency about the nature of childhood (Jenks 1996:7–10).

Culture is a social category (Jenks 1997:13). Culture at the level of local community and the individual is also the result of a community's interactions, developed in real situations to produce structures that have been negotiated in practice (Donald 1993:36). These structures may be tangible, such as the actual buildings of a school, and the provision of primers or reading schemes to assist the children to become literate. Such structures are designed to support contemporary notions of childhood.

The structures are also tacit, especially those structures associated with interaction and talk. Teachers ask questions to which they already know the answers, and the signal for this structure is usually a falling intonation as the teacher asks the question. Children are required to learn such tacit rules without being told; they respond respectfully, accepting the fact that the teacher will evaluate their response (Mehan 1979; Cazden 1988; Campbell 1996).

Such structures and customs are institutionalised everyday forms of interaction, but many become sites for contestation as societies change, and as the norms of cultural authority are transgressed and reworked (Donald 1993:37). For example, the view that adults should not intervene or interfere in the internal relationships of another family, particularly in larger and less cohesive communities, is currently being renegotiated. One of the contributing elements is our recent and overt recognition of the amount of child abuse that can be perpetrated by a small number of parents and surrogate-parents, and of our society's dawning recognition of the rights of the child.

The development and institutionalisation of statutory and regulatory sets of expectations of behaviours by adults towards children has implications for teachers and other professionally qualified persons who work with children. How adults interact with children will always be important, and the major and most obvious form of that interaction for the benefit of the child concerns the quality and style of the language used by the parties in a family, childcare centre or school. If children are to be put into a separated and dependent relationship in institutions such as childcare centres and schools, then we must ask about the benefit of the institution for the children. Children live in a social world (Jackson 1982:22), and all interactions in a social world imply particular obligations, including the question of where the child's interests are placed vis-a-vis those of the caregiver. Even positioned as a group set apart, children are assigned a social status, and a lowly one at that (Donald 1993:25).

CONVERSATIONAL PROPERTIES AND RIGHTS

Children's dependence upon adults is one of the taken-for-granted theories of childhood that position children as part of the invisible group par excellence in many contemporary societies (Qaurtrup 1990:78). Parents look after their children, and teachers employed in schools and childcare centres are aware of children and their needs; the teachers have to interact with the children every day. Yet even within these cultural institutions established exclusively for children's welfare and learning, adults can lose sight of the needs of individual children.

The effective use of language in interactions depends upon the development of more than the obvious expression of social and personal needs and wants in language. Of similar importance is the development of the tacit or implicit language of interpersonal relationships at any level. By focusing upon the implicit as they act unconsciously in their roles, parents and teachers give more than one message. The problem for some children emerges as they interpret the adult's response or evaluation of their utterances. Unnecessary or even unconscious non-acceptance or rejection of the young child's view can have consequences related to perceptions of the adult–child relationship. Naive realism is not only to be found in the immature perceptions of the young. Teachers and parents who fail to understand an individual child's perspective are also guilty of thinking that everyone else sees the world as they themselves do. The implications for children diagnosed with semantic–pragmatic syndrome become even more apparent. Children with this syndrome are often unable to understand the rules of conversation and appropriate interaction in context; the consequences of failure of adult sensitivity to their problems become acute for the child.

The problem of classroom Discourse for some children has been raised in Chapter 1, and that problem is exacerbated for the individual child by the implicit nature of classroom Discourse. The language that adults use in their everyday activities is also part of the taken-for-granted dimension of any social context. Speier (1976) has made the point that the usually unconscious theories (Painter 1985) which guide adult language-in-use are 'an ideological basis for adult interaction with children' (Speier 1976:99). The theory, or the ideology, is not contested by children. They are unaware of the system of language requirements used by adults, particularly when those implicit requirements are subtle. The request by a teacher to 'tell me a story' implies a recount of sorts with the noticeable beginning, middle and end of a topically-themed activity. The topic-associated string of events featured as stories by other cultures may not feature in the experience of the teacher (Michaels 1985).

Painter's impression of adult use of language in western middle class culture is that of language use for promoting explicit information about what things are, and about how and why things work (1985:39). Children enter this form of language interaction by asking questions or by making comment.

Hal: Giraffe garage. This one's a giraffe garage.
M.: Giraffes don't have garages, darling. Giraffes don't live in garages. Garages are only used for cars.

Many similar examples of the ways adults interpret and re-interpret experience for children have been provided by Tough (1977), Donaldson (1978), Heath (1983), Wells and Chang-Wells (1992), Corsaro (1997), Baker & Freebody (1989) and Danby & Baker (1998). Adult response to the observations of experience by the young child are important to the development of a child's thinking, language and self-concept. The following instance emerged some years ago. In the year Damien turned six, he and his younger brother each had infected tissues removed from the upper respiratory tract, necessitating an overnight stay in hospital. In the same year, his grandfather and great-grandmother each died in hospital after long periods of illness. Damien's observation, delivered with all the quiet reserve of someone expressing a view of life and death, was that 'Young people go to hospital to get better, and old people go to hospital to die'. No adult even remotely knowledgeable about the development of language for summing up general principles regarding experiences would respond with a statement about generalising from the particular. In everyday conversation, generalisations from individual experience are not challenged directly; to do so would be regarded as unfriendly and even rude. In the confines of institutional Discourses of places of higher learning, it is an acceptable and necessary part of discussion and debate to challenge generalisations. In the classroom for young children, the emergence of such a statement is a cause for quiet celebration on the part of a teacher that a child can use language so competently to express a view of life with such care.

Children get socialised or 'made into adults' by adults who teach culture, its norms, values, roles and behavioural systems (Speier 1976:98). This theory deserves contesting whenever it appears in those interactions when the child's half or portion of a conversation with an adult is not represented. The nature of children's cognitive and linguistic development is a culture of its own and deserves recognition as part of the social role that caring adults perform in working with children.

CHILDREN LEARNING LANGUAGE

If there is one feature or activity that sets people apart from all other living beings, then the development and use of an infinite variety of systems of communication is that singular feature. People in any society spend great amounts of time in communicative interaction with each other, continuously upgrading their skills and knowledge of language purposes and uses for the remainder of their lives. Language is more than just an important feature of living; language use defines persons as members of different social groups. Most noticeably, language defines the individual being.

The fact that language is simultaneously an individual and a social activity presents an immediate question for understanding how people develop language. Two snapshots showing children's uses of language in schools are presented below. Read each snapshot, then discuss or make notes in response to the following questions:

- Who exercises control in each scene?

- How does the adult in each scene assist each child's development of language?

- What do the children display about their knowledge and use of language?

Snapshot 3.1

Sarah is six years old. She is looking at a picture of children at a party. A teacher is asking questions of her.

T: What can you tell me about the picture.
S: They might be having a party?

T: Why do you think they are having a party.
S: Because they have party hats on, and they've got balloons and streamers up.
T: What do you think will happen next in the picture.
S: They might have a cake?
T: What do you like about birthday parties.
S: You get lollies, and you have a piece of cake, and you have a big play, and you invite your friends.
T: Why is it important to invite your friends.
S: Because, if you just had your family, and you were the only child, well, you wouldn't have anyone to play with. It wouldn't be very nice.

Notice that Sarah, who is in her first year of school, has already learned that when the teacher asks questions of her with a falling intonation, then the teacher is likely to be evaluating her response; Sarah responds with the rising intonation of the child under interrogation until she is more confident of the context. But there are other considerations here. How did Sarah learn to use the modal verbs 'might' and 'would'? How did she learn to use a double conditional clause so successfully in her last response? How did she learn to use language that relied upon her linguistic ability to talk about memories, experiences, feelings and relationships?

Snapshot 3.2

The following piece of writing was written by a nine-year-old boy in England some years ago. (I am indebted to Ruth and Jim Tracey for this sample.)

My father is on the broad side and the tall side.

My father was a hard working man and he had a lot of money. He was not fat or thin.

His age was about thirty years when he died, he had a good reputation, he is a married man. When he was in hospital I went to see him every Sunday afternoon. I asked him how he was getting on, he told me he was getting a lot better. My father was very kind to me and gave me and my cousins football cards. He likes doing woodwork, my father, for me, and he likes a little game of cards now and then or a game of darts. He chops the wood and saws the planks and he is a handsome man but he is dead.

He worked at the rubber works before he died.

The writer displays a wide range of understandings about the expression of a highly emotional personal experience. He has provided details about his father that let us know what he looked like, what he liked and how he interacted with his son. The writer has also created a character of himself by his choices of details about his father, and about his recall of their relationship. The text indicates many aspects of social mores that the writer sees as important. Yet consider how the writer has developed the language skills to be able to present so much information in such a small piece of writing. (There is another consideration, and this has implications for establishing positive classroom interactions to assist learning. The teacher's handwritten response at the end of the piece of writing is: 'Tenses; you keep mixing past and present'.)

As children develop, they display many interesting features of their language and its development. As you listen to them more attentively, you will be able to discern the most human of all activities, language use, and be able to gather further insights into the mix of individual and cultural knowledge that is available in any language display.

LANGUAGE: LEARNED, ACQUIRED OR DEVELOPED?
Behaviourism: language is learned

This theory emerged from the years of applying the Associationist theories of psychology to detailed studies of children's language development. The basic theory states that people learn because they associate the learned item with something from their earlier experience. By the middle of the twentieth century, this theory of learning by association had been changed among North American psychologists to behaviourism or learning theory. BF Skinner pronounced the theory that language is learned in his authoritative publication *Verbal Learning* in 1957. The behaviourist syllogism often used by his disciples goes like this: *Language is behaviour; behaviour is learned; therefore, language is learned.*

The process by which children learn their language is claimed to be a result of the application of operant conditioning; children are stimulated to imitate the language used by other language users in their environment. The response of these other people reinforces the child's use of language. For example, Damien (age 17 months) said 'big puppy' as he pointed to a cow. His parents told him that the large animal was really a cow, and he repeated the word. His success in learning the new word was rewarded by the parents; they showed pleasure in Damien's vocabulary development.

What can be observed in this interaction is the operant conditioning (stimulus–organism–response) model of BF Skinner. The cows provide a stimulus that is related to the experience of the organism (Damien) whose response (language behaviour) is accepted, then conditioned to approximate the correct word for the particular animal.

Behaviourists support their understanding of the nature of learning by invoking this example of the theory of imitation-reinforcement. The process of language learning and teaching is demonstrated when a child says something that is not the same as the accepted use, is given a model to copy, and by a series of successive approximations, the child is reinforced to learn the appropriate expression. For example, a child says 'tato'; the adult caregiver will then say 'potato'; the child now has the continuous attention of a willingly compliant adult, and repeats the word, gradually getting closer to the accepted pronunciation. For most young children, the attention of an adult is a reward system in itself, and providing other rewards such as sweets is neither necessary nor appropriate.

There is plenty of evidence in all language environments to support the theory that children learn language because the members of their environment provide models for them to copy. Those members also provide systems of reinforcement that support the development of language. Incorrect and inappropriate forms of language are not reinforced while desired ones are reinforced and praised in some way. However, there are a number of unsolvable problems inherent in this simplistic theory.

Most obviously, the behaviourist theory cannot account for the rapid rate of development in children's language. By the age of four or five, almost all children in any society can use language effectively, and have learned almost all the grammatical and syntactic information required to make meaning in their native or first language. The children have also developed a vocabulary that grows exponentially from their second year of life. It is significant that in those two or three years from about age two, children will develop almost half of their everyday working vocabulary. They will spend the rest of their lives learning the other half, as well as learning the specific vocabularies of their developing areas of interest and adult expertise. But more significantly, apart from some of the more involved aspects of grammar, the children have learned almost all there is to know about the grammars of their first language. The written language and other symbolic systems present similar yet different issues for learners.

To assume or theorise that children have developed so much knowledge and skill about their language through repeated interactions with enabling adults about every item of language is a quantitatively unrealistic assumption. There may be an argument for transference of learning, and the 'big puppy' example suggests that possibility. But there are too many separate language items that are learned too quickly by very young children. Given that one of the tenets of hard-core behaviourism is the notion that performance (what is on display) is the only indicator of the child's ability, then the performance demonstrated by the child far exceeds the input of the adults in the environment. That is, the child has greater competence for learning and learning language than can be demonstrated by performance alone.

Skinner's theory (1957) did not have long to wait for a response to this and other knotty problems about understanding the development of language in young children.

Nativism: language is acquired

The response emerged from Noam Chomsky and a legion of developmental linguists including McNeil (1970) and Slobin (1971). Their theories were not new, but then neither were the theories espoused by the behaviourists. Our first record of the nature–nurture debate applied to language acquisition and learning is to be found in Plato's *Cratylus*.

There is easily locatable evidence to show that children actually develop or generate their own rules for using language. 'My chair is broked', used by a five-year-old in a retelling of the famous *Three Bears* story, is not an expression that adults use. Children around four to six years of age are renowned for generating new rules for their language, and interestingly, these rules have a definable logic. For example, the irregular verbs in English do not add 'ed' to the present tense form to make the past tense. We can educate to be educated, but we teach to be taught, and we catch fish to eat and then talk about the fish we caught and ate. Teachers and caregivers of young children are constantly reminded of the young child's ability to generate little rules that are logically based upon the apparent rules of the making of the past tense of regular verbs in English. Yet no adult would seriously dream of stating the grammatical rule to a child. The usual evaluative response by the adult is to state the correct form, and interestingly, the young child will acknowledge this correction but not bother to use it.

So how do children have this facility for generating rules for the language they are learning and using to learn as they learn to use it? Chomsky (1965) suggests that the human infant is essentially an innate linguist, born with the ability to acquire the language used in its environment. He posited a theory of generative grammar, composed of language universals or deep structures that underpin all languages. Through a series of transformations, children derive all the rules that are unique to their first language or mother tongue (Tough 1977:17). The capacity of young children to initiate the construction of the rules of the language of their culture is clearly demonstrated, and scientific observation of the developing outcomes of that capacity supports the notion of the young child as a natural language learner. McNeil, one of the many linguists to work with Chomsky, suggested that children are born with a language acquisition device (LAD).

Such a theory, one that views children as creating language through their own innate and thinking capacities, is also essentially cognitivist. Children are thinking about language, relating meaning across different contexts (Painter 1998) in a manner described by Donaldson (1978) as disembedding language. The ability to detach language from meaning and function, that is, to move from using language instrumentally to using language as the object of its own use, is a peculiarly human ability. When young children ask about meanings and play with words, then they are demonstrating the use of language to 'conquer the immediate environment' (Donaldson 1978:133). Painter (1998) notes that the ability to relate one piece of language with another is to have a technique for learning at a potentially much greater speed than it is possible from observing the repeated use of words in local contexts.

But what has not been highlighted sufficiently in this discussion so far is the role of others in the development of children's language. Obviously, the environment in which children acquire their first language (and in many areas in the world, their first languages) is one that relies upon the assistance of adults. It is the much-studied importance of the role of parents and other adults that provides the environment in which children learn to talk and to mean. Bruner (1983) popularised the term language acquisition support system (LASS) in an effective attempt to highlight the importance of the social contribution to the development of language.

Interactionism: language is developed

There are many writers who have contributed to the theory that language is developed in social contexts in which the child actively initiates language interactions. The child later internalises the consequences of language use, internally initiating the processes whereby language is developed. Chief among these theorists is Vygotsky, whose seminal books *Thought and Language* and *Mind in Society* appeared in English in 1962 and 1978 respectively. Vygotsky had developed and written his ideas about language and learning in the intellectual, social and political ferment that permeated Russia in the 1920s. He died in 1934, but his influence on education internationally since the publication of *Mind in Society* has been both widespread and profound.

One of the many contributions Vygotsky has made to learning theories is his concept of a Zone of Proximal Development, that range of learning beyond what the child knows and understands, yet not so far away as to be beyond understanding. In education, the Zone of Proximal Development has been likened to the 'teachable moment', that time when the teacher realises that the child can learn a concept that can be grasped and learned with the support of a knowledgeable adult. What is so powerful about this apparently simple concept is the role of the knowledgeable adult.

Children use language because it gets results, and they develop their language abilities because language functions to get things, as well as functioning to get things done. It was Halliday who provided a coherent view of children's development of language when he published his model of the seven functions of language (1975). Although these functions are viewed in terms of the child's development of meaning, language development relies upon the active and supportive assistance of adults in all of the social contexts that represent the culture in which the child is growing.

LANGUAGE FUNCTIONS
Instrumental—the 'I want' function

Language is used to get things, to satisfy personal needs.

> David (aged 14 months) points to the refrigerator door and says 'Door'. (His favourite yoghurt is kept there.)

Regulatory—the 'Do as I tell you' function

Language is used to control the behaviour of others.

> Miriam says 'Daddy push', telling her father to push her along on her little tricycle.

Interactional—the 'Me and you' function

Language is used to begin or maintain interactions.

> 'Hello,' said Catherine, holding out her doll.

Personal—the 'Here I come' function

Language is used to express awareness of self; personal feelings.

> Andrew's room. Be where! Keep out!
> (Five-year-old Andrew's written warning to his older brother, with a hint of the regulatory function.)

Heuristic—the 'Tell me why' function

Language is used to find information and names, to seek knowledge, and to learn the how and why of people, things and events.

> John, aged four: 'Why don't the stars fall out of the sky?'

Imaginative—the 'Let's pretend' function

Language is used to create new worlds; used in and learned from stories.

> 'I'm He Man.' (Role play writing from Brad, aged six.)

Informative—the 'I've got something to tell you' function

Language is used to communicate information and express propositions.

> Mary, aged six: 'What did one ghost say to the other ghost?'
> 'Don't spook till you're spooken to.'

The value of this model of children's development of language is its emphasis upon the need for language to be developed in social contexts, thereby foregrounding the notion that language is essentially a social construct. Many students have thought that there was a further age-related developmental dimension to this model of development of language function, but observation of young children using language will show that many of the later functions emerge almost simultaneously. Certainly, there is no suggestion that any function disappears with age. All functions are further developed in social contexts in the manner suggested by Vygotsky, Halliday and Bruner.

The fascinating outcome of five years of living in a community of people who are generally supportive of the children's development is an impressive list of linguistic and social achievements. Carr (1999), Hymes (1972), Tough (1977) and Painter (1998) have supplied some details for the following list, and the list is not exhaustive. Between the ages of five and six years, most children display almost all, if not all, of the following linguistic and related cognitive abilities. The children:

- have a vocabulary of 4000–5000 words
- use talk to further their own learning
- can detach language from its function
- use talk to express feelings and opinions
- use talk for a range of purposes
- have control of most grammatical patterns
- use language for negotiating with/manipulating others
- adjust talk to suit context
- know when and how to join a conversation
- can talk about talk
- know the cultural rules for talking to different people
- have adult-like or near adult-like pronunciation
- derive pleasure from language
- use gestures, eye contact, intonation and pausing
- use the language of role and relationship
- make comparisons; state conditions; express reasons
- reflect on the meaning of experience
- draw inferences, and state generalisations and principles
- use language to discuss and apply rules
- develop schema for understanding relationships, connecting ideas learning connotations and expanding meanings
- become more verbally explicit
- use language to take up information beyond their own experiences

- demonstrate reflective awareness

- develop awareness of multiple meanings in written and spoken texts.

LEARNING LANGUAGE: CREATING OPTIMUM CONDITIONS

Children learn language and learn to learn because they have access to and get the attention of supportive adults and older siblings and peers. As mentioned earlier, the language outcomes demonstrated by children show that children and their adult caregivers are remarkably successful. The important question for teachers and parents concerns the processes whereby learning and language are developed within the language acquisition support system of the family, childcare centre, community and school. It is within these related systems of language use and support that children obtain the information and experiences that provide the input for internalising language and learning.

Holdaway (1979:102), following earlier writers on language and learning, discussed models for language and learning and teaching that called for teachers to attend to 'a range of problem-solving tasks integrating many skills in every moment of activity, and … the major task of teaching is to induce healthy activity in language, and to intervene in natural ways to sustain and clarify that activity'. Holdaway then explains the conditions under which teachers work with children, respecting the efforts which children make as approximations, but always to respect what the children bring to their own learning, and to respect 'the stumbling efforts of early performance' (1979:103).

Understanding and respecting the knowledge that children bring to language and learning is central to working and interacting with all children, regardless of the individual mix of ability, language background or special needs that any child may have.

A few years later, Cambourne presented his model of the conditions that support children's learning, and in particular those conditions which support learning language and literacy. His model of learning has appeared in a number of forms, but it is most clearly demonstrated in his 1988 book on teaching language, *The Whole Story*. In summary, the conditions for language learning are:

Immersion

Learners need to be immersed in supportive environments that provide resources and opportunities for interaction with knowledgeable others.

Demonstration

Learners need to observe and be given many demonstrations of learning, use of language and literacy. The knowledgeable others need to be conscious of what they are modelling for children.

Engagement

Many teachers include this as a condition together with Cambourne's original seven conditions. The value of immersion and demonstration emerges powerfully when the learners are actively engaged in their environment of resources and people.

Expectation

Teachers and caregivers, the knowledgeable others, expect that learners will learn. 'We achieve what we expect to achieve' (Cambourne 1988:33).

Working with learners is based upon activities that the child is capable of learning with adult support within the zone of proximal development. Learning activities are planned so that positive learning outcomes are expected; unreasonable and unrealistic expectations are never present.

Responsibility

Learners need to be given opportunities to make their own decisions about learning; to be given time to realise how the various bits of information go together to help solve a problem; to take responsibility for their learning; and to take responsibility to seek assistance with their learning.

Use

'Learners need time to use, employ and practise their developing control of learning in functional, realistic and non-artificial ways' (Cambourne 1988:33). Practice also requires access to the support of teachers and other adults.

Approximation

Teachers and parents respect the 'stumbling efforts of early performance' (Holdaway 1979:103). Learners' efforts are seen as approximations of the desired models, and their efforts with their learning are respected rather than controlled by just 'fixing the error'.

Response

Learners must be given feedback that is relevant, timely, appropriate, non-threatening, and readily available with no strings attached (Cambourne 1988:33).

The approach to teaching and learning which allows the operation of these conditions for learning is one that respects learners and their capabilities and potential. It assumes that all children are interested in improving their language and understanding of the symbol systems of their world. Teachers who work with learners therefore observe and interpret positively what learners bring to every learning opportunity. These teachers provide opportunities to support learners by modelling what is to be learned within a program that empowers learners to take responsibility for their own learning activity. Instruction is provided as required and as requested, and always in a manner that respects the realistic attempts of the learners.

Summary

Learning one's first language is the foremost and most successfully undertaken intellectual task of the human person; and the sheer quantity and quality of what young children learn in their first few years of life is a tribute to their learning capacities, to their potential, and to the efforts of the adults who have supported their learning of language. At the same time, the children have acquired many dimensions of learning itself. Teachers and parents, especially those who are aware of the processes whereby this learning has been so successful, will be wary of teaching approaches that regard the child as an empty vessel or little mug into which all knowledge can be poured from the big jug of the teacher.

So how is formality, status and power organised by talk? And for the benefit of children in learning and care institutions, how are such dimensions organised? Teachers generally operate from their stated concern to maintain control of the learning activities in a classroom of 25 or more children (Campbell 1996). But teachers also operate from a stated concern for the welfare and benefit of the children. Possible contest between control and sensitivity to individual learning can be avoided when the teacher's focus is a professional one of awareness of the nature of language development and use.

Rather, knowledgeable adults not only know what learners need to know; such teachers also know how learners learn the symbol systems of spoken and written language, and all of the information that accompanies using language to learn about people and objects in the environment. Such teachers weld the theories of Vygotsky, Cambourne, Halliday, Holdaway, Heath, Chomsky and Skinner into programs of classroom interaction that support and respect all learners.

Activities

1. **Discuss the following pieces of children's spoken and written language, noting which functions of language are being displayed. Use Halliday's model of functions of language as a guide. In some instances, you will need to create a context to support your perception.**

   1. Don't pull my hair or kick me!
   2. Mum's telling the children to go out and play and not to hit the cat. And the dad's going to wait a bit. (Child describing a picture; Tough 1977:97.)
   3. Get out; get out of the way. It's going to crash. (Tough 1977:18.)
   4. Why do the wheels go round?

5. There is only six pepel alowd to play in the room. No more than six pepel.
6. Wanted to swap: A geometry set for a football.
7. People don't like you if you take their things.
8. Steven: I wonder where you get tiger food.
   Big Bro: Tigers eat meat.
   Mother: (teasing) Give it a little boy.
   Steven: (2.4 seconds later) Is a boy meat? (Painter 1998.)
9. I've got one of those … but it's not like that one. Mine's not got an Indian painted on it like that.

2. **Look at photos in old family albums and see where the young children are actually/literally positioned in whole-family and adult–child group photographs. Use your own childhood photos.**

Annotated bibliography

Don Holdaway 1979 *The foundations of literacy*. Ashton Scholastic, Sydney.
The text is an old one, but has not dated. Holdaway provides one of the most succinct introductions into the range of theories underpinning the classroom reading program, and offers a system of teaching that supports and respects learners. He clearly shows how and where the role of the teacher shifts from supporter to instructor/teacher and back again. The book describes approaches to teaching literacy such as shared book reading, language experience approach, and the teaching of phonic knowledge.

Corsaro, WA 1997 *The sociology of childhood*. Pine Forge Press, Thousand Oaks, California.
Corsaro provides readers with a well-presented discussion about the nature of childhood, drawing upon historical, cross-cultural, developmental and ethnographic approaches to his consideration of the socialisation of children. Short case studies and vignettes are provided as examples. The book is useful to both undergraduate and postgraduate students as a starting point for reading. An added bonus is provided by the writer's careful analysis of observations and of the literature he reviews.

Shirley Brice Heath 1983 *Ways with words*. Cambridge University Press, Cambridge, UK.
One of the most outstanding books in language studies using ethnography as a major research tool. Heath lived in three separate communities in the western parts of Carolina, and presents her findings and interpretations of language use and multiple literacy resources and use in Maintown (middle class), Roadville (white, working class Bible-belt), and Trackton (working class African–American). The results provide teachers and language researchers with techniques and insights into understanding how language is used in different communities. The implications for teaching will never be dated.

References

Bruner, J 1983 *Child's talk*. Norton, NY.

Baker, CD & Freebody, P 1989 *Children's First School Books: Introductions to the culture of literacy*. Blackwell, London.

Cambourne, B 1988 *The whole story*. Scholastic, Auckland.

Campbell, R 1996 *Teaching grammar*. Unpublished PhD Thesis. University of Queensland, Brisbane.

Carr, J 1999 [Personal correspondence].

Cazden, CB 1988 *Classroom discourse*. Heinemann, Portsmouth, NH.

Chomsky, N 1965 *Aspects of the theory of syntax*. MIT Press, Cambridge, Mass.

Chomsky, N 1975 *Reflections on language*. Pantheon, NY.

Corsaro, W 1997 *The sociology of childhood*. Pine Forge Press, Thousand Oaks, CA.

Danby, S, & Baker, CD 1998 ' "What's the problem?": Restoring social order in the preschool classroom'. In I Hutchby & J Moran-Ellis (eds) *Children and Social Competence: Arenas of Action*. Falmer Press, London.

Donald, J 1993 'The natural man and the virtuous woman: Reproducing citizens'. In C Jenks (ed.) *Cultural reproduction*. Routledge, London, 36–54.

Donaldson, M 1978 *Children's minds*. Fontana, London.

Halliday, MAK 1975 *Learning how to mean: Explorations in the development of language*. Edward Arnold, London.

Heath, SB 1983 *Ways with words*. Cambridge University Press, Cambridge, UK.

Holdaway, D 1979 *The foundations of literacy*. Ashton Scholastic, Sydney.

Hymes, D 1972 'Models of the interaction of language and social life'. In JJ Gumperz & D Hymes (eds) *Directions in Sociolinguistics*. Holt, Rinehart & Winston, NY, 35–71.

Jackson, S 1982 *Childhood and sexuality*. Basil Blackwell, Oxford.

James, A & Prout, A (eds) 1990 *Constructing and reconstructing childhood*. Falmer, London.

Jenks, C 1982 *The Sociology of Childhood*. Batsford, London.

Jenks, C 1996 *Childhood*. Falmer, London.

Jenks, C 1997 *Culture*. Falmer, London.

McNeil, D 1970 *The acquisition of language*. Harper & Row, NY.

Mehan, H 1979 *Learning lessons: Social organisation in the classroom*. Harvard University Press, Cambridge, Mass.

Michaels, S 1985 'Hearing the connections in children's oral and written discourse'. *Journal of Education*, 167:1:36–56.

Painter, C 1985 *Learning the mother tongue*. Deakin University Press, Geelong, Vic.

Painter, C 1998 'Preparing for school: Developing a semantic style for educational knowledge'. In F Christie (ed.) *Pedagogy and the shaping of consciousness*. Cassell, London.

Plato (n.d.) *The Republic*, trans. AD Lindsay. Heron Books, London.

Qaurtrup, J 1990 'A voice for children in statistical and social accounting: A plea for children's rights to be heard'. In A James & A Prout (eds) *Constructing and reconstructing childhood*. Falmer, London, 78–98.

Skinner, BF 1957 *Verbal learning*. Appleton-Century-Crofts, NY.

Slobin, D 1971 *Psycholinguistics*. Scott, Foresman, Springfield, Ill.

Speier, M 1976 'The child as conversationalist: Some culture contact features of conversational inter-actions between adults and children'. In M Hammersley & P Woods (eds) *The process of schooling*. Routledge & Kegan Paul, London, 98–103.

Tough, J 1977 *The development of meaning*. Allen & Unwin, London.

Vygotsky, LS 1962 *Thought and language*. Cambridge University Press, Cambridge, Mass.

Vygotsky, LS 1978 *Mind in society*. Harvard University Press, Cambridge, Mass.

Waksler, F (ed.) 1991 *Studying the Worlds of Children: Sociological Readings*. Falmer Press, London.

Wells, G & Chang-Wells, GL 1992 *Constructing Knowledge Together: Classrooms as Centres of Enquiry and Literacy*. Heinemann, Portsmouth, NH.

Chapter 4

Oracy: the cornerstone of effective teaching and learning

Rod Campbell and Nicole King

> *Teachers are explorers. As they explore the world and the lives of their students, they cast lines to different ways of thinking. Teaching is often bridge-building; beginning on one shore with the knowledge, experience, know-how and interests of the student, the teacher moves towards broader horizons and deeper ways of knowing.*
>
> — *Ayers 1993:66*

THIS CHAPTER AIMS TO:

- enhance appreciation of the importance of oracy for communication, teaching and learning in the classroom

- explore the links between students' funds of knowledge and teachers' skills in the development of successful classroom interactions

- provide frameworks to support continuity between the background experiences of diverse learners and language use in the classroom

- provide models for using oracy effectively in the classroom.

INTRODUCTION

A crucial dimension for learning in the classroom is the nature of the relationship between teacher and students, and this relationship is characterised by forms of language interaction operating between and among teachers and students.

However, language is a medium used within all cultures to aid communication, confusion and conflict equally, if not concurrently. Given the universal practice of oracy in the home, in society and consequently in the classroom, teachers as professional educators must also be very knowledgeable about the use of spoken language as an implicit barrier and an explicit bridge to learning in their classrooms.

Communication uses symbols in order to create a medium for expression of ideas and feelings, but the act of sharing that expression also involves understanding, otherwise there is no communication. Hence, language is a social activity, one where individuals and groups from and within different cultures share meaning. If one individual or group is unable to understand the communication systems in place in the classroom, that individual or group quickly becomes alienated and excluded from the classroom learning experience. To develop the notion stated in Chapter 1, schools are places from which children are unable to escape, and the problems for some children are compounded if the discourse processes of the classroom are not designed to accommodate all the children.

When there is continuity, and even congruence, between children's competence with the language, Discourses and the requirements of formal education in formal learning settings, then the match between home language and home expectations fits more closely with the language and expectations of the school. However, should there be discontinuity between home and school, and the teachers are unable to accommodate and use the child's language and funds of knowledge, then the learning experiences of that child at school are in jeopardy. The differences and failure to be accommodated within the learning contexts of the school become even more problematic, and the child is placed into a form of double jeopardy. Not only is the school unable to assist, the child is unable to escape.

One of the distinguishing features of school language is the fact that teachers' talk is not always reliant upon the immediate context. Donaldson (1978) has explored the notion of disembedded thinking, one of the most important requirements of learning in a formal setting. Schooling values the ability to use language to talk about things in other contexts. Indeed, education has often been a site for vicarious learning, mediated by the interpretations of the syllabus committees, the textbook writers and the teachers. And vicarious learning is centred on the abilities and the attitudes necessary for learning about peoples, places, events and ideas mediated by others. Human language is admirably suited for talking about concepts; the entire structure of syntactic systems, carried by their dependence on grammatical function word classes and word order, verb tenses and vocabularies, lends itself to disembedded thinking and abstract conceptualisations.

Problems arise for many students whose backgrounds, interests, language use systems and home support systems do not gel with those dimensions of the school system and with teachers' values and attitudes. Sometimes, lack of information about the students' life-worlds becomes the barrier to teachers' appreciation of the students' references to their own experiences.

Therefore, school culture, language, teacher talk and classroom Discourse practices are not always in tune with those of many students, and do not occur within a familiar setting and routines in the same ways that home language uses do. In many classrooms, teachers do most of the talk, often talking to large groups of students. This type of talk differs markedly from the turn-taking ebb-and-flow of conversation in a one-to-one adult to child interaction. In the school setting, the teacher controls the topic and the direction of talk, and the students have few opportunities to initiate conversation and discussion. At home, opportunities have always existed for adults to provide for and respond to child-initiated talk.

If the teacher is to be able to cast lines to different ways of thinking, then the exploration metaphor presented by Ayers also reflects the lines that each child brings to the classroom shores. Different ways of thinking are brought by the children to the classroom, and the teacher's classroom-based activities need to take the children's language and thinking into new realms of communication, higher-level thinking and deeper intellectual quality. But in order for the children's experiences to be used for further learning, teachers have the especially challenging task of moving the children's oracy into the broader spectrum of public language. In effect, there are many children for whom the teacher must construct a bridge from home language to public language while simultaneously building bridges for oracy to contribute to the learning of each child.

ORACY

Oracy is the capacity to express oneself in speech, fluently and appropriately to setting; and fluent expression is the product of knowledge, experience, positive self-esteem and a supportive learning environment. Familiarity with the expectations of how language is coded and used in that learning environment is also vital for success.

Classroom oracy or talk is the significant element in students' learning; it is both the form in which learning is presented and delivered, and the vehicle by which learning is interpreted. Oracy is the pathway to solid success as a learner, and the means of feeling success as a learner. Learners must be communicators and thinkers before they can be effective readers and writers.

It is no small wonder that, as teachers, we tend to assume that written language is the only respectable medium through which to learn. But speech comes first, by some millions of years; and it comes first in our life history as individuals. We may have learnt to read and write, but we still go on talking and listening; and we still go on learning by talking and listening (Halliday 1985:vii).

Competency with oracy ensures that learners can:

- take some responsibility to initiate and direct their own learning
- select options and outcomes
- make inferences
- self-question and monitor their own learning
- work collaboratively with peers
- reflect on the learning journey.

The most effective approach to involving students in developing oracy skills is by incorporating their interests and experiences within the matrices of contemporary classroom planning. But as discussed in the introduction to this chapter and in Chapter 1, the most important elements in the development of students' classroom participation are the students and the funds of knowledge they bring with them, gained from their experience. Teachers who involve student talking and listening around interesting and challenging topics and themes also provide the vehicle for developing student thinking, problem-solving and creativity.

METACOGNITION

Metacognition refers to the higher-order thinking processes involved in understanding and applying knowledge. A commonsense definition is the ability to think about thinking. Metacognition allows learners to use the substance and content of an area of knowledge, and this use is demonstrated in the ability to articulate that knowledge with confidence. It is also demonstrated in the ability to manipulate knowledge in new ways, to make novel connections and links with established systems of thinking.

Metacognition is developed when learners are encouraged, supported and enabled to take responsibility for the planning and pacing of, and active engagement with, their own learning. Metacognitive abilities are further developed as learners reflect about their learning, demonstrating the skills of the self-directed learner.

Part of the active learning cycle of the self-directed and reflective learner is increased risk-taking during classroom learning activities. Successful risk-taking supports self-esteem as a learner; the learner is able to initiate and negotiate learning within the parameters of the interactive learning environment established by the teacher. Such a negotiated approach to curriculum implementation respects and encourages children's contributions as participating in collaborative learning.

Teachers can thus facilitate metacognitive possibilities by orchestrating the session timetable for literacy, mathematics, art and other learning areas into larger blocks of time. Within such allocations of time, there are opportunities for focused learning episodes for those elements that require further instruction and learning. There are also opportunities for students to have time to practise learning by undertaking contracted tasks and in rotational group work. Reflective talk time at the end of the session allows learners to explore and consolidate their learning experiences collectively and individually, thus supporting metacognitive opportunities.

TEACHER TALK: BRIDGES AND BARRIERS

Barriers: issues concerning teacher talk in the classroom

The role of the teacher is to assist students to learn the cueing systems and skills needed to participate in classroom discussion and learning. Difficulties and inequalities emerge when the teacher is unaware of the needs of the children, and of the funds of knowledge that each child brings to the classroom. The difficulties for student learning are compounded when the teacher controls the learning in the classroom with too great a focus on curriculum-based outcomes rather than providing assistance for the students to learn how to learn.

Of course, there are elements of learning the curriculum that are necessary before real discussion and reflection on learning takes place; learners need to have a foundation upon which to build the concepts for learning in a particular curriculum area. But teachers can help students to learn how to learn, to develop and use the metacognitive capacities needed to understand and use information to acquire knowledge. The most effective teaching is that which assists learners to make connections between existing knowledge and the acquisition of new knowledge.

Freebody et al. (1995) have offered a taxonomy of troubles or difficulties that teachers can create for students. The central issue concerns the nature of the interactions between teacher and students, and the unconscious maintenance of a program of 'interactive trouble' of various kinds. Interactive trouble occurs when teacher's questioning is focused upon 'getting the one correct answer', usually the one in the teacher's head and which the students are trying to locate. The distinguishing feature of this activity is carried by the basic instructional sequence of Initiation–Response–Evaluation (Mehan 1979; Cazden 1988; Perrott 1988; Campbell 1996). Students quickly learn that whenever the teacher asks a question (*initiating* the classroom discourse practice of instruction by questioning) with a falling intonation, then the teacher has an answer in mind. The student *response* is often made with a rising intonation, as the students search for the answer they believe the teacher wants them to provide. The sequence is completed with the teacher's *evaluation* of the student response, usually a positive 'yes' or a 'good try' type of evaluation.

Freebody et al. (1995) classified the resulting troubles for students under the following headings:

1. **Epistemological trouble** arises when the knowledge being sought or the classroom discourse strategies are not shared by both teacher and students. In the regular classroom there are students with diverse cultural and knowledge backgrounds, and so the IRE sequence immediately leads to some of the students not knowing what the lesson is about.

2. **Organisational trouble** occurs in the classroom lesson when the responses of some students may be appropriate in response to the questions asked, but which the teacher has to 'put aside' or 'on hold' because of the nature of the task being undertaken and the teacher's focus on the lesson. Semantic maps or concept webs or graphic organisers are arguably one of the best strategies for making the learning task explicit, yet these strategies can become classic instances of organisational trouble, compounded by the use of questions designed to get student thinking 'on to the same track' as that of the teacher.

3. **Reasoning trouble** emerges when the teacher is unable to use student responses as sources of information into the thinking and reasoning of the other students. When students have their ideas and contributions 'put aside', they are less likely to offer further ideas. The trouble is particularly damaging where the quality and length of the student's response indicates that the student has thought about the response.

4. **Pedagogical trouble** is a common occurrence, brought about by the teacher's lack of clarity in explaining the requirements of the lesson or activity, and often compounded by student inattention when the explanation is being given. The result is student inability to become involved in the lesson, particularly when the student has not offered any responses for some minutes and is suddenly asked to do so.

5. **Relational trouble** appears regularly when the teacher shifts expectations from correct answers to seeking other ideas and responses, to speculation, to understanding humour or to any of a number of shifts that happen during a lesson. The students need time (that is, many weeks) to get to understand the cues the teacher uses as the lesson proceeds. As students are learning how to learn from the teacher in the learning-controlled instructional sequence, there are many opportunities for unintended learning outcomes.

6. **Stylistic trouble** results from the differences between the teacher's background and that of the students. The teacher's language style (the ways words are chosen and used in particular linguistic structures) presents troubles for a significant number of students in many classrooms. The trouble is particularly damaging for the learning and self-esteem of students with different language and cultural backgrounds.

Therefore, the necessary practice of using oral language as the central element of classroom instruction and learning presents teachers and students with a number of issues, and it is the teacher who needs to address these issues. The teacher who relies upon traditional classroom discourse practices and basic instructional sequences characteristic of these practices, has a number of issues to address before there can be real learning all of the time for all of the students in the classroom.

Bridges: guidelines for teacher talk in the classroom

A number of teachers use frameworks established upon principles that value the individual, that build upon the funds of knowledge and experience, and therefore the strengths of learners, that eliminate barriers to learning, and that construct all the students and the teacher as learners together. The classroom then represents a practical demonstration of practices that reflect principles of effective learning and teaching:

- consistency in managing students' contributions to classroom interactions
- cueing systems for interactions are explicitly taught and practised by all
- teacher talk is explicit so that all students understand requirements
- sufficient scaffolding has been provided to support learning
- strategies and tactics for learning are carefully modelled, using the students' experiences as part of the scaffold and model for learning
- opportunities are provided for students to reflect upon their learning with the teacher, with regular sharing of lesson content and learning processes available to assist all learners.

In this learning environment, students' use of oracy shifts in quality and quantity; the students contribute more, and they contribute more substance as evidence of their participation. The classroom therefore reflects collaboration and learning. Such valuing and participatory classroom frameworks for learning capture the students' social and community capital. The result is 'productive cultural action' within the classroom community.

Involving students in the teaching and learning process occurs within the following activities and procedures:

- offering choice
- offering open-ended tasks
- encouraging cooperative learning and group interdependence
- enabling students to establish and monitor their own goals
- allowing students to assume responsibility for their own learning

- planning with an appreciation of the students' learning styles in mind
- modelling and scaffolding questioning
- modelling and scaffolding self-questioning and monitoring one's own learning
- linking learning experiences to past, current and predicted events explicitly
- reflecting on thinking and learning regularly
- employing written reflection activities such as journals and self-monitoring tasks.

Effective learning settings facilitate the development, and update the use, of metacognitive practices. The teacher approaches learning from a student-centred perspective, ever mindful of the relevance of supportive classroom processes and strategies. Oracy practices form a major part in developing thinking and metacognitive strategies. Planning well for oracy therefore ensures that oracy is given due recognition as the umbrella activity for learning.

EXPLICIT TEACHING

The notion of explicit teaching is more than making the learning or object of instruction clear to the students. Explicit teaching also involves consideration of all the information needed for learning, and that information includes access to the teacher's expectations in terms of the processes of acquiring the knowledge from the lesson. Explicit teaching for effective learning considers each of the following eight dimensions.

Prior knowledge

In this stage, there is much use of interactive language, with particular forms of question and discussion to make connections with and gain access to the funds of knowledge that students bring to their learning.

Time (in teaching blocks)

In both literacy and mathematics sessions, as well as for other learning areas in the teaching program, time needs to be given over to whole group reflection about the learning in which the students have participated.

Discovery/exploration

The students need to explore and discover for themselves, individually and collectively, what it is they are learning. This focused use of precious time allows the meaning-making and analytical practices of the language repertoire to be accessed by the learner within the learning environment established by the teacher.

Scaffolding

The teacher provides scaffolds for the children through the use of:

- a question matrix use of combined open questions
- stories and examples that support learning the concept
- experiences through active exploration of learning as it develops.

Modelling

The teacher actively models strategies and processes for undertaking learning and practice activities, using their own and students' background knowledge and experiences.

Coaching

The teacher provides specific support to individual students as they are engaged in their learning and practice activities. Sometimes, coaching involves working with selected groups of students on lessons that are focused upon specific aspects of the learning.

Apprenticeship

Within the learning area, apprenticeship occurs when the learner has the time and opportunities to manage transfer of skills. This may be managed through exploring the ideas or learning for another purpose or in another context. The Guided Reading model is an example of the apprenticeship model as the teacher scaffolds, models and instructs learners as they engage with the reading text and develop the learning strategies to be applied to understanding, using and analysing the text.

Encouragement

The teacher encourages the learner's ability to manage more of the learning task independently, so that the learning is continually nurtured. Motivation thus shifts from that extrinsically provided by the teacher to the student's intrinsic motivation to learn and apply new knowledge with confidence.

The following snapshot is provided for you to 'hear' a teacher's learning about her own work while helping young learners to become participants in classroom activities (Campbell & Garrahy 2000).

Snapshot 4.1: Reaching new depths for floating and sinking

Janice Moore is one of a number of teachers who undertook a project designed to assist their own professional self-development. The project sought to assist that process by involving the teachers in taking the extra time needed to work with those young children who did not contribute effectively in classroom learning interactions. As the teachers worked through the project, they became aware of the values and possibilities of explicit teaching.

Janice was working with children in her Year 1 class in a primary school. In the following snapshot, she explains the processes whereby she realised the value of explicit teaching. Initially, a teaching mentor observed her lessons while audiotaping one of the lessons. The taped lesson was then transcribed, with assistance from field notes, to produce a transcript of her talk or classroom discourse. She published the following:

All teachers would benefit from the experience of seeing their teaching reduced to a black-and-white transcript—it made me aware of my own needs for improvement.

One of the findings from the transcript was the frequency of classroom interruptions. These interruptions cause havoc with our lessons, with both the teacher and the children losing focus and attention. Valuable time is lost trying to recreate the mood, if you do at all. One suggestion was to use a closed-door policy with a notice:

Introduction in Progress! Enter after the First Act!

Another issue that emerged during my study of the transcript was the need for me to become more focused and explicit when framing my questions. I had a tendency to ask questions that encouraged the children to 'guess what's in the teacher's head'.

Sample of transcript:

(The teacher and children have just finished reading the book *What makes Light?* together.)

T:	… now today, we've talked about in the last couple of weeks all the different things that make light, now we're going to look at something that's very special, that we use. Sometime, in fact last night, when I was leaving the classroom I used one. I wonder what it might have been?
Girl:	A ruler?
T:	No, it wasn't a ruler, I was leaving the classroom. The sun had gone down, I flipped off the lights, it was very very dark in here. What do you think I needed to take with me downstairs and out through the library?
Ruth:	The light?
T:	I needed some light, and what do you think I might have used?
Boy:	A torch?
Girl:	Torch.
T:	Why do you think I used a torch?
Neil:	To see in the dark?

The interchange lasted two minutes, with pauses, and partly demonstrates how the children had to keep offering ideas to find out what I wanted them to tell me.

(Janice then planned a series of lessons to assist a selected group of students who rarely contributed to classroom interactions.)

As I moved on with this project, I became aware that while small groups are the best way for children to interact, experiment, talk and play, the children also needed explicit instructions to guide their interactions. I also needed to vary the working groups. Sometimes I used mixed ability groups to allow the more able students to spark ideas for the less willing students. At other times I used same ability groups to allow the less able/willing students to gain confidence to express their opinions. In these latter groups, each child had to talk.

I began a unit called 'Floating and Sinking', prepared to become more of a guide or mentor during an experiment. To see how I achieved my outcomes, a lesson was videotaped. A small group of five children retold the story Who Sank the Boat (Pamela Allen), using plasticine for the boat and marbles to represent the animals. During the lesson the plasticine became too moist and would not retain its shape as a boat. I was distracted as I worked with two children who were intent on squeezing out the moisture. It was only later when I had viewed the videotape that I became aware that one child had recreated the story using the felt board. The lesson outcomes had been achieved but it was a little different from how I had envisaged it!

After viewing the tape, I became increasingly concerned about three children who needed to develop the confidence and skills to interact with others in group sessions. These children now began to build on their background knowledge by playing, experimenting and discussing their findings with their peers. Their confidence grew as they became more confident problem-solvers, taking responsibility for their own learning. Our unit culminated with an activities session: making a floating and sinking bottle, blowing bubbles, making hot chocolate with a floating marshmallow, and popping corn.

During these activities, one of the three children made the comment: 'How does a submarine work? It floats and sinks'. This became the basis for my next session with these three students. We found a diagram of a submarine and it showed how water is released from baffles to allow it to float. The baffles are filled with water to allow the submarine to sink. As a group we did an experiment using raisins and carbonated lemonade, in order to mimic the rising and sinking (submerging) of a submarine. The raisins initially sink, but then gather carbonated bubbles that lift the raisins to the top. The bubbles pop, air is released, and the raisins sink again.

This experiment also encouraged these children to suggest new questions such as: Can we use water? Can we use water and lemonade?

The video of this session clearly showed the children's interest, and the use of these questions after performing the experiment and seeing the raisins rise to the surface. They had the confidence to take risks with their learning, and were able to sum up their learning experiences using the knowledge and language they had developed during the unit. The outcomes were achieved: the children under study for unwillingness or inability to participate in classroom interactions were able to contribute, and their confidence was developed and displayed. They were excited by their learning and felt valued.

This project was also aimed to help me to develop professionally, and I found these dimensions valuable:

- having opportunities to work with other teachers

- sharing ideas about classroom practices

- identifying ways to assist young children to talk and contribute during focused learning activities

- using videotape for self-evaluation of teaching

- analysing classroom talk and questioning

  - How much teacher talk occurs?

  - What is the quality of children's responses?

  - Which children are missing from the classroom talk?

  - Are children really contributing if they are 'guessing what is in the teacher's head'?

Activity

1. How has the teacher used and developed the eight dimensions of explicit teaching?

2. How has the teacher addressed the problems associated with teacher talk and the need to get the non-participating children involved in classroom discourse?

3. Discuss the principles of explicit teaching and the use and importance of oracy in classroom learning.

PACKAGED ORACY PROGRAMS

There are many oral language programs available to teachers, and these programs offer a wide variety of choices in the form of pre-packaged programs, planning instruments and curriculum intervention strategies. The professional judgment of the teachers is needed in order to discern which program, instrument or series of strategies will assist oracy development in their classrooms. Among issues to be considered are:

- needs of individual students

- needs of the school community

- cohesion with whole school planning

- accessibility to staff in terms of organisation and resources

- the fit of the program to school and learners' requirements.

All of these issues are investigated and negotiated within an overall appreciation of all perspectives.

Of paramount concern are the ways of talk that are to be facilitated by the teacher within the program of choice, with resources and materials appropriated when needed to fit a number of connected program needs. That is, the talk used by the teacher must resonate with the program and with the learning requirements, experiential knowledge and language of the learners. But even the most carefully developed program will not fulfil the day-to-day as well as incidental needs of all learners in the classroom. Planning ensures that the philosophy and structures are in place to ensure that the incidental elements of the oracy program resonate with the objectives and strategies of the overall program.

All oracy or oral language programs are not alike. They differ across a number of dimensions. The following programs exemplify a range of programs currently available, as well as indicating possibilities for the development of a school's individual program such as the *Gateways to Literacy Program* (2000) presented at the end of this list.

1. Early years: Speakers and Listeners (1999)

This packaged program supplies a full complement of strategies, performance indicators, learning activities and related resources. The package is nested within the SAID framework, which provides the teacher with a teaching construct around which to scaffold many speaking and listening activities. The SAID framework has four parameters:

STIMULATE

- engage students' interest and enthusiasm
- find out what they know
- introduce the purpose of the activity
- outline, with some detail, expectations.

ARTICULATE

- clarify the task
- draw attention to what is to be learned, and how it is to be learned
- check students' understanding of task requirements.

INTEGRATE

- ensure students know when to use their new learning
- bring the elements of the learning together by reminding the students of previously learned strategies and how these strategies fit together with the new strategy.

DEMONSTRATE

- show the fluent behaviour that incorporates the focus strategy

- explore deeper levels of understanding

- provide students with opportunities to demonstrate learning; ask questions and clarify student understandings and application of the learning.

2. The Oral Language Developmental Continuum (1994) and The Oral Language Resource Book (1994)

This program offers different emphases about oral language. The focus is upon a three-point construct, with many of the elements combined in each component:

- the language of social interactions

- language and thinking

- the language of literacy.

The *Developmental Continuum* provides a comprehensive set of developmental indicators for assessing the development of oral language in children. The program presents eight phases of oral language development, from beginning language, through early and exploratory and emergent phases in young children to the consolidation phase. The final three phases of extended, proficient and advanced language use are particularly useful for teachers in the middle and upper primary classrooms.

There is a strong thread linking the program to literacy, and the supporting *Resource Book* is highly regarded by those teachers who have accessed it.

3. The Magic Caterpillar Building Blocks to Literacy Programme (2002)

This program incorporates all the micro-skills for constructing the bedrock for strong language and literacy development. The oral to literate framework incorporates a hierarchically arranged experiential program for children in the early years of kindergarten, preschool and primary school. Gross, fine and perceptual motor skills form a major strand within this program. All important elements for foundational language skill development are included through a framework built upon the following domains: Talking, Listening, Looking, Moving and Concepts of Print. Each of the domains consists of micro-skills and forms a dynamic system of learning. Within the Talking Domain, oracy is constituted by three Strands: Processes of Talk, Performance of Talk and Classroom Cuing. The interactions and talk of classroom management are included in the Classroom Cuing Strand as part of the Talking Domain.

Each specific skill in the program has to be finessed in order to play its integral part among the whole dynamic system of learning language and literacy. By exploring the Strands of Processes, Performance and Cuing, links are developed between all three strands of the use of talk and interaction.

The *Magic Caterpillar Programme* hinges upon the effective and dynamic use of the child's funds of knowledge, thus ensuring that teacher-child interaction operates within the zone of proximal development. The child's funds of knowledge provide the core around which the teacher focuses learning, thereby eliciting motivation and intrinsic engagement on the part of the child as learner. Activities are grounded in the learning conditions stated by Cambourne (1988; see Chapter 3), and are constructed in order to develop learner autonomy. Because the *Magic Caterpillar Programme* is constructed in terms of outcomes for the learner, the individual needs of the learner are central to this program, and pivotal in the implementation of the program. The program offers an innovative futures perspective to scaffolding the curriculum to suit the learner.

The *Magic Caterpillar Building Blocks to Literacy Programme* links with the *Magic Caterpillar Handwriting Programme* and the *Smart Start Perceptual-Motor Programme* as part of a complete First Years of Schooling Program.

4. Gateways to Literacy: Millner Primary School (2000)

The staff of the school has produced a stand-alone package which details the practices and strategies used for providing a combined program for the development of oral language, phonological awareness and sensory motor skills. Millner Primary School in Darwin is a prime example of a school that has planned and implemented programs to support student learning in a school with more than 60% of its population comprising indigenous and ESL students. Millner Primary School was the Northern Territory winner in the 1999 National Literacy Week Awards for Literacy and Numeracy Achievement.

The Program has the following objectives:

- to enhance oral language skills appropriate to each child's needs, according to their individual assessments

- to further develop effective communication skills in social interactions, in literacy development and in thinking skills

- to provide practical opportunities for students to practise oral language skills in relation to meaningful physical experiences

- to further enhance understandings that children have about themselves, their abilities, and the world

- to help develop appropriate problem-solving skills

- to organise and enhance the self-esteem of children succeeding at appropriately programmed activities and experiences

- to have fun as well as learning new skills.

The underpinning view of language learning places emphasis upon content, form and use of oral language, and the activities are nested in this view. Interactive language activities are linked to speech and phonics and the use of stories and other texts as part of the frameworks devised to implement the program.

The *Gateways to Literacy* program is the result of the work of classroom teachers, speech pathologists and occupational therapists working constructively together over a period of four years to produce the program. Ron Argoon and Nancy Batenberg provided the leadership, direction and management of the development of the program. Student performance in Territory-wide benchmark tests has shown increasing improvement in recent years.

Summary

Proficient use of practices for teaching effective use of oracy for learning and thinking is founded upon respectful interactions between learners and teachers. These processes need to be designed to support learners to become responsible for their own learning within well-established codes of classroom behaviour that also support the development of metacognition. Oracy is the umbrella learning process, and teachers negotiate a curriculum with the children to enhance the possibilities for many levels of thinking to be developed simultaneously because of the nature and explicitness of the classroom talk for all purposes.

In the process of prioritising oracy at the centre of the curriculum for learning in the classroom, teachers permit all children to acquire and use the secrets of classroom discourse practices. In the same process, children gain ownership of learning and of the curriculum, become more willing and confident about taking risks with their learning, look for novel ways to apply new learning, and gain the fluency and confidence needed for success at school.

Annotated bibliography

Oral language Developmental Continuum 1994. Longman, Melbourne.

Oral Language Resource Book 1994. Longman, Melbourne.
These books provide excellent starting points for teachers to use in assessing and teaching oracy in all grades of the primary school. Both books are available in the teacher reference sections of most schools' libraries, and are easily obtainable from the publisher.

A number of oracy programs owe much to the pioneering work of the Western Australian teachers and academic staff who developed the First Steps Project resources in the years prior to publication in 1994.

Magic Caterpillar Building Blocks to Literacy Programme 2002. The Magic Caterpillar Company, Brisbane.

Magic Caterpillar Building Blocks to Literacy works in unison with the Magic Caterpillar Hand-writing process, using the framework stated earlier in this chapter to overlay all oral language experience through the Talk Process. Performance of Talk and Classroom Cueing liberates much cognitive energy in the classroom.

References

Ayers, X 1993 *To teach: The journey of a teacher*. Teachers College Press, New York.

Brann, B & King, N 2002 *The Magic Caterpillar's Building Blocks to Literacy Programme*. The Magic Caterpillar Company, Brisbane.

Campbell, R 1996 *Teaching grammar*. Unpublished PhD Thesis. University of Queensland, Brisbane.

Campbell, R & Garrahy, B 2000 'The Darling Downs Project'. *Practically Primary*, 5:3:34–45.

Cambourne, B 1988 *The Whole Story*. Ashton Scholastic, Auckland.

Cazden, CB 1988 *Classroom discourse: The language of teaching and learning*. Heinemann, Portsmouth, NH.

Donaldson, M 1978 *Children's minds*. Fontana, London.

Early Years: Speakers and Listeners 1999. Longman, Melbourne.

Freebody, P, Ludwig, C & Gunn, S 1995 *Everyday literacy practices in and out of schools in low socio-economic urban communities*. Centre for Literacy Education Research, Griffith University, Brisbane.

Gateways to Literacy: Millner Primary School 2000. Millner Primary School, Darwin.

Halliday, MAK 1985 *Spoken and written language*. Deakin University Press, Geelong, Vic.

Mehan, H 1979 *Learning lessons: Social organisation in the classroom*. Harvard University Press, Cambridge, Mass.

Moore, J 2000 'Reaching new depths for floating and sinking'. *Practically Primary*, 5:3:41–42.

Oral Language Developmental Continuum 1994. Longman, Melbourne.

Oral Language Resource Book 1994. Longman, Melbourne.

Perrott, C 1988 *Classroom talk and pupil learning: Guidelines for educators*. Harcourt Brace Jovanovich, Sydney.

Chapter 5

Text types, grammar and style

Rod Campbell and Graham Ryles

> *Teachers and students ... need a metalanguage—a language for talking about language, images, texts, and meaning-making interactions*
>
> — *The New London Group 1996:77*

THIS CHAPTER PRESENTS AN introduction to information that teachers and writers will find useful in order to become explicitly knowledgeable about their language and how the written language works. In the two parts of this chapter, you will have opportunities to learn about grammar, and gain further knowledge to increase the power of your writing.

Every text, spoken or written or in any form, is derived from a culture and from the social purposes and practices that give rise to the text. Knowing and understanding a system of text types (or genres) is useful for members of a literate community. The choice of text type helps in making decisions about what to write, and also raises important questions about the choice of language features and word use. One of the most important dimensions of a text type is the structure and organisation of the information it contains. Letters do not look like reports, and reports are structured very differently from narratives. This chapter introduces selected text types, and introduces some of the ways in which style, grammar and word choice function to make writing more effective. The aims of this chapter are to:

- introduce the text types of narrative, report, procedure, transaction, explanation and argument

- study some of the linguistic features of these text types

- study the ways in which traditional and modern linguistic understandings of grammar contribute to the expression of meaning in the clause and sentence

- extend your knowledge of the ways in which language choices affect understanding of text, and how choices can be used in composing texts

- present a metalanguage for examining the function of grammars and styles used by writers

- introduce a model of grammar, style, punctuation and vocabulary.

PART A: TEXT TYPES: CONTEXTS AND PURPOSES

The words we choose to use in any piece of writing are determined by the purpose of the writing. When environmental scientists write about the effect of chlorofluorocarbons (CFCs) and other gases upon the earth's ozone layer, they will usually not mention words such as corgi and spaniel. When we write personal letters to a friend, the choice of words can be as broad as we intend it to be for the audience. In the former example, the scientist will ensure that the report uses certain words, grammatical rules and punctuation correctly, and a number of drafts of the report will be worked over before the report is sent on. Meanwhile, the personal letter writer will usually write one draft only, and often there will be a few errors. Chat rooms on the Internet are a modern example of the misuse of grammar and spelling as writers express themselves in a first and only draft, writing words as they would say them. We do not advocate a widespread acceptance of inappropriate spelling and grammatical forms, but in effect the purpose and audience of any text will determine what type of text is to be used, and therefore the kind and amount of effort required in writing the text.

Read the following text types. Then discuss them using the questions below as discussion starters.

Text 1

Marcia Conte has much pleasure in inviting James Brown and friend
to her 21st Birthday Party to be held at The Tudors Reception House
on Friday 12 June 2000 at 8.00 p.m.
RSVP 1 June 2000
1 Elm St
Ridgeview 3001

Text 2

29 May 2000

Dear Marcia

Thanks for your invitation. My friend and I will see you on 12 June and look forward to a great night.

Regards

Jim

Text 3

If men are to govern themselves well, they must be trained. The education of the aristocrats often produced men of great ability. But the poorer citizens, who could not afford schooling, were much less fitted to govern … the real power in the government stayed in the hands of the educated, experienced aristocracy. A further limitation on democracy resulted from citizenship restrictions, which barred a majority of male inhabitants from ever becoming citizens (source: *Story of Nations* 1960:80).

(Note: the word 'Athens' has been deleted from the above passage.)

Text 4

Suburb

The city's traffic

Snarling through the day;

The freeway's monsters

Moaning far away.

(source: Rod Campbell 2000)

Use the following questions as a guide to discussing the above texts.

1. What is the purpose of each text?

2. Who are the participants in each text?

3. What are the roles and relationships of each participant?

4. What degree of formality exists in each text?

5. What kind of atmosphere or mood does each text give?

6. How do the words contribute to the effectiveness of each text? Why?

7. What is the problem of Text 2 in relation to Text 1?

8. Discuss the contexts that gave rise to the development of each text.

9. How do the writers use word choice, grammar and punctuation to assist their purposes in writing their texts?

10. How is each text organised in order to achieve its purpose?

11. History is presented as expository or explanatory text, but the very nature of the power associated with knowledge leaves its content open to contest. On what grounds would you contest the information contained in Text 3?

USING GRAMMAR ACCORDING TO PURPOSE: RECOGNISING TYPES OF TEXTS

The following list of text types or genres provides only a sample of some of the language features that are used in each type of text. Fiction writers tend to use many genres simultaneously, so there is often a blurring between genres. Reasonably proficient writers are aware of their choices as they move between genres and the identifying language features of each.

The terms 'text type' or 'genre', as used in modern classrooms for talking about forms of writing, refer to the way information is organised and structured, using the language features that are appropriate to the purpose and context of the text to be produced. Any consideration about choices of vocabulary, punctuation, usage, grammar and style depends upon the genre in which the writing is to be presented. (This principle applies also to other forms of presenting information: spoken, visual and gestural.)

All texts serve a purpose, but each purpose has a particular form or style to assist communication. The text-context theory presented in Chapter 1 provides a foundation upon which writers can build the structures for the different text-types of writing, with the associated vocabulary and grammatical choices they wish to use. There are many different ways in which various teachers and linguists have organised types of text. One of the most common ways is to list six or seven main generic forms, and to provide examples for each. The following list owes much to the work of Martin & Rothery (1984), Collerson (1988), Derewianka (1990), and Campbell & Ryles (1996). Each text-type is followed by a brief introduction to one or two of its major language features.

There are many different kinds of texts, and the uses of each are determined by purpose and context. Some are specific to school classrooms, such as school reports written by teachers, and projects and essays written by students. There are other genres specific to cultural pursuits, and many of the community or environmental texts are very suitable for classroom use. Advertisements, newspaper and magazine articles, and the various forms that fill up our lives provide real-life and worthwhile texts for classroom analysis and use. As students become attuned to the forms of each type of text, they will understand the language features and requirements of each text.

Narrative

Narrative texts are essentially about stories. A major purpose of narrative is to entertain, while at the same time providing information about real and imagined worlds, and contributing to the maintenance and evolution of cultural values personally and globally. The major features of a narrative concern people (characters), in one or more places (setting), doing things with or to each other (plot). The organisation of the events of the narrative is usually sequential, but may also be cumulative, discursive or reflective, or even a mixture. Finally, a narrative follows a sequential pattern of orientation (introducing the characters and plot), development of the plot towards a complication, or series of complications, and the resolution of complications in some manner. Narrative texts include fiction, fantasy, myths, legends, historical fiction, romance, mystery thrillers and science fiction.

LANGUAGE FEATURES

(Note: in each section on the linguistic features of each type of text, you will be introduced to the metalanguage, the terms used to talk about the linguistic features. You can locate definitions and details in this chapter by using the book index.)

Most narratives are written about events that have occurred, and therefore the past tense of verbs or material or other verb processes are used when writing about events that have occurred. Verb tense may change when dialogue is used or if the writer introduces description to write about things or places that exist. For example:

> The Long River <u>flows</u> (present tense verb) through valleys and gorges to the sea, and here Shervington <u>established</u> (past tense verb) his trading business in the nineteenth century.

Linking words such as *and* and *then* consequently appear to reinforce the notion of time in the sequence of events. Adjectives and metaphors are used in order to assist description of characters, settings and events. For example:

> Shervington's nose presented traceries of <u>fine, purple</u> (adjectives) lines among the red skin, a <u>delta</u> (metaphor) of varicosed capillaries overworked through drinking <u>heavily</u> (adverb) for too many years.

THE DROVER'S WIFE

(A retelling of the story by Henry Lawson)

> Out in the bush, in a dusty clearing hewn from the stunted mallee scrub, stood a two-roomed slab timber shack with a split-slab floor. The multi-trunked trees seemed grey and almost colourless except for some dark, green trees along the creek bank. The nearest neighbours were twenty miles away and relatives did not visit often. The drover was away with the sheep, and his wife and children had been left alone at home.
>   The children were playing late one afternoon when one yelled 'Snake! There's a snake!' The drover's wife raced from her kitchen, picked up the baby and grabbed a stick. She screamed at the children to keep away from the woodheap near the house.

The family dog-of-all-breeds broke its chain and rushed after the snake which was disappearing down a hole under the house. The wife and her oldest son chained the dog, too valuable to lose, to its kennel.

The children were made to sit on the table, and when they had eaten their supper, she went further into the house and gingerly snatched some pillows and blankets for them. The children would be safe using the table as a bed. With a long stick at her side, the woman sat reading by candlelight. She brought the dog inside when a storm arose later and raged around the house.

The dog kept its eyes glued to a crack in the wall. He was an untidy dog but he was afraid of nothing. The dog became interested in the crack again, and the woman realised that the snake was there. The dog hated snakes and had killed many. One day, she felt intuitively, a snake would kill him. The woman placed a hand on the dog's head.

Near daylight, the dog drew himself closer to the wall. The head of a brown snake appeared from the crack in the wall, and the woman raised her stick. The dog darted in as the snake came out, grabbed the snake in its jaws and stopped it from going back. The eldest boy awoke and wanted to help.

Thud! Thud! The drover's wife hit the snake. The snake reared its head to strike. Thud! Thud! The snake's back was broken and its head crushed. The woman lifted the snake from the floor and threw it onto the fire. With her son and her dog at her side, she watched the snake burn. Her son told her that he would never go droving; her tears glistened softly, each drop on her face reflecting the dying flame.

Activity

When you have read this story, re-read it and discuss it with a colleague. Consider its structure as a narrative: how many complications are there? What is it really about? How do the writer's choices of words contribute to your understanding of the story? Can you see the characters? The setting? Can you feel the mood of the story? How does the writer help you to achieve your understanding of the characters, the settings and the moods of this story? How does the writer use language and word choices to help you read, participate in and analyse the story?

Report

The purpose of reporting texts is to inform, usually objectively, but even persuasively, depending on the purpose of the writer. Reports can be used to communicate ideas and information, to inform and report on events, issues and phenomena without irrelevant details. Information is researched and presented in a report in an organised way by using paragraphs, maps, diagrams and charts. The information provided must be accurate and is often supported by references to other reports. Examples of reports include all kinds of science reports, newspaper articles, professional articles and reports, work analyses and reviews of books, films and other human activities. The central feature of a report is the presentation of information in a logical and reasonably objectivised form. In some reports, the writer is allowed to intrude personal opinion if there is an established convention; reviews are a good example of the necessary use of personal opinion. Frequently, reports are blurred or enmeshed as part of explanation and argument genres.

An information report has an opening paragraph in which there is a general statement that positions the topic under report. The following paragraphs present detailed information in such a way that each paragraph develops more detail about a different element of the topic. The final paragraph provides a general statement that glosses the topic in some way.

LANGUAGE FEATURES

Verbs tend to be in present tense, depending upon the existing state of the topic. For example:

> Animals (generalised participants) such as horses and lions (specific participants) live (present tense verb) by eating plants or other animals. Dinosaurs also ate (past tense verb) plants and other animals and dinosaurs.

Generalised participants are used, especially in the opening paragraph, although specific participants will appear as examples. Often the timeless present tense is used; *Food is necessary for energy and growth.* Technical vocabulary is often used (*herbivores and carnivores*). Description is needed to examine the components of the topic, so adjectives, similes, metaphors and the language of comparison and contrast are employed by the writer. For example:

> The adult blue (adjectives) whale is larger than (comparative language) any other animal, its massive bulk supported by the water like a wooden block in a tub (simile).

WHALES AND PEOPLE

There are many species of whales, and the Blue Whale is the largest living animal in the world. Whales are mammals; the young, or 'calves', are fed on milk produced by their mothers until they are old enough to feed themselves.

The Humpback Whale is one of the largest whales, and it is particularly popular among the people and tourists in the eastern states of Australia. Each year, these whales migrate from the feeding grounds in the Antarctic Ocean to the warm waters of the Coral Sea. Here the whales give birth to their calves, and after a few weeks among the islands of the Coral Sea and the Great Barrier Reef, the whales return to the Antarctic to begin feeding again.

Along the way, the Humpbacks seem to play in the protected waters of Moreton and Hervey Bays. Their spectacular breaching and playful pec-slapping are features of the display that can be seen by tourists and fishermen.

The size of these animals appeals to people. The fact that these animals do not attack people and boats also has an appeal. Tourists on the whale-watching boats quickly develop a strong attachment to the whales that entertain them. Perhaps the awesome size of these creatures that allow people to enter their habitat is one dimension of the new relationship that has developed between people and whales in recent years. The 'Save the Whales' campaign has also contributed.

Activity

Write a report on your favourite food. You may want to research the topic for specialised and generalised information.

Procedure

The purpose of a procedural text is to provide instructions or directions for undertaking a task. The most common examples of procedural texts are recipes, rules of games, 'how-to' manuals and instructional kits. The procedural text is usually organised in three parts: goal (usually the title of the direction or activity), list of ingredients or things to use (in order of use), and method (the steps to undertake the activity, very carefully listed in sequence).

LANGUAGE FEATURES

The most easily recognisable feature of the verbs of procedure is the use of imperative mood as action verbs used in present tense. For example:

> Break eggs into a bowl. Blend eggs, milk, pepper, grated cheese and herbs in a bowl. Heat butter in pan. Pour the mixture slowly into the heated pan. Stir carefully using spatula. Prevent eggs from sticking to the pan.

(The underlined words are verbs realising action processes in the imperative mood. Imperative mood includes verbs that order, tell or command.)

Other features include the use of generalised and specific participants as nouns (*ingredients* is a generalised participant; *eggs, milk, cheese* etc. are specific participants). There are also adjectives and adverbs used to provide detailed information about the items or participants (*grated* [adjective] cheese; *slowly, carefully* [adverbs]).

Activity

Write down your favourite recipe, or one you would like to write about. Next, list the ingredients and the procedure separately. Note your choice of verbs and abbreviations.

Transaction

The purpose of this type of text is to transact ideas or information about things or events between people involved in the transaction. The best examples of transactions are letters, memos, facsimiles, email, invitations and notes. Transactions also include responses to all of the above. This genre is the one most commonly used by people in their everyday lives, and there are particular conventions depending on the degree of formality required. Writers consciously consider relational aspects of the text–context model as they plan and write transaction genres. A personal letter to a friend will include a range of topics and be informal. A letter asking for an interview for a job requires a high degree of formality or tenor, and the content or field will also be very carefully presented. Formal invitations have specified conventions, ending with the letters RSVP, placing a requirement upon the invited person to reply to the invitation, usually by phone or formal acceptance letter.

There are other transaction genres such as advertisements, for sale notices, lost and found notices; each has its own conventions, and you can find examples of these genres in local newspapers.

LANGUAGE FEATURES

Addresses are written using open punctuation, particularly in formal and business letters; that is, capital letters are required but there are no commas and full stops used in the addresses. Note the placement of salutations and closure remarks, the addressee or name, and the use of paragraphs. The opening paragraph states the purpose of the letter clearly, but be aware of the need for formal closure in formal letters. *Yours faithfully* and *Yours sincerely* have conventions of use. If the addressee is given as a position such as *The Manager* or *The Director*, *Dear Sir* or *Dear Madam*, then *Yours faithfully* is used. Use *Yours sincerely* only if the addressee is named. Abbreviations appear often in letters, and there is never a full stop after an abbreviation that ends with the last letter of the word; for example, *Mr* and *Ms* and *Qld* do not have full stops; *Vic.* and *Tas.* need full stops, unless they are used in addresses in letters and on envelopes.

FORMAL ACCEPTANCE

James Brown and Mary Otto have much pleasure in accepting
your invitation to attend your 21st Birthday at The Tudors
Reception House on Friday 12 June 2000 at 8.00 p.m.
25 Riverside Place
Placewood 3003

Activity

Reflect on the last 24 hours and list the different transactions you have noticed. Compare your
list of transaction genres with those of three of your colleagues.

Explanation

The purpose of explanation is to show, describe or explain how something works.
Some examples include the ever-popular *How and Why* types of books and texts.
Explanations occur in school textbooks where writers explain items of knowledge and
information such as: revolutions and rotations of the earth and how these are connected with seasons and tides; why a steel ship floats; the latest theory about the
Bermuda Triangle. Again, this genre is used together with other genres in newspapers
and novels.

LANGUAGE FEATURES

A variety of processes is shown, used together with generalised participants realised
as nouns, or some form of nominal group. For example:

> The seas (generalised participant) <u>contribute</u> (action verb; material process) greatly to the
> welfare of the people on the planet, whether those people are <u>fishermen* who rely upon
> the sea for a living</u> (nominal group) or <u>city dwellers</u>* (nominal group).

*specific participants
Often the timeless present tense of verbs is used:

> The earth <u>revolves</u> around the sun.

Passive voice may be used:

> Copper <u>has been used</u> by people for thousands of years.

Cause–effect, comparison and contrast, and time relationships will be used to provide structure to the text at a top level of organisation.

MAGNETS

Any object that shows magnetic properties is called a magnet. The invisible force that attracts objects to the magnet is called magnetism. Every magnet has two poles where most of its strength is found. These are called the north pole and the south pole. When it is suspended, a magnet orients itself along a north-south axis or line.

Magnets can be made by stroking a piece of metal such as a strong needle with another magnet, thus magnetising the needle.

A remarkable property of the magnet is that, when broken, a north pole will appear on one of the broken ends and a south pole on the other. Each piece has its own north and south poles. This polarity allows magnets to establish a magnetic field, a principle that is applied and widely used in many modern appliances, and in any industrial process requiring electromagnetism.

Activity

Think of a natural phenomenon or physical item about which you are reasonably knowledgeable: for example, volcanoes, cyclones, rocks, skiing, drama, football, painting, etc. Explain this topic to a friend, recording your explanation on an audio cassette. Play the tape back, and study the choices you have made in terms of structural organisation, grammar, and choice of participants and processes.

Argument

The purpose of argument is to persuade or convince others of a particular point of view. There are different ways to structure an argument, but the goal of convincing, persuasion or propaganda must be kept in mind. Usually the opening paragraph is a thesis statement, placing the point of view up front, then evidence and illustrations are presented logically in the following paragraphs, after which follows a final paragraph summarising the thesis.

Another structure is to present a thesis statement, provide evidence to support it; then provide the opposite point of view (the antithesis), together with its evidence and illustrations; a synthesising statement (synthesis) is presented in the final summary, where the original thesis is shown to be of superior merit or quality.

LANGUAGE FEATURES

Emotive terms may be used to try to involve the audience or reader, as well as conjunctions of reason (*because, since, as*) and condition (*if*) in particular. There is movement between active and passive voice (*The floods ruined the farmers* becomes *The farmers were ruined by the floods*), and verbs may be nominalised (*The settlers acted quickly to save the farm* becomes *The quick actions of the settlers saved the farm*).

Many figures of speech (tropes) such as metaphor, simile, alliteration, assonance and personification will be used. A variety of rhetorical structures will be used to support arguments, such as rhetorical questions (no answer required, and rarely used in formal written argument but too often used in spoken debate), or parallelisms (*Around the town! Around the country! Around the world! The Spinifex Bank takes care of your savings*).

WHO NEEDS WHO? MAGAZINE?

What is living? What is the purpose of living? To become noted? To be granted honours and high office? Achieving? Achieving what? This introduction is laced with the questions, often rhetorical, that pepper the lives of anyone who ever read a magazine about people, a front page about other people, or watched television news about yet more people who have become famous. The rhetoric of fame is trumpeted in a glossy affront to living and literature peddled in a magazine called *WHO?*

The message clearly given by the conspirators of *WHO?* Magazine is that recognition comes with achievement and fame. The conspiracy involves many players, and together they actually determine that recognition becomes a game between three groups of people, all of whom must be unsatisfied with the conditions of their individual existences. The members of each group include those celebrities whose needs for public notice are high, the hack writers who are willing to invent and relay porkies to help them, and a public that joins the conspiracy to promote dramatis personae for an ongoing drama of life to relieve the monotony of the mundane.

Living is more than being famous, much more than identifying with the famous, and far beyond the need to pander to the needs of the members of either of the groups in the conspiracy. The pleasant condition of life is to remain incognito, passing through the avenues and rituals of friendships, unremarked by the cares and envies of others who are essentially unhappy with their own lives.

'Bene qui latuit, bene vixit'; 'one has lived well, who has lain hidden'. Living is being, being at one with the world without depending upon the acclaim of others. Isn't the truly integrated person one who relies on others for the everyday practices of living in harmony?

Fame! Who needs it? Or should that be 'Fame! *WHO?* needs it!'

Activity

What is the main thesis of this argument? List the various techniques used by the writer, and give examples of these.

Texts: a basis for learning about language

Using various types of texts in a practical and purposeful manner provides language learners with opportunities for developing their understanding and use of language. Writers and speakers are empowered by knowing that they can use relevant words and structures to meet the purposes of their communication. Much of this knowledge is already available to children and adults; they see examples of the many genres or texts with which they are familiar in their everyday lives. Genre has a social and cultural base. Nobody would write a poem as a job application, yet it is possible to corrupt the social understandings of the use of certain linguistic features of the various genres. For example, a person could write invitations to a party by using limericks or any short form of poetry, particularly if the recipients of the invitations were aware of the writer's creative abilities.

Geertz (1973) introduced the notion of blurred genres, and Stock & Robinson (1990) have used this notion of blurred genres to describe how few genres are clearly distinguished from each other. The point we wish to make here is that the freedom to blur genres for purpose and effect derives from a developed or learned knowledge of the possibilities that such knowledge provides the writer or communicator. But of equal importance in empowering the writer and reader is knowledge about the language features and conventions of written English.

PART B: GRAMMAR AND STYLE: CONVENTIONS AND THEIR USE

'I must say,' her mother said, 'I don't understand school ways these times. Why, when I was her age, I could say every cape and bay in the right order from Cape York to Melbourne. And grammar! The teacher couldn't catch me in it. Between you and I, if you'll excuse me saying so, I think there ain't half enough grammar taught now.'

That is the worst of this formal grammar—it is useless. A girl can be so very good at it and yet say 'between you and I'. Correct speech is a matter of the ear.

'How are you going to correct errors in speech and composition if you do not teach formal grammar?' the pro-grammarites ask. I say we can teach it by informal grammar (Helen Sinclair 1929:184–5).

The (1998 Writing K-12) Syllabus is based on the educational assumption that children will learn the writing conventions 'naturally' through use. If children are in an environment in which they want to write for a purpose, so the argument goes, their writing will develop in a natural way.

This assumption, however, is flawed. A child learns to write in a very different setting— a school—and in very different ways to a baby learning to speak. Writing has to be learned in a different way to speaking. It is for this very purpose that schools as we know them were established in the late 19th century. Generalisation and abstraction about language resources such as grammar or spelling are efficient tools for learning which are available once oral language has been acquired.

The point is that few students can develop their own understanding of how language works and how to write just through doing lots of writing. With no textbooks or curriculum materials, teachers are left to teach the language conventions in an ad hoc and incidental way as their students seem to need them. Not only does this suggest an unstructured and fragmented approach to language learning, but it places an unrealistic and unfair burden on teachers (Mary Kalantzis & Gunther Kress 1989:18).

The above statements reflect a small part of a long history of argument that is at the core of education and schooling: what are the basics of teaching writing and learning about language? And how could and should these basics be taught and learned? The debate on these questions is an activity for you to undertake with your colleagues at university and in the school. We take the view that in order to learn to write with understanding and style, writers need to be able to talk and think about the choices they make as they improve, edit and reshape whatever they have written. We also take the view that all teachers and the children in their classes are writers, all learning to improve their writing together, with the teacher providing the knowledge and opportunities for skill development for the children.

As you read and study this chapter, you will be introduced to many terms about language. Most of these words will be explained by definition within the text.

Why teach and learn grammar?

All peoples talk about their language. We talk about capital letters, words, print, adjectives and metaphors. Poets choose whether or not to use rhyme, and make sure that there is some form of rhythm, if not regular metre. Poets, writers and readers also make use of such tropes as alliteration, personification, simile, metaphor, metonymy, hyperbole and onomatopoeia. As users of language, we can respond to the content of the poem and to the writer's style. But what assists us to become more knowledgeable about language is reading it, writing it and talking about it. People everywhere talk about language and use metalinguistic terms as they talk about language. At the level of commonsense knowledge, people talk about dialect variations in accent, grammar and words.

The term 'grammar' has many meanings, and the following definition from the Concise Oxford English Dictionary provides a clue about the general confusion concerning the nature of grammar.

Grammar: 'the art and science dealing with a language's inflections or other means of showing relation between words as used in speech or writing, and its phonetic system, and the established rules for using these' (1976:465).

Grammar can then be understood as the overarching term for any comment about the use of language, but writers and teachers need a workable model for understanding how the parts come together to provide a framework for writing. The following model (Table 5.1) displays various elements of language and their relationship to each other. The superordinate element is style, what writers bring to their creation by virtue of their personality and knowledge of their subject. Knowledge and control of elements of writing contribute to that style.

Before embarking on a discussion of the elements of the model in Table 5.1, there is another term that has been historically linked with grammar for over 2500 years. 'Rhetoric' is concerned with the ways in which a text is structured and organised to achieve its purpose. In the classical curriculum from Ancient Greece and Rome, and in the Universities of the Middle Ages in Europe and to the 20th century, the trivium of grammar, rhetoric and logic were studied by all students beyond the primary years of schooling. Rhetoric includes the development or invention of an argument or

Grammar and style

STYLE
(choices for writing and speaking)

RHETORIC
(structure of a text to achieve purpose)

TRADITIONAL TERMS
(descriptive terms)

MODERN FUNCTIONAL GRAMMARS
(relationships and functions of language)

PRESCRIPTIVE GRAMMAR AND USAGE
(expectations of standard written English)

PUNCTUATION
(marking boundaries and relationships)

VOCABULARY
(choosing suitable words for writers' purposes)

Table 5.1   *(Source: Campbell & Ryles 1998)*

debate, its organisation, the deliberate use for effect of linguistic devices such as figures of speech, memory and delivery of the argument. The Roman writers and orators Cicero and Quintilian are regarded as outstanding exponents of rhetoric. In modern English, rhetoric has been revived to provide writers with models for making their writing more effective. Speech writers, journalists and special feature writers are well versed in rhetoric. These writers may have contributed also to rhetoric's acquired connotation of unreality or even untruth in contemporary commonsense understandings of language terms, reflected in the familiar phrase 'rhetoric or reality'?

GRAMMAR: FUNCTION, DESCRIPTION, USAGE AND STYLE

You have already used a large amount of grammar and knowledge about language in reading to this part of the book, and in the process of reading and thinking about your language, you have become aware that you know many of the terms used. One of the features of an educated person in any society is the ability to use the language of language whenever required. Yet learning all the many details about grammar presents problems for many students and writers. That is because grammar is one of those areas, like calculus and computer technology, where the principle of COIK applies: Clear Only If Known. In this section, you will be introduced to grammar through a number of understandings of grammar: function, description, usage and style. While learning about these elements of grammar, we will also consider punctuation, a noticeable feature of any written language. Prescriptive grammar, punctuation and vocabulary choice will also be addressed.

Functional grammar: making language function

Language works because words are ordered and structured in systems that vary from one language to another. The central and universal linguistic structure of a group of words in a language is the clause.

Clauses: insights from contemporary and systemic functional grammar

Clauses work by placing whatever is being talked about (the participants) with an expression that shows what is, or is being done or said (the process). For example:

> The children / played / many games.
> (participant) / (process) / (participants)

The term 'participants' allows us to talk about *who or what* is involved in the clause, while the term 'process' allows us to talk about *what is going on* with the participants or what the participants are doing. Participants in the English clause are usually realised through the use of nouns and pronouns. Processes are realised by verbs.

There are other functional groups of words that are used in clauses: circumstances and nominal groups. The term 'circumstance' allows us to talk *about how, when, where* or *why* something is going on. For example:

The children played excitedly   for fun   in the field   all afternoon.
                    (circ: how) / (circ: why) / (circ: where) / (circ: when)

(Note: that example of a one-clause sentence has been contrived to show how a clause can be expanded by adding new information in the form of different kinds of circumstances. You will notice that three of these circumstances have been structured using two or three words. These small or circumstantial structures are called 'phrases'; the major difference between a clause and a phrase is that a phrase will rarely have a process together with a participant.)

Clauses vary in their structure (but a clause will always have a process) and usually have one or more participants. For example, the processes in the clauses below are underlined.

1. Run! (Process only, but there is an implicit participant: who/what is to run?)
2. Run quickly! (Process and circumstance, implied participant/s.)
3. Everybody   must run   the race   to the tree   very quickly.
   (participant) / (process) / (participant) / (circumstance) / (circumstance)
4. The older children must be able to run their races   faster.
        (participants) /   (process)   /   (participants) / (circumstance)

In clause 4, the participants (*children*) have been described as 'older', and the information packaged in a phrase (*the older children*). Another name for this structure of information about the main participant in a phrase is 'nominal group' or 'noun group'. A nominal group can include phrases and other clauses.

Also in clause 4, you will notice that all the information that incorporates the process of what is to happen (*must be able to run*) is packaged as a single verb phrase. A second piece of information or goal of the participants (*their races*) appears as a phrase, and finally the single word *faster* appears as a circumstance. Information is added to each of the parts of the clause by packaging the information in phrases and nominal groups that are embedded in the clause.

There are other systems for packaging more information. Another method is to develop one or more clauses around the participants and the circumstances, and to embed these clauses within the main clause of the sentence. For example:

5. The older children who have been training for their events in the school sports
   (participants: relative clause [see 'Clause types' below] giving further information about
   the participants)

<u>must be able to run</u> all their races *as fast as they can.*
(process) / (participants) / (circumstance as dependent clause [see 'Clause types' below] of manner)

People who speak English as their first language are able to use their awareness of their language to create an infinite variety of structures within a clause. How many ways can you say or write using the words *children, run, race* and *fast*? Sentences using a variety of clauses allow an infinite possibility of responses.

Many people see themselves as writers, and because teachers must see themselves both as writers and teachers of writing, it is useful to be more than just aware of your skills in expressing information about any topic in so many different ways. It is helpful to be conscious of the ways you structure the parts of your clauses and even to have a system of describing how you do this. Having a few terms to talk about language allows you to become more knowledgeable about the quality of your writing.

Phrases

A phrase may be any group of two or more words that does not include a complete verb.

Often phrases are named according to one of the parts of speech that are prominent in the phrase. For example:

People, Cars, The nations, Those feelings   noun phrases.
The *old* car, *modern* nations, *hard* feelings   adjective phrases
down the road, *across* the street   prepositional phrases

Noun and adjective phrases are also examples of the nominal group.

Clause types: insights from traditional and functional grammars

The clause is a group of words that contains a verb. Clauses can be categorised as independent and dependent; and as complete and incomplete. Relative clauses are considered as a special form of dependent clause. The relationship of dependency between clauses is shown explicitly in the use of conjunctions.

Knowing about conjunctions is important for understanding and talking about grammar. Conjunctions are mainly of two kinds: coordinating and subordinating. Those terms themselves provide you with the first clue.

1. INDEPENDENT CLAUSES AND COORDINATING CONJUNCTIONS

Coordinating conjunctions (*and, but, or*) are used to join two or more clauses that have an equal and coordinating relationship. For example:

We went to the city <u>and</u> the bus broke down on the way.**
We wanted to go to the city <u>but</u> the bus broke down on the way <u>and</u> we came home.**
We went to the city <u>or</u> we played on the beach.**

The words *and*, *but*, and *or* are used to join clauses together. The clauses in each sentence are independent of each other. You can remove the coordinating conjunctions and replace them with full stops and capital letters. For example:

We went to the city.* The bus broke down on the way.*
We wanted to go to the city.* The bus broke down on the way.* We came home.*
We went to the city.* We played on the beach.*

Each clause is of equal status, and therefore we say that the clauses are independent clauses. You would have noticed that by removing the coordinating conjunctions, a number of one-clause or simple sentences (indicated by *) have appeared. For your further information, a sentence with two or more independent clauses, without the use of dependent clauses, is called a compound sentence (indicated by **).

Most importantly, the conjunctions also introduce a semantic element into the relationship. *And* has an additive relationship, and provides additional information; *but* provides an adversative relationship; *or* provides an alternative relationship between two clauses. *Yet* and *however* provide a limiting relationship between clauses. (*However* can operate as a coordinating conjunction, a subordinating conjunction, or as a linking word, depending upon its use. A sound stylistic principle is to use 'however' as sparingly as possible.) An understanding of the semantic relationships that conjunctions (joining words) bring to the sentence is part of the grammar of any language.

2. DEPENDENT CLAUSES AND SUBORDINATING CONJUNCTIONS

Subordinating conjunctions are used when there is a dependent relationship between one clause and another. For example:

We went to the city <u>*because*</u> *we wanted to buy shoes*.
The children played <u>*until*</u> *the sun went down*.
<u>*If*</u> *you want to see the movie*, you need to go to that cinema complex.
<u>*Wherever*</u> *you go*, your shadow goes with you.
You can leave <u>*as soon as*</u> *you finish*.

The dependent clauses are in italics, and their subordinating conjunctions are underlined. If we rewrite any of these clauses as simple sentences leaving the conjunction attached to their respective clauses, then the resulting statements appear odd. In effect, the dependent clauses depend upon the independent clauses to make sense. For example, *Until the sun went down* becomes meaningful only when it is part of a larger statement, or is understood to be part of a specific statement. We often use dependent clauses in spoken language without the independent clause because the context of the meaning is understood between the speakers. A dependent clause left as a complete sentence on its own in written language is one form of sentence fragment. Sentence fragments are never to be used in formal writing, unless the writer is deliberately using them for effect.

Sentences that contain one or more dependent clauses are known as complex sentences. The use of subordinating conjunctions and dependent clauses makes language more powerful. The conjunctions bring their own meanings to the relationships between the clauses. The following table lists the semantic relationships.

Semantic relationships

SUBORDINATING CONJUNCTIONS	RELATIONSHIP
because, as, since	cause/effect, reason
when, as, while, before, after, until	time
as soon as, since	time
if, unless, whether	condition
in order that, so that	purpose, reason
though, although, however	limiting
where, wherever	place
as if, though, although	concession

Table 5.2

Generally, the use of dependent clauses allows greater power in writing. A text that is little more than a list of independent clauses joined by *and* is an early form of writing development in young children. Mature writers make use of dependent clauses by choosing conjunctions where the meaning of the conjunction gives power to the purpose of the text. *We are going to the beach and the weather is hot* has a different meaning to *We are going to the beach because/when/as soon as/if/ the weather is hot.*

There is another trick of writing style which mature writers use: deciding whether to place the dependent clause before or after the independent clause.

If the weather is hot, we are going to the beach.

This construction is called a **periodic sentence**, and you will realise that the dependent clause at the beginning of a sentence has a comma acting as a punctuation item or boundary marker. This is an example where grammar, punctuation and style work together so that writing conventions and style are in harmony.

Starting the sentence with the independent clause is known as a **loose sentence**:

We are going to the beach <u>if the weather is hot</u>.

Knowing a little about the grammar of clauses gives writers choices for writing, choices which will add to the writing style.

3. RELATIVE CLAUSES

The relative clause is a special form of dependent clause. The relative clause is used to add information about a participant as a clause. For example:

The old **man** **who** <u>lived down the road</u> owned a **dog** **that** <u>barked often</u>.

In the above example of a complex sentence, the dependent clauses are underlined. The rest of the sentence is the independent clause. The relative pronouns *who* and *that* are usually placed next to the participant (also the referent) to which they refer or relate. Each relative pronoun and its 'referent' (the word to which the relative pronoun refers) is indicated in bold print. The relative clause is therefore introduced by a relative pronoun that joins the clause to the participant in the other clause. There are instances when writers choose to keep the relative pronoun and its referent apart, but such a practice often confuses readers who will have to stop reading to look for the correct or intended referent. (See also Nominal group, below.)

4. INCOMPLETE CLAUSES

Incomplete clauses are usually dependent clauses. These clauses have a verb, but that verb is stated in an incomplete form. For example:

<u>Speeding</u> along the road, he was unable to see the danger.
<u>To watch</u> the sun rise, the children got up well before dawn.
<u>Having eaten</u> a big meal, they were feeling uncomfortable.

Incomplete clauses do not have to appear at the beginning of the sentence, but for the purposes of explanation, we have placed them here so that you will be able to apply the test for an incomplete clause. Remember that a clause must have a verb, and in each of the three incomplete clauses in italics there is a verb, underlined. However, these verbs are incomplete or non-finite. The test for an incomplete clause is to place it after the independent clause, and then to fill in the gaps from your own meta-linguistic knowledge of your language. For example:

He was unable to see the danger <u>because he was</u> speeding along the road.
The children got up well before dawn <u>so that they could</u> watch the sun rise.
They were feeling uncomfortable <u>as they</u> had eaten a big meal.

Note that by changing from the periodic sentence starting with an incomplete clause, you can say almost the same thing by using a loose sentence and completing the verb and the clause. (For your information, some linguists call the underlined clauses 'participial phrases', because the present and past participle form of the verb is used [see the section 'Verbs' below]. The second sentence used a form of the verb known as the infinitive—'to watch'.)

However, not all participial forms are incomplete clauses. Consider the following examples:

<u>Speeding</u> is dangerous.
<u>To be or not to be</u> is the question.
<u>Swimming at that beach</u> was not advised by the lifeguard.

You will realise by now that the test for an incomplete clause cannot be applied to the examples just listed above. There is no dependent relationship between two clauses. In each example, the underlined statement is actually the participant in a single independent clause, and acts in the same way as a noun. These constructions are examples of nominal or noun groups, and we will consider the nominal group structures now.

Nominal group

This structure is one of the most commonly used structures in English. A nominal group may be one word or may contain as many words, phrases, dependent clauses and other nominal groups as a writer chooses. The main feature is that all the information is about the main participant or head noun in the clause. Note the following examples:

<u>Fruit</u> is good for you. (Noun as single participant as nominal group.)
<u>Stone fruits</u> are better for you. (Adjective phrase including noun participant.)
<u>Stone fruits which are ripe and fresh</u> are the best for you. (Dependent relative clause included in the group.)
<u>Fresh and ripe bananas grown on eastern hillsides so that they receive the morning sun</u> are good for you.

The main participant or head noun in each nominal group is: *fruit, fruits, fruits, bananas.*

It is possible to add more and more to the nominal group. But knowing the possible forms of nominal groups is only an introduction to understanding the function of the nominal group. Halliday (1985:70) provides an example from science, showing how the nominal group is widely used in scientific and other forms of report writing and description.

> In the Newtonian system, <u>bodies under the action of no</u> forces move in straight lines with uniform velocity.

The introductory circumstance, *In the Newtonian system*, sets one piece of given information and the boundaries for the movement of the physical item, *bodies*. *Bodies* is the major participant or head noun in the underlined nominal group, and the rest of the group defines another limitation upon the bodies: *no forces are acting upon those bodies*. The verb acting is nominalised to *action* (see section 'Nominalisation' below). In effect, the nominalisation results in only one process remaining in the clause: *move*. Knowing the structure of the clause allows the reader to unpack the meaning of the definition about the effect of force upon a body. *A body moves in a straight line at uniform speed if there is no force acting on it, according to the theory of Sir Isaac Newton.* (Yes, there is more to gravity than falling apples, and that example of Halliday's also demonstrates how meaning is formed from prior world experience and from understanding the form and function of language.)

Understanding how the nominal group and its component parts function together with the rest of the sentence is important in understanding the details to be found in that sentence: *Bodies (unaffected by any external force) move in space (in straight lines) and in time (at uniform velocity), according to Newton's system.*

In summary, the important consideration for understanding how language works is to realise that knowing the **form** of the grammar is insufficient. Understanding how the forms contribute to the **function** is more useful in becoming an informed writer. And the function of the grammar is to contribute to expression of meaning.

Nominalisation

Nominalisation is the process by which a word or expression, usually a verb, is turned into a noun (nominal) expression. For example:

> He <u>behaved</u> inappropriately when asked to blow in the bag.
> His <u>*behaviour* was</u> inappropriate when he was asked to blow in the bag.

The verb *behaved* has been changed into its nominal (noun) form, *behaviour*, and there has been a subsequent alteration in the grammar of the independent clause. The effect of nominalising the verb in the original sentence has been to formalise the statement. One change has been to shift the focus of perception from the man who behaved inappropriately to the man's inappropriate behaviour. In the first sentence, the man is the agent of the behaviour. In the second sentence, the behaviour has been made into the agent.

Freeborn (1995:146), rewrote a formal statement as follows:

> In this book <u>we aim to study</u> how to work out an empirical method by which we can <u>analyse</u> what people <u>assume</u> when they <u>converse together socially</u>.
>
> Actually, the original authors wrote the following:
>
> <u>The aim of this study</u> is to work out an empirical method of conversational <u>analysis</u> capable of recovering the social <u>assumptions</u> that underlie the <u>verbal communication</u> process.

You can see how the verbs underlined in the first statement have been nominalised in the second or original statement. You will become increasingly aware that the genre of much textbook writing incorporates nominalisation as a usual and expected writing practice.

TRADITIONAL GRAMMAR: COMMON NAMES AND TERMS

There are many different interpretations of traditional grammar. For the purposes of this chapter, and in accordance with the model presented earlier in Table 5.1, we have separated grammar into three areas: functional, traditional (common terms including parts of speech), and prescriptive grammar and usage. In the section on functional grammar, we have already incorporated the functions and forms of traditional grammar. All schools or theories of grammar are essentially functional in that they describe how language functions to assist the communication of intended meaning. The central core of any understanding of the function of grammar is the clause, and we have incorporated the notions from Halliday's systemic functional linguistics together with the terminology of traditional grammar taught in schools in all English-speaking countries.

The traditional grammar of the British and Australian school grammars discusses the functions of the clauses in terms of how they function adverbially or adjectivally. The traditional American grammar considers the functional relationship between clauses to be those of dependence and independence, and this theory allows greater flexibility and educability in the transition from linguistics studies to classroom applications. Writers do not need to be trained linguists, but they do need to articulate an understanding of language use, rather than relying too much on their tacit understanding of how language functions in print.

Parts of speech

The parts of speech comprise groups of words that function together to make phrases and clauses in spoken and written language. In this section, we are introducing these terms briefly, using some of the notional definitions that teachers and children have been stating for years; for example, a verb is a doing word. Such notional definitions are insufficient for a complete understanding of the parts of speech, but knowing the function of these words in clauses and nominal groups is important.

The most common parts of speech can be classified unto two groups: open class words and closed class words. The parts of speech in each class give clues to their function in that mixture of vocabulary and grammar that is the result of our writing choices.

OPEN CLASS PARTS OF SPEECH

Open class words include nouns, verbs, adjectives and adverbs. More words can be added to the parts of speech in this class, so they are open-ended. We can add words from other languages, such as *sushi*, make up words such as *hoover*, and use adjective forms derived from proper names: *Newtonian*. The open class words tend to function mainly as vocabulary words (lexical items) in the clause. Open class words comprise nearly all of the half million or so words available for use by users of English.

Nouns are words that are the names or titles of any thing, place, person, idea and feeling. Nouns can be common (car, person, country), proper (Thomas, Canada, Persephone), concrete (rock, star, water), abstract (thought, perception, angst), and be a name for anything tangible or intangible. The participants in the clause are usually realised by nouns, or by words representing nouns; e.g.:

<u>Swimming</u> is forbidden. <u>She</u> spoke loudly.

Swimming is the participial form of the verb *swim* (and for your information, the verb form used as a noun has the special name of gerund). *She* is a pronoun that refers to a woman or girl.

Adjectives are words used together with nouns to add information or describe the noun; e.g.:

the <u>old</u> dog; a <u>breathtaking</u> concept; an <u>outstanding</u> example of <u>contemporary</u> art.

Adjectives are also used after the noun they talk about in such expressions as *The dog is <u>old</u>*.

Adverbs are words that are used together with verbs to add information to or describe the verb; e.g.:

she ran <u>swiftly</u>; he drove <u>fast</u>; they speak <u>quietly</u> and <u>comprehensively</u>.

Adverbs are also used with adjectives; e.g.:

a <u>really</u> old car; a <u>breathtakingly</u> simple design.

Note: modern writing style suggests limited use of adverbs and greater use of more powerful verbs; e.g.:

> They <u>drove quickly</u> around the streets. → They <u>careered</u> around the streets.

Verbs are words that realise the process being performed or shown in a clause. The verb is the part of speech that 'drives' the clause. Verbs are classified according to a number of their **forms**—*tense*, *participle*, *infinitive*—and their **functions**—*tense*, *mood*, *voice* and *transitivity*.

Verbs: Forms and processes

PROCESS	TENSE		PARTICIPLE (USED WITH have, be, do)	
	Present	**Past**	**Present**	**Past**
Action/Material	walk	walked	walking	walked
	give	gave	giving	gave*
	come	came	coming	come*
	go	went	going	gone*
	do	did	doing	done*
	run	ran	running	run*
	catch	caught	catching	caught*
	buy	bought	buying	bought*
	depend	depended	depending	depended
	receive	received	receiving	received
	sneak	sneaked	sneaking	sneaked
Saying	talk	talked	talking	talked
	tell	told	telling	told*
	speak	spoke	speaking	spoken*
Perceiving/ Thinking/Feeling	see	saw	seeing	seen*
	think	thought	thinking	thought*
	know	knew	knowing	known*
	teach	taught	teaching	taught*
	feel	felt	feeling	felt*
Having/Being Relational	have/has	had	having	had*
	is/am/are	was/were	being	been*
*irregular verbs				

Table 5.3

Regular/irregular verbs: irregular verbs in the list above are starred. These verbs are called irregular because there is variation between tense (*is, was*), and between the tense and participial forms (*is, being*). Many irregular verbs are the most commonly used in English, and have been part of this language since the 5th century. Regular verbs are more numerous, and tend to be developed from other languages such as Latin.

The **infinitive form** of the verb is the present tense form with 'to' in front: *to strive, to seek, to find and not to yield* (Tennyson: *Ulysses*).

Voice may be **active** (*I drove the car.*) or **passive** (*The car was driven by me*). The effect of moving from active voice to passive is to shift the agency of the action process from the beginning of the clause. The general meaning is the same, but there is a shift in emphasis, particularly if there is a stated context for the process. For example:

<u>I drove the car</u> that won the race. <u>The car</u> that won the race <u>was driven by me</u>.

The term **Mood** is used to indicate the varieties of expression that reflect manner or intent carried by the verb in the clause. There are four verb moods:

Indicative/Declarative:	*The lady went to the shops.*	(statement)
Interrogative:	*Did the lady go to the shops?*	(question)
Imperative:	*Go to the shops!*	(order/command)
Subjunctive:	*If I were able to go to the shops, I would.*	(wish)

The subjunctive mood is also marked by specific words: *can, may, could, would, should, might*. These words are known as modal auxiliaries, as they are used with a verb to indicate the mood. For example:

He <u>could</u> go on the trip.

Verb transitivity is concerned with the kinds of processes involved. See Table 5.3.

The notions of **transitive and intransitive verbs** refer to those verbs that may take a **direct object** (*She walked a kilometre.*) or **indirect object** (*He struggled with the idea.*) In the latter instance, *struggle* is an intransitive verb that can never take a direct object. We cannot *struggle something; struggle* must be followed by a preposition and the object of the process of struggling.

CLOSED CLASS PARTS OF SPEECH

The closed class words include the **prepositions, pronouns** and **conjunctions**. These 100 or so words function to make sentences and phrases work, and as cohesive systems in and between clauses and sentences. These words are also known as grammatical words and as function words; they function grammatically. All have their derivation in Old English, and are the linguistic cement around which the open-class words are placed.

Conjunctions (joining words) are words that are used to join one clause to another. **Coordinating** conjunctions are used to join two or more independent clauses; **subordinating** conjunctions are used to join dependent clauses to another clause. (See the section Clauses above.)

Prepositions (position words) are words that are used to locate something in terms of time and space. They may be used in prepositional phrases (<u>over</u> the moon, <u>under</u> the sun, <u>before</u> noon) as circumstances in the clause, or may be used after some verbs to make a prepositional phrase or verb (take <u>out</u>, take <u>in</u>, take <u>off</u>).

Pronouns (referring words) are words that are used to refer to, and take the place of, one or more words or phrases. Pronouns can refer to words in other sentences or parts of a text.

The couple owned a dog that had won many prizes. <u>They</u> took <u>it</u> to shows everywhere.

Case chart of pronouns

SUBJECTIVE	POSSESSIVE	OBJECTIVE	POSSESSIVE	REFLEXIVE FORM
I (s)	my	me	mine	myself
we (p)	our	us	our	ourselves
you (s)	your	you	yours*	yourself
you (p)	your	you	yours*	yourselves
he (m)	his	him	his	himself
she (f)	her	her	hers*	herself
it (n)	its*	it	its*	itself
they (p)	their	them	theirs*	themselves
one	one's*	one	one's*	oneself
who	whose	whom	whose	—

*possessive pronouns ending in 's' DO NOT have an apostrophe, EXCEPT FOR one's!
(s)=singular number; (p)=plural number; (m)=masculine gender; (f)=feminine gender; (n)=neuter gender.
Note 1: there are a special group of pronouns known as relative pronouns: *who, whom, whose, which* and *that.*
Note 2: demonstrative pronouns or adjectives *this* and *that, these* and *those* are used in much the same manner as pronouns for referring to other words and phrases: *This rose is more distinctive than those (roses over there).*

Table 5.4

They refers to the couple (*couple* is the referent for *they*); *it* refers to a *dog* (that had won many prizes).

The pronoun operates as one of the main forms of cohesion within and across texts by referring to words within and outside of texts. The pronoun is the only part of speech in English that is inflected to mark number (singular or plural), gender (masculine, feminine, neuter), case (subjective, objective, possessive) and reflexivity (myself, yourselves). An example for teaching the term 'pronoun', as well as a method of assisting writers to be careful editors with pronouns, is available in Chapter 8.

PRESCRIPTIVE GRAMMAR AND USAGE

These terms are used as a general way of referring to the so-called rules of English. In the past, much grammar instruction has focused upon these conventions rather than upon the actual functions of the language. The examples below are provided for your consideration and careful use and understanding. As a general principle regarding their use, it is wise for all writers to be aware of usage and to abide by the expected conventions. This list is not exhaustive.

1. Subject–verb agreement (also known as false concord)

RULE 1: A PLURAL SUBJECT TAKES A PLURAL VERB; A SINGULAR SUBJECT TAKES A SINGULAR VERB

A dog eats meat.   Dogs eat meat.

That dog has fleas.   Those animals do not have fleas.

Few writers for whom English is the first language have difficulty with this rule. The troubles begin with the following instances.

When the subject is a collective noun. The number of each collective noun is determined by current usage. (See Fowler 1996.)

Flock, herd, school, team, side and *group* are all singular:

The side is winning. That team is losing.
(Usage in USA says team is plural!)

Everyone, everybody, anybody, anyone, none, no one: always singular (for verb):

Everybody is bringing their friends.

Each, every, one: always singular.
Number: the hard rule is always singular. Plural usage is creeping in.
Some: always plural.

<u>Some</u> are coming.

Majority/minority: always plural.
Any: singular or plural, depending on the number of the group to which *any* refers.

<u>Any person</u> is welcome; <u>any ideas</u> are welcome.

Correlatives: *Either … or*; *Neither … nor*: Depends on the number of the second noun.

Either that car or those <u>animals</u> are to go.
Neither those toys nor that <u>drum</u> is to go.

Summation nouns such as *scissors, binoculars, glasses*: plural.
Aggregate nouns such as *media, data, news*: singular. (USA: *data* takes plural.)

RULE 2: AGREEMENT WHEN THERE IS MORE THAN ONE SUBJECT
Type 1:

(a) The <u>train</u> and the <u>bus</u> are coming.
(b) The <u>horse and cart</u> is coming.

(Determine how many items are involved; (b) is one form of transport.)
Type 2:

(c) Only one or two copies are available.
(d) Several small drinks or <u>one large drink</u> is enough.

(The number of the second subject determines the number of the verb.)
Type 3:

The <u>children</u>, not the teacher, are responsible for their own books.
(Ask 'Who is responsible etc …?')

RULE 3: WHEN SUBJECT AND VERB ARE SEPARATED BY OTHER INFORMATION IN THE CLAUSE
<u>People</u> from the other side of town where there is little public transport drive cars.

(Use a denial word after the subject: People don't what? (or won't, can't, didn't, etc.).

2. Agreement of noun and pronoun

The general rule is that the pronoun must agree with its referent noun in person, gender and number. Problems can be avoided by using plurals as much as possible.

> The <u>teacher</u> tells <u>her/his</u> class about <u>a child's</u> work.
> Teachers tell their classes about <u>children's</u> work.

In modern inclusive English, it is now permitted to use the plural pronoun *their* to refer to a singular noun which is not specific. Again, we suggest that plurals be used in preference; the convention can then be maintained.

> <u>Every student</u> is changing <u>their</u> enrolment.
> <u>All students</u> are changing <u>their</u> enrolment<u>s</u>.

However, the following example of two notices is worth study.

> Each <u>worker</u> should be aware of <u>their</u> responsibilities.
> <u>Workers</u> should be aware of <u>their</u> responsibilities.

The first notice asks each worker to be aware, rather than the generalised meaning of the second notice. Context and purpose should be the determining factor in making the choice between using plurals or the inclusive plural for the singular noun.

3. Splitting the infinitive

The term refers to placing an adverb (usually) between the 'to' and its verb.

> The children wanted <u>to constantly play</u> marbles.

The sentence could just as appropriately be stated as:

> The children wanted to play marbles constantly.

Or:

> The children constantly wanted to play marbles.

The meaning shifts as the adverb is shifted, but the generally accepted principle about the application of this old 'rule' is to avoid splitting the infinitive unless its placement there 'sounds comfortable'.

A perennial problem appears when the adverb of choice is 'only'. The principle here is to think about where you believe 'only' works best to express your meaning.

She wanted <u>to only read</u> the book.
She wanted only to read the book.
Only she wanted to read the book.
She wanted to read the book only.
She wanted to read only the book.
She only wanted to read the book.

4. Between you and I/me

This example of usage versus rule continues to excite debate among those committed to discussing the minutiae of grammar; the debate also wastes hours. *'Between you and me'* is grammatically correct, and should be used in formal English, both written and spoken. (Reason: pronoun case after a preposition is objective.) *'Between you and I'* is very widely used in spoken English in general conversation.

5. It's I/me

The rule is that the pronoun after the 'being' verb (verb 'to be') is subjective case, therefore *'It's I.'* is correct. That expression is maintained in a couple of dialects of English. The more widely accepted and used expression is *'It's me.'* Since the expression is spoken, it never appears in written English, except in dialogue.

Usage rules this one … definitely *'It's <u>me</u>!'*

6. Could of/could have

Could have is correct and appropriate, and must be used in formal written and spoken English. Ditto: *should have, would have, must have.*

(The problem emerges from the spoken expression *'could've'*, and children's replacement of *''ve'* with *'of'* is understandable. But teachers must insist on <u>'have'</u> in the students' writing.)

7. Different to/from/than

NEVER use *different than*. <u>*Different from*</u> avoids any problems.
Different to is used when two comparisons are contextually connected.

The food in Spain is <u>different to</u> the food in Moldova.

8. Try to/and

<u>*Try to*</u> every time, especially in formal written and spoken language.

9. Because at the beginning of a sentence

It is perfectly reasonable to use *because* at the beginning of a sentence. Writers need the freedom to choose between the use of loose and periodic sentences.

10. And/But/Or at the beginning of a sentence

It is not usual for these coordinating conjunctions to appear constantly at the beginning of a sentence. Writers choose to use a coordinating conjunction at the sentence beginning for effect.

11. Preposition at end of sentence

Which is it?

> This is the car I learned to drive <u>in</u>? or
> This is the car <u>in which</u> I learned to drive.

The best principle is choose according to context and purpose, together with the notion that what you decide 'sounds right'. The notion of formality or tenor of the relationship between you and your reader or listener is worth keeping in mind. But for fun … How would you remove the prepositions from the end of the following statements?

> What are you going to cut down on? (Crystal 1984)
> This is a situation I will not put up with. (Churchill: apocryphal?)
> What did you bring that book I don't want to be read to out of up for? (Burchfield)

If the final preposition is sounding comfortable, leave it there (Fowler 1931).

12. Sentence fragments and run-on sentences

A sentence begins with a capital letter and ends with a full stop or other accepted boundary marker. A sentence also must express an idea and/or its subordinate and other relationships in a complete unit. Since a sentence contains at least one clause, there must be a verb. Leaving out the verb is one example of a sentence fragment.

The problem in the following sentence fragment is caused by letting the relational clause (underlined) become a sentence in its own right.

> The whole place was jumping. <u>Which said a lot for the band playing its first gig.</u>

The full stop after 'jumping' should be replaced with a comma, and the capital *W* with a lower case *w*.

(Note: there are a number of fiction writers who are using a few sentence fragments for style; but as a general principle, never use fragments or run-on sentences in formal writing, especially in reports.)

The run-on sentence occurs when the writer does not use an appropriate boundary marker between clauses this causes the reader a problem because readers use the convention of sentences unconsciously when reading they become confused because the writer's mistakes obscure the meaning of the text.

NUMERALS

Numerals are used for numbers above ten, but never used at the beginning of a sentence, with the exception of a year. For numbers below ten, use the word.

> Twenty-seven children were in the room. 1999 was going to be a good year for this 26-year-old teacher and his eight-year-old charges.

PUNCTUATION

Punctuation is used in written English to show relationships and to act as boundary markers. Punctuation is therefore essentially a system of conventions for writers and printers. The first item of punctuation is word space. For detailed information about all aspects of punctuation, please refer to the *Australian Style Manual*, revised and published periodically (see annotated bibliography). A couple of useful items to note are outlined below.

Open punctuation

Used in addresses in all contexts now. That is, the only item of punctuation used is the capital letter. NO dots, lines, or punctuation marks on envelopes or in the letter address.

> The Editor
> Sunday Spreader
> Murdoch St
> Adelaide SA 5000

Apostrophe

1. APOSTROPHE OF OMISSION: USED TO INDICATE A MISSING LETTER OR LETTER IN A WORD

- MUST be used with usual contractions: *Isn't; won't; wouldn't;*

- NOT NEEDED in *govt, dept, Qld, Cwlth*; use in such abbreviated words only to avoid ambiguity, such as *A'asia*. Not needed in *1990s*.

- AVOID the use of greengrocer's apostrophe, where people confuse the abbreviation as needing an apostrophe of omission (*avo's for avocados*).

2. APOSTROPHE OF POSSESSION: USED TO INDICATE POSSESSION

Use the three-step method to form **singular possessives** with apostrophe:

1. Write base word: *boy*
2. Add apostrophe: *boy'*
3. If there is no 's', add 's': *boy's*

Use the same method for **plural possessives**:

1. Write base word: *teachers*
2. Add apostrophe: *teachers'*
3. (There is already an 's')

Irregular plural possessives:
The following are already plural, therefore add apostrophe and 's':

children's; men's; women's; mice's.

Singular nouns ending in 's':
(a) with one sibilant sound:

James's bike; Thomas's train; Dickens's novels

(b) with two sibilant sounds:

Jesus' Teaching; Moses' Law; Ulysses' epic.

Special instances:

princess' (singular); princesses' (plural)
my uncle and aunt's birthday (if joint ownership, use on the latter or last noun)
Mozart's and Puccini's operas (both: ownership is not joint)
for goodness' sake
someone else's job.

Possessive pronouns:
NEVER take an apostrophe: its, theirs, ours, yours, hers.
(Exception: *one's*)

Commas

There are many conventions for using commas, and a thorough understanding of the clausal system is required for their use.
1. In a list of items, whether words, phrases or clauses. No comma before the last item in the list; 'and' is used instead.

We bought apples, oranges, a large watermelon, two dozen ripe bananas, an aubergine <u>and</u> zucchinis.

However, a comma should be used in the following instances:

2. Between two independent clauses where the subject of each is different.

The <u>parents</u> rested in the shade, and the <u>children</u> played in the sun.

3. Between two long clauses in order to avoid ambiguity and to assist the reader.

We had been on the beach for many hours that day, and (we) decided that it was time to find shelter.

4. Between the <u>dependent clause</u> and the independent clause (periodic sentence).

<u>As there were few sales,</u> the item was taken off the market.

5. When a sentence begins with an introductory adverb or circumstance.

Suddenly, the rain pelted down.
Late in the afternoon, the storm hit the city.
Before introducing the winner, may I congratulate all finalists.

6. As parenthesis to show <u>restricted relational clause</u> (even though still part of the nominal group).

John, <u>who used to be at school with me</u>, is now in Perth.

7. To separate adjectives.

Fit, highly-trained, well-conditioned athletes are required.

8. In direct speech—note the patterns:

'It's all snow and ice,' she said.
She growled, 'I'm not going with you'.
'That's my car,' he said, 'when I win the lottery'.

Quotation marks

Use single quotation marks to denote speech or a quotation.

'I don't think they're coming,' Tom stated sadly, 'or they would have been here last night'.

(Note: all punctuation that is part of the quoted statement is included inside the quotation marks.)

Kipling stated that 'cricket is for mad dogs and Englishmen' (Coward 1937).

Use double quotation marks inside another quotation.

Coward wrote that he 'believed that Kipling had originally made the statement "Mad dogs and Englishmen stay out in the midday sun."'.

Abbreviations

Abbreviations do not take an apostrophe except to avoid ambiguity.

Use a full stop where the abbreviation does not end with the same letter as the original:

Mon. Tues. Wed. Thurs. Fri. Sat. Sun.
Jan. Feb. Mar. Apr. Aug. Sep. Oct. Nov. Dec.
(May, June and July should not be abbreviated.)

Unless used at the end of a sentence, DO NOT use a full stop after:

- an abbreviation that ends in the same letter as the original: Dr, Mr, Ms, Mrs, Fr,

- contractions: Dept, vols, St, Rd

- symbols of measurement or currency: km, g, ml, Hz, N, AUD, USD, Yen

- acronyms: ANZAC, NATO, UNESCO

- abbreviations of most countries and states: USA, UK, NZ, SA, WA, NSW, NT, ACT, Qld (But Tas. and Vic. take a full stop)

- ordinal numbers: 1st, 2nd, 3rd, 4th, 15th, 33rd, 24 August 2002.

COHESION

Cohesion involves the systems of references that link clauses and sentences together across the paragraphs of a text. Different linguistic theorists have presented models for the various reference systems that assist cohesion of any text. Understanding these systems and checking for their careful use is one of the many aspects involved in editing texts.

Lexical cohesion

The sentences and paragraphs of any text are linked by the choice of words that are appropriate for that topic. Each text, particularly reports and other informational texts, has a lexical (vocabulary) set, or set of words appropriate to the topic. For example, a report on herbs would contain names of herbs, as well as ideas for growing, using and preserving them. (See *Whales and People* above in this chapter.)

Pronoun reference

There are four kinds of pronoun reference, depending on the position of the referent noun or word group in relation to the pronoun. Two are discussed here.
(a) the referent appears before the pronoun (anaphora):

The <u>car</u> was heard down the road well before <u>it</u> could be seen.

(b) the referent appears after the pronoun (cataphora):

<u>They</u> had never known that the waves could be so dangerous, even though the <u>children</u> had seen the *Endless Summer* movies on video in their homes near Alice Springs.

Pronoun reference systems need to be studied as part of editing and proofreading a text. Difficulties arise for readers where the writer has been less than careful. For example, the following statement is from an out-of-date science book for children.

The spider traps its victim in a net. Then it eats it, and traps other victims, keeping some of them for later or for its babies as they hatch to eat them.

(The reader has to keep going back to work out which it or them refers to what animal.)

Substitution

Substitution is used often in English. The use of pronouns is the most obvious example of substitution. Less noticeable but very often used is the stylistic substitution of one word with another for effect. In the following example, the word 'animals' has been substituted for 'sheep'.

The farmer was worried about the effect of the drought on the <u>sheep</u>. The <u>animals</u> were suffering.

Logical sequence

Sentences are written in sequence according to event and time. Young children use *and* and *then* to foreground the logical order of their recounts of events. As students read and write more, and as they are taught by knowledgeable teachers, they become more mature in the styles they adopt to show sequence.

Signal markers

Signal markers, sometimes known as 'linking words' by many teachers, are generally used to assist logical sequence. Signal markers are often used at the beginning of clauses, sentences and paragraphs, and they operate as circumstances. Examples of some signal markers, categorised according to function are:

Time/order:	firstly, secondly, thirdly etc.
Additive:	as well as, in addition (to)
Alternative:	nevertheless, on the other hand, alternatively.

Ellipsis

Ellipsis occurs when writers and speakers leave out words, but the meaning is still intended. The ellipsis, or elided words, are shown in brackets in the following example.

> Initial fears that the player would need surgery were eased by X-rays (which were) taken at the hospital.

(For your information, ellipsis is also a form of punctuation; the three dots … are used to indicate that part of the original text has been left out deliberately.)

VOCABULARY (LEXIS)

Writers choose words carefully, and during the editing phase of their work, they will spend time deciding whether changing some words will assist in improving their piece of writing. In respect of word use, there are many aspects to be considered as you undertake the editing and reshaping of your writing. Perhaps the most useful advice provided to would-be writers is to eschew the utilisation of a Sisyphean surfeit of superfluousness. In plain English, use words that your readers know, and use those words sparingly. More bluntly, consider the first question for writers: Who is your audience?

English is a mongrel tongue, according to Brandreth (1979:9), and has evolved as arguably the richest language in the world. The largest French dictionaries account for about one hundred thousand words. English has half a million and growing, continuously taking words (called 'loan words') for permanent use in English. Some examples are permanent, like *angst*, *deja vu* and *judo*; others reflect the passing political moment, like *glasnost*. English has also added many words to other languages. Russians say *ice-cream*, and Japanese and Chinese are likely to use the English word *beer* as often as their own words for beer.

The result of more than 1500 years of unfettered development of vocabulary is an English language that has collected words from everywhere, and has even based its vocabulary on a masterful intermingling of Old English, Norman French, Latin and Greek. The implication for writers is to choose words that are known and understood, and to use less well-known words where necessary for stating meaning precisely for a particular audience. For example, 'committing an error', 'making a mistake' and 'performing a faux pas' are variations upon similar meanings.

There are many books available to help writers with word choice, but the best starting place for developing a healthy vocabulary is to read widely. Then use the dictionary and thesaurus reasonably often until the need to know more about your language and its vocabulary becomes habit-forming. Crosswords are invaluable and challenging approaches to personal vocabulary development.

STYLE

Good writing style is developed from years of experience of reading different kinds of texts, and from the development of confidence in successful writing for a purpose. The next support for developing good writing style is to build knowledge and confidence in using words. Understanding the clausal systems of English is a third area of skill development that contributes to style. These aspects of confidence, experience and development have profound implications for the role of teachers in helping their students to become confident readers and writers.

Most students have been told the following about style.

1. Vary the length of your sentences.

2. Write one idea per paragraph, with examples.

3. Don't repeat the same word. (Work on improving word choice.)

4. Don't start a sentence with coordinating conjunctions (and, but, or).

All pieces of advice are useful, but only partially. Varying sentence length is a good start; sentences of the same length become boring for the reader. One idea per paragraph is great advice for report writing, but most novelists vary paragraph length between one word and almost a page! Repeating the same word is overcome by using a thesaurus and making use of the cohesive device of word substitution. And finally, choose when to use a coordinating conjunction for effect at the beginning of a sentence. Some other stylistic devices are:

5. Vary the use of loose and periodic sentences.

Starting every sentence with the independent clause can produce dull writing. Periodic sentences bring a variation into the pattern of your text. Be careful, however, that any changes do not mask meaning.

6. Consider what to put first in a clause.

Information placed at the beginning of the clause becomes the 'theme' of the clause, containing the given information that will be used to introduce the new information presented later in the clause. Working from given to new information is a necessary feature of written and spoken language. Look at the way the same information can be moved around in a one-clause sentence (often called a simple sentence).

> The whole town came to see them leave next morning.
> Next morning, the whole town came to see them leave.
> To see them leave, the whole town came next morning.

This approach to style uses the grammar to determine what is to be themed information that appears first in the clause or sentence. In the sentences above, the themed information is underlined. What appears towards the end of the clause or sentence, and which is more likely to be remembered by your readers, is the new information.

Summary

This chapter has introduced models for understanding the organisation of different kinds of texts. It has also introduced the linguistic features that support the effectiveness of each text and its purpose. The chapter has also introduced the conventions, trends and rules associated with formal writing, and with formal speech. One of the longstanding outcomes of education from the earliest recordings in the *Upanishads* and elsewhere has been proficiency in language use and convention. Nothing has changed in the years since. Study the requirements for persons seeking professional employment in the Careers Sections of weekend newspapers, and note how many of the advertisements for career opportunities demand high levels of spoken and written communication.

Activities

1. Describe the genre used by the seven-year-old child in the following text. List the features in terms of use of verbs, general and specific participants, and descriptive words and statements. Note the use of invented spelling and punctuation. What understandings of the conventions of written language does she demonstrate?

> I wos going Dawn caBell terast (Terrace) on my Big Bieck. It wos a Stiep Hill, and my Brakcs pat up (packed up) wen I wos Haf the wai Dan the Hill and I broacd my collaBoan (collar

bone), and I had to go to the hosPtall to get a slliea (sling) on It. I'ts getin beta, ten I can ride I't a gain

2. Rewriting for clarity and logic

Your writing needs to present information logically from one clause to the next. Study the text below, and rewrite it to remove the problems. Discuss your choices with others in your study group.

Witnesses call

Police are investigating a single car accident which happened at Lyttleton on Friday night in which one person was killed and the other injured after a car collided with trees. A Canterbury Road man, the driver of the vehicle, a blue/grey Honda sedan, died at the scene while his 23-year-old female passenger was treated for injuries. The accident happened at the intersection of Galloway Road and Ayrshire Road. Any witnesses are urged to contact Sen Con Renmark of the Christchurch Traffic Investigation Squad on (067) 4569 7709.

(Hint: list the clausal and other constructions down a page, then number and group them before rewriting.)

3. Activities with a verb and a thesaurus

Select a verb, such as *walk* or *said*, and then list as many synonyms for that verb as you can, working alone or in a group. Then match the walking action or talking sound to each of the animals listed below. (You can use your own list of animals.) For example:

aardvarks amble, elephants tramp, tigers prowl … cats purr, dogs bark, magpies sing …

Make a book of Animal Walks or Animal Squawks:

Aardvark, bear, cat, dog, elephant, fish, goat, horse, iguana, jumbuck, kangaroo, lion, monkey, numbat, otter, pig, quokka, rat, snake, tiger, unicorn, vole, wombat, xiphias, yak, zebra. (Xiphias is a swordfish.)

4. Grammar glitches (Knowing your writing conventions)

Find and repair the problems in the following texts. Discuss your responses with others in your study group.

- Don't use commas, which aren't necessary.

- Its important to use your apostrophe's correctly.

- When dangling, watch your participles.

- About them sentence fragments.

- Don't write run-on sentences they are too hard to read.

- Just between you and I, case is important too.
- Don't use no double negatives.
- Make each pronoun agree with their referent. (Or antecedent.)
- Verbs has to agree with their subjects.
- Try to not ever split infinitives.
- Proof-read your writing to see if you any words out.
- Correct spelling is esential.

Annotated bibliography

Campbell, R & Ryles, G 1996 *Grammar in its place*. Oxford University Press, Melbourne.
A text for teachers that provides examples of different text types and teaching activities to facilitate student learning. Also includes a number of activities which teachers may undertake to teach the children to learn to talk about language.

Freeborn, D 1995 *A course book in English grammar*. 2nd ed., Macmillan, London.
A comprehensive guide to English grammar. Definitely a book for linguistic studies at university level, perhaps at post-graduate level. The book is still accessible to students with an initial working knowledge of grammar.

Derewianka, B 1990 *Exploring how texts work*. Primary English Teachers' Association, Sydney. This book contains step-by-step instructions for working with children as the teacher and students explore, as the title states, how texts work. Details are provided for developing understanding of a number of text types: recount, instruction, narrative, information report, explanation and argument. The theory is firmly based in a functional approach to using grammar. The text is accompanied by a video that shows teachers working with their students, and a workshop manual for teacher inservice programs. The package remains one of the most useful resources for teachers.

Halliday, MAK 1985 *Spoken and written language*. Deakin University Press, Geelong.
The book provides a clear introduction to systemic functional grammar, providing teachers with many reasons for understanding how written texts work. Such knowledge will help teachers to assist their students to develop reading and writing skills.

Jarvie, G 1993 *Grammar guide*. Bloomsbury, London.
One of many useful guides to understanding how language works as well as providing writers with a handy reference for knowing which conventions to use where. Not as definitive as any of the more recent editions of Fowler's *Modern English Usage*, but accessible.

Style manual 2002 6th ed., John Wiley & Sons, Canberra.
This is the definitive guide to all matters concerning the conventions associated with publishing in print.

References

Brandreth, G 1979 *Pears book of words*. Pelham, London.

Campbell, R & Ryles, G 1996 *Grammar in its place*. Oxford University Press, Melbourne.

Campbell, R & Ryles, G 1998 *Teaching grammar, learning grammar: A workshop for teachers*. NSW State Conference of the Australian Literacy Educators' Association, Lismore, 4th April.

Collerson, J 1988 *Writing for Life*. PETA, Sydney.

Concise Oxford English Dictionary 1976. OUP, London.

Crystal, D 1984 *Who cares about English usage?* Penguin, Harmondsworth, UK.

Derewianka, B 1990 *Exploring how Texts Work*. PETA, Sydney.

Fowler, HW & Fowler, FG 1931 *The King's English*. 3rd ed. OUP, London.

Fowler, HW 1983 *A dictionary of modern English usage*. 2nd ed. Revised by E Gowers, OUP, Oxford.

Fowler, HW 1996 *The new Fowler's modern English usage*. 3rd ed. Revised by RW Burchfield, OUP, Oxford.

Freeborn, D 1995 *A course book in English grammar*. 2nd ed. Macmillan, London.

Geertz, C 1973 *The interpretation of cultures*. Basic Books, NY.

Halliday, MAK 1985 *Spoken and written language*. Deakin University Press, Geelong, Vic.

Kalantzis, M & Kress, G 1989 *Education Australia*, Issue 5.

Martin, JR & Rothery, J 1984 *Choice of genre in a suburban primary school*. Paper presented at the Annual Congress of the Applied Linguistics Association of Australia, Alice Springs.

New London Group 1996 A Pedagogy of Multiliteracies: Designing Social Futures. *Harvard Educational Review*, 66:60–92.

Rogers, LB, Adams, F & Brown, W 1960 *Story of Nations*. Henry Holt, New York.

Sinclair, Helen 1929 *Tales out of school*. Angus & Robertson, Sydney, 184–5.

Stock, PL & Robinson, JL 1990 'Literacy as conversation: Classroom talk as text building'. In JL Robinson (ed.) *Conversations on the written word: Essays on language and literacy*. Boynton/Cook and Heinemann, Portsmouth, NH, 163–240.

Strunk, W & White, EB 1979 *The elements of style*. 3rd ed. Macmillan, NY.

Chapter 6

Children and print: reading

David Green

> *The overall mandate, as I see it, is to ensure that students leave <u>each level</u> of schooling with a developed and reflective sense of their own reading strategies, with a range of insights into how texts work, and with an array of strategies for resisting, contesting and re-writing texts*
>
> — *Corcoran et al. 1994:23; emphasis added*

THIS CHAPTER HAS TWO AIMS:

- to explore some of our underlying beliefs about the nature of reading
- to look broadly at the implications these beliefs have for literacy practices in the classroom.

INTRODUCTION

Before you can begin to consider how to approach reading in the classroom, you must have a notion of what reading is. Take a moment to reflect upon your own view of reading, and be prepared to modify that view as you progress through this chapter.

To begin our exploration of reading, consider the following poem:

Jabberwocky
T'was brillig, and the slithy toves
Did gyre and gimble in the wabe;
All mimsy were the borogoves,
And the mome raths outgrabe.
'Beware the Jabberwock, my son!
The jaws that bite, the claws that catch!
Beware the Jubjub bird, and shun
The frumious Bandersnatch!'
He took his vorpal sword in hand:
Long time the manxome foe he sought—
So rested he by the Tumtum tree,
And stood awhile in thought.
And as in uffish thought he stood,
The Jabberwock, with eyes of flame,
Came whiffling through the tulgey wood,
And burbled as it came!
One, two! One, two! And through and through
The vorpal blade went snicker-snack!
He left it dead, and with its head
He went galumphing back.
'And hast thou slain the Jabberwock?
Come to my arms, my beamish boy!
O frabjous day! Cullooh! Callay!'
He chortled in his joy.
'Twas brillig, and the slithy toves
Did gyre and gimble in the wabe;
All mimsy were the borogoves,
And the mome raths outgrabe.
(Lewis Carroll)

If you were asked to relate what happened in this poem, you would have little trouble in giving an acceptable account. Primary school children are able to dramatise the poem indicating that they, too, are able to make meaning, despite the fact that nearly 50% of Carroll's poem consists of nonsense words. Any theory of reading has to account for this phenomenon and must recognise that reading involves more than the recognition of words or what Goodman (1967) called 'barking at print'.

Now read the following text:

> The boy's arrows were nearly gone, so they sat down on the grass and stopped hunting. Over at the edge of the wood they saw Henry making a bow to a small girl who was coming down the road. She had tears in her dress and tears in her eyes. She gave Henry a note which he brought over to the group of young hunters. Read to the boys, it caused great excitement. After a minute, but rapid examination of their weapons, they ran down to the valley. Does were standing at the edge of the lake, making an excellent target (source unknown).

Notice how you had to self-correct as you read this text. Look again at one of the places that you had to self-correct. What made you do that? The answer is probably that it didn't make sense the way you first read it. So here is the first important point we have to make about reading:

READING IS MEANING MAKING

So how do we go about meaning-making? We use four basic cue systems: semantic, syntactic, graphophonic and paralinguistic. A semantic cue involves our prior knowledge of the topic we are reading. If, for example, I am reading a text about dinosaurs, I would be anticipating words like 'brontosaurus' or 'herbivore'. In the second sentence of the text above, the semantic cues actually led you astray. Because the young hunters had arrows, you anticipated that 'bow' would be the weapon for firing those arrows.

A syntactic cue involves our understanding of the patterns of the language. Readers carry a template in their brain of the types of words that occur in the language and the order in which they are likely to occur. If a sentence begins with: 'The old lady ...' you would anticipate either a verb telling you what the old lady did (The old lady fell ...) or a phrase telling you something about the old lady (The old lady with the sore back ...). In the sixth sentence of the text above, the expression 'After a ...' caused you to anticipate a noun rather than an adjective. 'After a minute' is also a common English phrase which you would have heard many times.

Graphophonic cues refer to the sound–symbol relationships in the language. In the case of a text about dinosaurs, you probably only need the first two letters of the word 'brontosaurus', plus the visual length of the word to guess the word. The paralinguistic cues are the punctuation, pictures, font and layout all of which can contribute to the meaning of the text, especially in the kinds of picture storybooks that young readers are likely to encounter.

Of course, children read many different types of texts other than storybooks, and it is quite likely that some children use their knowledge of the generic structure of texts to aid their predictions in reading. In other words, whether they are reading a story, a factual report or a recipe, different types of texts change the anticipation of what might come next in the text:

> *Genre, the different ways in which language patterns are realized in written texts to meet various social and communicative goals, serves as the powerful engine that drives the expectations or guesses in this selection process (Pappas & Pettegrew 1998:36).*

There are two points you should consider at this stage, and to which we will return later:

- How are children most likely to acquire facility with these cue systems?
- What kinds of texts will they require?

Now, you are probably thinking that this notion of reading as 'meaning-making' just sounds like commonsense. If it was commonsense teachers wouldn't spend so much time on oral reading. Oral reading is a form of word calling done in public. Unfortunately many children learn in the early grades of school that public show is what they are meant to be doing. I have asked 26 children, in the first week of Year 2, to read the following sentence:

> The cowboy jumped on his house and rode out of town.

Seventeen children read the sentence as it appears (group A). Four children substituted 'horse' for 'house' without realising they had made a substitution (group B). Two children originally read 'house', realised it didn't make sense and pointed out the error in the text (group C). Three children were unable to tackle the text.

I then interviewed the children individually and asked what they thought they were doing when they were reading. Nineteen gave answers that showed a 'word' orientation to reading: 'Saying what the words are'; 'Knowing the words.' Six children gave answers that showed a concern for meaning: 'Finding out what happens in the story.'

I checked these responses against the teacher's initial assessment of the children's reading ability based on a cloze activity and a miscue analysis. This check revealed that 16 children in group A who read the original sentence as it appeared, and who gave interview answers that showed a 'word-recognition' view of reading, were rated as 'poor' readers by the teacher (an experienced and well-informed lower primary teacher). The six children in groups B and C, who self-corrected the original sentence and who gave 'meaning-centred' answers in the interview, were rated as either good or very good readers by the teacher. Significantly the children in group A had all spent their first year of school in the same classroom: a 'Skills based' classroom that had relied heavily on the oral reading of the Endeavour Primer Series. The children from groups B and C had not come from that classroom. Although the group A children had both graphophonic and word recognition knowledge, these clearly were not enough for them to be able to make sense of the text.

The notion of reading as meaning-making raises another question, one that was discussed in Chapter 1: Where does the meaning come from? Consider this text:

> 'It is very difficult living in a penthouse with a man who practises the violin till midnight' she said, as she handed the pistol to the policeman (Mellor 1984).

I have asked various people to read this text and tell what happens in it. Some of their answers have been:

- she killed him

- she was scared he was going to kill her

- he killed himself because she nagged him.

Now these are interesting responses because the text itself doesn't mention killing. My respondents were universally surprised when I pointed this out. What they had done is fill the gaps in the text, and all readers do this with all texts because all texts have gaps (although probably not as many as this one). Because we all have different values, life experiences and reading histories, we all fill the gaps differently.

So reading is much more than simply extracting the meaning from the text. In fact, by using the text for cues, readers compose their own meaning. This is complicated even further by the Discourse in which the reading takes place (see Chapter 1). The following is part of a transcript from a shared book experience in a Year 1 classroom. As you read it, consider how the children are being positioned to see their role, the teacher's role, the nature of the text and the nature of reading.

> **T:** Oh. I can guess what Tony is doing next and I think he's having trouble doing it. What do you think he's doing, Brett?
> **B:** He's doing a puzzle. (up)
> **T:** Doing a puzzle. That's right. Let's read the story.
> (The teacher might wait to consult the text before pronouncing a student 'right'.)
> **T:** What other animals are there?
> **S:** Hippopotamus. (whispered)
> **T:** A bit hard to tell when they're dressed up in clothes, isn't it. Andrew?
> **A:** ( ) See, ummm, there's a hippopotamus there?
> **T:** Umhm. And what do you think the other one is? Daniel?
> **D:** ( )
> **T:** Bill?
> **B:** A hippopotamus?

T: Possibly, we'll find out when we open the story. Let's start now. SMALL HIPPO AND
    BIG RHINO, you were right, LIVED DEEP IN THE FOREST …
(Baker 1991:105)

Teachers ask these kinds of questions to encourage children to predict. And prediction
is an important strategy in reading. But the questions here are doing more than this.
They are contributing to a Discourse in which texts have a single meaning, and that
meaning is to be found in both the text and the teacher who, as the arbiter of correct
answers, has already 'correctly' interpreted the text. As Baker points out, 'Some students offer answers in interrogative intonation, acknowledging that they could be
wrong and/or asking if they are right' (Baker 1991:105).

The Discourse of the classroom teaches children what reading is and what it is for,
and reading is clearly much more than saying words. Meaning is not only in words.
Consider the meaning of this word: *bugger*. In fact, like most words, the meaning
depends on the context in which the word is used. Here are some of the ways in which
this word is commonly used. Consider the meaning of the word in the context of each
sentence:

The bugger won't fit.
He's a miserable bugger.
You clever bugger.
Now you've really buggered it.
Bugger it!
Stop buggering around!
Bugger off!
I know bugger-all about this.
Don't play silly buggers with me.
I'm buggered.
How have you been, you old bugger?
Well bugger me!
Go to buggery.

Incidentally, the word originally meant a Bulgarian heretic.

But if you think this word is unusual in having multiple contemporary meanings,
consider a very ordinary word like 'run'. The Macquarie Dictionary lists 170 meanings for 'run', depending on how it is used: a cricket score, a ladder in a stocking, a run
on the stock market, running your fingers through your hair, a car engine running and
so on. How many more can you think of?

This clearly makes a nonsense of memorising individual words from flashcards
as a way of learning the meanings of words. So, how do we learn to make meaning
from texts? In the following section, we will look at the three main approaches to the

teaching of reading that have been adopted in the last 30 or so years. I will treat the approaches separately here, but in reality many primary classrooms have evolved a mixed strategy that borrows from each of these approaches.

APPROACHES TO READING

As with any profession (law, medicine, engineering), teachers and academics attempt through research and experience to improve their practice. It is interesting, therefore, to look back at where we have come from in the field of reading education, partly to acknowledge the work of our predecessors and partly because at least some aspects of past practices remain in our classrooms.

Behaviourist approaches

These approaches were also known as 'skill-based' approaches because the child was initially expected to learn what were assumed to be cognitive skills for decoding print, the 'skills' of reading. Usually these skills involved recognising the sound–symbol relationship of letters or groups of letters (phonics approach) and/or memorising a sight vocabulary of common words (whole word approach) (Chall 1967). Both approaches to learning to read involved an initial introduction to print through decon-textualised print, often presented on flashcards, which the child was expected to memorise. These approaches presented essentially a transmission model of teaching, with teacher as expert and children as passive receivers of the teacher's knowledge. Children were introduced to carefully devised basal readers or primers with language controlled and contrived around a fixed vocabulary, phonic elements and a simplified syntax. In later primary grades some literary texts were used, usually in compilations as class readers. But the transmission model was continued with the focus on vocab-ulary development, oral reading and literal comprehension based on the teacher's interpretation of the story.

Naturalistic approaches

Such approaches were a logical development from the personal growth theories that gained acceptance in the late sixties but which had been around at least since Dewey in the late 19th century. They attracted labels like 'Whole Language' and 'Top Down' methods because of their focus on whole texts as the primary unit of meaning, rather than words or graphemes. Two of the ways by which initial literacy was developed were 'shared book' experiences as promoted by Don Holdaway (1979), and language experience approaches as promoted by Sylvia Ashton-Warner (1963). With shared book approaches, large versions of literary texts were prepared so that children could join in with the teacher's repeated readings of favourite stories. Once the children were familiar with a text, more attention was paid to the text at the sentence, word and grapho-phonic level. This approach reversed the order of learning promoted by the 'skills model'.

In Language Experience approaches teachers take the role of scribe to turn children's oral language into written text. These texts then form part of the reading program.

Apart from 'personal growth' models, three other theories underpinned naturalistic approaches to reading. Firstly there was a growing recognition (Goodman 1967; Smith 1978) that reading involves more than a decoding of print into sound, and that it involves at least three cue systems—semantic (word meaning), syntactic (word order) and graphophonic (sound–symbol connection).

The second set of ideas that influenced whole language pedagogy came from New Zealand. Here attempts were being made to replicate in beginner grades the bedtime story setting of pre-school children (Holdaway 1979). Holdaway observed that children who were read to frequently in their pre-school years developed 'reading-like' behaviours such as turning the pages of a book and retelling the story to themselves. The children also gained familiarity with books, with book language and syntax, with story structures, and a positive attitude to books that facilitated their easy transition to school reading (Berg 1977). In the classroom this translated to 'shared book' experiences using big books.

At roughly the same time, other theorists were making links between literacy learning and the child's initial learning of oral language. The most visible of these theorists in Australia was Brian Cambourne (1988). Building on the work of Smith (1978), Goodman (1967) and others (Rosenblatt 1978), he produced his now famous 'conditions of language learning': immersion, demonstration, approximation, expectation, responsibility, feedback, employment and engagement (see Chapter 3). Cambourne argued that as these conditions were present in the learning of the mother tongue, they needed to be present also in learning to read and write.

Significant advances were made in many classrooms as a result of Whole Language theories. These advances included an encouragement of risk-taking in both reading and writing, an emphasis on meaning-making rather than on the surface features of texts, an incorporation of literary texts into the mainstream of primary teaching, and a recognition of enjoyment as an important ingredient of language learning. However, criticisms of whole language approaches soon emerged. One criticism was that primary schools focused on narrative texts to the exclusion of the factual texts children need to succeed in high school and beyond (for a balanced critique of 'whole language' see Richardson 1991; Reid 1987; and Green in Baker & Luke 1991:228-30). Writers emerged (Morris & Stewart-Dore 1984) who not only pushed for the inclusion of factual text in the primary curriculum, but also wanted a change in the teacher's role—to explicitly teach the top-level structure of factual texts as an aid in their comprehension. Some texts are structured as problem–solution texts, others as lists, cause–effect or comparison–contrast. Being aware of which structure applies to the text you are reading facilitates comprehension.

A second criticism of whole language approaches was that they ignored the social aspects of language learning and lacked direct intervention by teachers to 'scaffold' the learning experience for children (Painter 1985). The combined effect of these factors was said to privilege the already privileged (those children from homes where literacy scaffolding was already supplied), and to disadvantage children who did not come from such homes, including various working class, ethnic and other minority groups. These views were grouped under the banner of 'sociological approaches'.

Sociological approaches

Is reading just concerned with making individual interpretations of texts or finding authorised meanings in texts? Promoters of sociological approaches claimed that we are positioned to find meanings because of our own social history. The form and content of the text (itself a social construction) and the learned reading practices of an 'interpretive community' (Fish 1980) also contribute to making meaning. This means that texts are inherently ideological, and consequently literacy learning/teaching is a political act. For a fuller discussion of this point see Chapters 1 and 2.

What was being suggested here was that language learning is a culturally determined act rather than something we just do naturally, like breathing. If it were natural, it would require only a conducive environment for everyone to have an equal opportunity to become fully literate, and differences in achievement could be ascribed to differences in 'natural' ability. Instead language learning becomes 'cultural capital'—particular, culturally determined ways of doing things; not the only ways, but the ways that happen to be valued by dominant groups in the society.

It was argued that some children who came from social backgrounds that practised literacy in these particular ways found the transition from home to school a comfortable experience. At the same time the school recognised, approved and rewarded them. Other children, however, brought to school language practices that did not receive this recognition even though such practices had worked very well in their home communities. It was asserted that these children were not illiterate; they simply used their literacy in ways different from the ways valued by the school.

Critical social theorists added two new dimensions to reading pedagogy:

1. A focus on the way that language operates in the real world. So when we read we need to ask:

    - Whose world view are we being asked to accept?

    - Through whose eyes are we being shown this world view? Why?

    - Whose voices are we not hearing?

    - What are the other gaps in the text? Jenny O'Brien, for example, used junk mail with her five to eight-year-olds and asked, 'Who makes these ads? Why? Is your family here? Why not?' (O'Brien 1994).

2. A particular way of looking at texts.

Critical social approaches foreground the following characteristics of texts:

- they are socially constructed; that is, texts are constructed by someone whose particular world view is embedded in the text

- they position readers, providing a particular point of view from which it seems most natural to read the text (Kress 1985:36)

- they are polysemic because they all contain gaps which can be filled by the reader (Iser 1978).

In short, all texts are problematic and in critical literacy classrooms readers are encouraged to interrogate and resist texts in order to foreground the ideologies embedded in them. For examples of primary classrooms focused on critical literacy practices see: Comber 1994; Kempe 1993; O'Brien 1994; Knobel & Healy 1998.

So how are we to make sense of these diverse approaches to reading in the primary school? One of the most useful attempts to do so has been made by Freebody and Luke (1990) and Freebody et al. (2001). They claim that an effective reader has to adopt four roles:

- a code breaker—working out the sound/symbol relationships of the text

- a text participant—working out the meanings of the text

- a text user—working out what this particular type of text is for

- a text analyst—dealing with the ideological dimensions of the text.

Significantly, Freebody and Luke argue strongly that we do not learn these various roles sequentially. We should, in fact, learn all four roles together from our first contact with texts.

Adopting such a model enables us to avoid many of the arguments that have filled professional journals over the last three decades. However, before concluding this chapter, it is important to clarify the code breaker role, especially as it applies to novice readers.

WORKING WITH NOVICE READERS

Well-informed infant teachers adopt two key strategies when developing code breaking skills with novice readers:

1. A 'whole–part–whole' strategy: the teacher begins with a whole text, whether a big book, the words of a song or a piece of junk mail, and the initial focus is on the meaning of the text. After this is established, the teacher might work on part of the text to develop code breaking skills before returning to the whole text (see snapshot below). Such a strategy maintains the centrality of meaning in reading while the operational skills are being developed.

2. Moving from shared/modelled reading to guided reading to independent reading:

    - **Shared reading**: here the teacher works with a large, mixed ability group and the teacher does most of the reading. The children join in as they become more familiar with the text. The focus is on relating the text to the childrens' own experiences; exploring the meanings of the text; and exploring the language patterns and vocabulary of the text. A common strategy is to use semantic and syntactic cues to encourage prediction.

    - **Guided reading**: here the teacher works with a smaller group of children with similar ability. Mostly the teacher would use multiple copies of a new text to develop meaning-making strategies such as: thinking ahead/thinking back; asking questions such as 'Does it make sense?'; using background knowledge; and rereading.

For a detailed exploration of shared and guided reading you should read David Hornsby's excellent book, *A Closer Look at Guided Reading* (2000).

We hope you have concluded by now that reading is not an activity that can be divided into developmental bits and taught one bit at a time. It is a social practice that must be engaged in in its entirety in a sympathetic and supportive environment in which the purpose is made clear and the focus is on meaning. In summary, it would seem that children can best be led to full and effective reading by:

- focusing on meaning at a text and sentence level

- using those texts for real purposes

- problematising the ideologies of those texts

- exploring the codes of the words (phonics) and of the language (syntax) within the context of meaningful texts.

Snapshot 6.1

Context: a year 1 class, third term, undertaking a unit on fairy stories.

A large, mixed ability group sits on the floor in front of the teacher. The teacher holds up a large book version of The Gingerbread Man (created by the teacher). The teacher points to the cover: 'Does anyone know who this is?' Some children recognise the character. One child refers to the movie *Shrek*. The teacher points to the title and reads it twice. She turns to the title page and reads the title again.

The teacher now reads the story, running her finger continuously under the lines of text as she reads them. As the story progresses some children join in with the repeated line: Run, run, as fast as you can, you can't catch me I'm the gingerbread man. The teacher pauses only briefly on a

couple of occasions to encourage prediction. At the conclusion of the reading the children are asked to retell the story to the person beside them. The children then draw one scene from the story.

Over succeeding days the story is read several times with increasing numbers of children joining in the repeated line. The teacher takes the chance during these subsequent readings to:

- encourage prediction by covering some words and asking children to work out what they are.

- use some of the vocabulary in a different context by making gingerbread men.

- explore the children's interpretations of the text—'Did the gingerbread man deserve his fate?'

After one reading of the story, the teacher puts on the wall a large strip of card containing the repeated line from the story. The children are asked to read it. Pairs of children are given a smaller version of the strip. They are asked to cut this into phrases: Run, run/ as fast as you can/ you can't catch me/ I'm the gingerbread man. The sections are shuffled and the children have to put them back in the correct order. They test this by reading the sentence. The sentence is then cut into individual words and the process is repeated.

In a subsequent session the teacher focuses on the word run and the initial consonant 'r'. The children search magazines for things that begin with this letter. The pictures and words are attached to a graffiti board.

Finally the children work on a presentation of their story to the rest of the class. Different children read key sentences and the whole group reads the repeated refrain.

Snapshot 6.2

This is a small group of advanced readers in a year 4 class discussing *The Watertower* by Gary Crew. The text had been read to them a couple of weeks earlier by the teacher librarian and they had just read it silently to themselves. The letter D refers to me, the other initials refer to children in the group. As you read this transcript, consider the attitudes of these children to the text and to the act of reading. If you have not read this text yourself, it would be useful to do so before going on.

D: What did you think of this book?

K-A: I thought the story and the words didn't give you as much detail as the pictures. The pictures told you more about what the book was written for ... and pretty much the whole story.

D: And what was it written for?

K-A: I think, by the shape of the watertower, it looks like a sort of an egg, and it looks like something would hatch out of it, or something like that … (D: So you think it's a science fiction story?) Yeh.

SH: Um, in the watertower, they've got this eyeshape on top of the watertower and all the people, they seem to have that shape on their hand, their eye, their hat, and it's like it's controlling all of them, somehow, it's got that picture on their head or their hand or in their glasses, and they're always looking at it …

L: I was just going to say it's like a pattern, say everyone in the village except for Spike and Bubba have been in the watertower, which you can see because of the look in their eyes, and so I thought Spike's mum had probably been in the watertower and she probably told Spike that it was safe to go in the watertower so he was confident that it's alright to go in there, and so he passed it on to Bubba after he'd come out, saying that it's safe and so Bubba went in. So I thought it's like a circle and it keeps getting passed on to everyone that it's safe to go in the watertower but it controls you after you've been in.

S: I reckon that, because at the beginning it says no one remembers when it was built and who built it, because they might have known before but when they've been in no one remembers because it's hypnotised them or something and that egg shape could have been some kind of outerspace spaceship or something …

D: Right, so a number of you are thinking the watertower is not a watertower, it's something else, right?

M: I think the watertower is probably a watertower but it's not just a plain watertower. I think that everyone who has swum in the watertower has that really scary look in their eyes, because when Bubba came out he had the look in his eyes and he said it was all right to swim in there so I think it looks kinda like a spaceship in a way and like it's landed and everyone who swims in it gets that look in their eyes and is controlled by it.

D: Does anyone else want to say anything about that look in their eyes because that does get your attention doesn't it?

A: They're all looking towards the watertower all the time so there must be something from the watertower that went inside their body to make them look at the watertower the whole time.

B: Their eyebrows show that they're angry, because when they look at the watertower you can see that their eyebrows are down and they look really mad.

D: What's interesting to me is that all of you are talking about the pictures. Nobody's said anything much about about the story itself. (Stephen did.)

S: Yeh, I said that at the beginning no one remembered who built it and when it was built because they had gone into the watertower …

D: That's right, you did too.

A: They make you think, the whole story just makes you think and …

D: Makes you think what?

A: Makes you think why it was written and what was <u>in</u> the watertower and … the water only swirls like that if there's something in it and all the noises he heard, it makes you think, what were they? And there's no right or wrong answer, it's just what you think.

B: Yeh, just what you think, but also it had a beginning and a middle but it left you … it didn't tell you why, it didn't tell you when, well it did tell you when it happened but like it didn't tell you the conclusion, like it didn't tell you the end part, it just left you, oh the books over now …

K-A: Yeh, it sort of, at the end of the story left you dangling not knowing why, when, where, how …

D: So what do you do then, do you fill that bit in yourself?

Several: Yeh, yeh.

L: Yeh, like Steven was saying, it looks as like they're hypnotised, it looks like that on the front cover too because the names, Gary Crew and Steven Woolman are upside down from each other and it's like things are whirling around like you're hypnotised and you don't know what's going on and you don't care what's going on …

K-A: And on the water tower on the front cover it's like there's light coming down through the middle and like there's swirls around the outside like (M: it's a space ship) there's something about to come out or something …

L: Yeh, and I was going to say, if there were no illustrations you wouldn't have a clue what the book was about.

D: Now I find it interesting that you said you have to make up your own version because the book leaves you up in the air … so what I'd like to know is how you did that, I'd like to know how you decided what's really happening.

K-A: We've already told you that.

D: Have you?

K-A: Yeh, I told you it's like an egg and it's going to hatch and it's hatched or something's inside it making the whirl in the water …

D: But what about at the end, how does it end? I mean, if it ends up in the air, you write the ending … and decide what happens in the end.

A: Well, if there was a sequel, I don't know what it would be like because there's heaps of different endings, they could find out what was in there they could just, like keep passing, being safe and people would keep swimming in there or, I don't know.

D: We've only got about a minute left, has anyone got something to say we haven't heard so far?

B: In the watertower, the man who, if someone built it, then that man or the person who built it might be in the water making it swirl (others: yeh), he might be dead, just floating around making it swirl.

D: You don't think it's an alien …

L: No-one knows …

A: There could be a curse on that man and he's just waiting around on the bottom of the thing and making it swirl and there's a curse on him.

M: And anyone who goes in there, they get the angry look.

B: Yeh because when Bubba comes his eyes are all right but when he comes out they're like all the other people.

L: You don't know the guy in the water is dead, I mean, he might be still alive and he might be threatening the people not to tell anyone.

D: But you don't know it's a person.

L: Yeh, but if it was a person, he could be threatening the people that's going in there not to tell anyone he's in there.

A: Since all their eyes are like that, that could be like someone coulda tried to kill the man and his eyes, when he died, or if there is a man, were like that so anyone who goes in there gets his eyes.

SH: It's like the watertower's a mother to them and it keeps saying 'look at me' and it's a secret, and they keep on looking at it it's like a secret and somethings telling them to just keep on looking at it.

KA: In this picture (of the town and the man with the fork) he's got a fork and in another picture where Bubba's looking at the tower and he's hiding in the bushes, he sees this big sort of claw thing and it's just like the fork.

At this stage, the bell went and we had to finish but several of the children came up to me at later stages in the day to show where the claw/fork appears in other parts of the book.

Activities

1. Return now to the definition of reading you wrote down at the start of this chapter. Do you wish to modify it? Share and discuss your definition with other people who have read this chapter.

2. Newspapers and talkback shows frequently run what are known as 'back to basics' campaigns. The following letter is typical of those published during such campaigns. Use your informed perspective on reading to write a response to this letter.

BACK TO BASICS

We could solve the problem of illiteracy in our schools if teachers were trained to teach phonics.

When I was a child all teachers used this method and all children learned to read. It's logical and simple—teach the sounds of the letters, then the letters become words and once they know words children can read.

I think the government should make this approach compulsory before more children's lives are ruined.

Angry mother of four.

Annotated bibliography

Freebody, P & Luke, A 1990 ' "Literacies" Programs:Debates and Demands in Cultural Context'. *Prospect,* 5(3).
Introduces the important concept of multiple reader roles and stresses the notion that all roles must be developed simultaneously. The concepts have been updated and broadened in recent times, but this is still the best introduction to the notion of the four reader roles.

Freebody, P Luke, A & Gilbert, P 1991 'Reading Positions and Practices in the Classroom', *Curriculum Inquiry* 21:4.
Reviews contemporary theories of reading and then argues for a critical social view that links reading practices to classroom Discourses.

Hornsby, D 2000 *A Closer Look at Guided Reading.* Eleanor Curtain, Armadale, Victoria.
Clear, practical and very thorough account of shared and guided reading practices in the primary classroom. Greatly appreciated by classroom teachers for its numerous practical examples.

Knobel, M & Healy, A (eds) 1998 *Critical Literacies in the Primary Classroom.* PETA, Sydney.
Presents a wide range of classroom applications of critical literacy from teachers such as Jenny O'Brien, Chris Searle and Ray Misson as well as the two editors.

O'Brien, J 1994 'Critical Literacy in an Early Childhood Classroom'. *Australian Journal of Language and Literacy,* 17:1.
A unique insight into the thinking of an early childhood teacher as she tries to promote a critical approach to texts in her multi-age classroom.

References

Ashton-Warner, S 1963 *Teacher.* Bantam, New York.

Baker, C 1991 'Classroom Literacy Events'. *Australian Journal of Reading,* 14:2.

Baker, C & Luke, A 1991 *Towards a Critical Sociology of Reading Pedagogy.* John Benjamins, Philadelphia.

Berg, L 1977 *Reading and Loving.* Routledge & Kegan Paul, London.

Cambourne, B 1988 *The Whole Story: Natural Learning and the Acquisition of Literacy in the Classroom.* Ashton Scholastic, Auckland.

Chall, JS 1967 *Learning to Read: The Great Debate.* McGraw-Hill, New York.

Comber, B 1994 'Classroom Explorations in Critical Literacy'. *Australian Journal of Language and Literacy,* 16:1.

Corcoran, B Hayhoe, M & Pradl, G (eds) 1994 *Knowledge in the Making: Challenging the Text in the Classroom.* Boynton/Cook, Heinemann, Portsmouth, NH.

Crew, G & Woolman, S 1994 *The Watertower.* ERA, Flinders Park, South Australia.

Fish, S 1980 *Is There a Text in This Class?: The Authority of Interpretive Communities.* Harvard University Press, Cambridge, MA.

Freebody, P & Luke, A 1990 '"Literacies" Programs: Debates and Demands in Cultural Context'. *Prospect,* Vol. 5(3).

Freebody, P Luke, A & Gilbert, P 1991 'Reading Positions and Practices in the Classroom'. *Curriculum Inquiry,* 21:4.

Goodman, K 1967 'Reading: A Psycholinguistic Guessing Game'. *Journal of the Reading Specialist,* 6, 126–135.

Goodman, K 1986 *What's Whole in Whole Language?* Scholastic, Toronto.

Holdaway, D 1979 *The Foundations of Literacy.* Ashton Scholastic, Sydney.

Hornsby, D 2000 *A Closer look at Guided Reading.* Eleanor Curtin, Armadale, SA.

Iser, W 1978 *The Act of Reading.* Routledge and Kegan Paul, London.

Kempe, A 1993 'No Single Meaning: Empowering Students to Construct Socially Critical Readings of the Text'. *Australian Journal of Language and Literacy,* 16:4.

Knobel, M & Healy, A (eds) 1998 *Critical Literacies in the Primary Classroom.* PETA, Sydney.

Kress, G 1985 *Linguistic Processes in Sociocultural Practice.* Deakin University Press, Geelong, Victoria.

Mellor, B 1984 *Changing Stories.* Chalkface Press, Perth.

Morris, A & Stewart-Dore, N 1984 *Learning to Learn from Text: Effective Reading in the Content Areas.* Addison-Wesley, Sydney.

O'Brien, J 1994 'Critical Literacy in an Early Childhood Classroom'. *Australian Journal of Language and Literacy,* 17:1.

Painter, C 1985 *Learning the Mother Tongue.* Deakin University Press, Geelong, Victoria.

Pappas, C & Pettegrew, B 1998 'The Role of Genre in the Psycholinguistic Guessing Game'. *Language Arts,* 75:1.

Reid, I (ed.) 1987 *The Place of Genre in Learning: Current Debates.* Deakin University Press, Geelong, Victoria.

Richardson, P 1991 'Language as Personal Resource and as Social Construct: Competing Views of Literacy Pedagogy in Australia'. *Educational Review,* 43:2.

Rosenblatt, L 1978 *The Reader, the Text, the Poem: The Transactional Theory of the Literary Work.* Southern Illinois University Press, Carbondale.

Smith F 1978 *Reading.* Cambridge University Press, London.

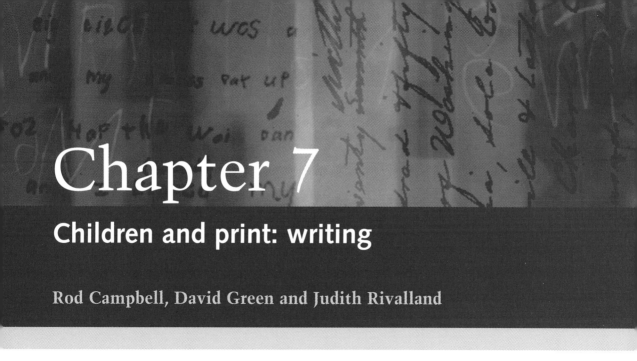

Chapter 7

Children and print: writing

Rod Campbell, David Green and Judith Rivalland

INTRODUCTION

Writing is essentially a cultural artefact. Different cultures have developed systems of writing that can be classified as alphabets, syllabaries and characters. European languages are based upon the old Greek alphabet, adapted by the Romans to produce the Western European phonetic symbols for the limited number of vowels and consonants with which we are so familiar. The Cyrillic alphabets of Eastern Europe are also derived from Greek. Arabic and Hebrew use syllabaries in which the symbols represent syllables rather than individual letters. The Japanese hiragana and katakana are other examples of syllabaries. The Japanese also use Chinese characters. Chinese writing makes use of characters as logographs representing actual words and complex concepts in visual form, as well as representing sounds.

The cultural and social development of writing is also manifested in the history of writing. In many early cultures, writing was initially used for commercial and administrative purposes. The possibilities for writing poetry and narrative emerged over time. The Bible, particularly those books known by Christians as the Old Testament, has formed the basis for three major religions. Other poetry and sagas of earlier cultures are also available today in translation.

Writing, regardless of the symbol system used, allows us to have contact with the ideas and activities of other cultures across space and time. In very recent years, technologies have allowed the immediate use of spoken and written language. Email, for example, is a very recent form of writing which provides an example of a technology that bridges some of the features of both written and oral language. Writing, however, continues to maintain pre-eminence as a widely preferred form of record-keeping and reporting, as well as of narrative and poetic expression.

The 19th century introduction of compulsory education for children heralded a social and national demand for universal literacy in many countries. Writing became one of the most important objectives of education. But people have different abilities, needs and perspectives on writing, and the history of writing education has been a site for multiple contests for many years. Debates about grammar, spelling and handwriting have been the most obvious areas of contest, with these debates often masking the realities of writing and writing instruction.

By focusing upon the visually obvious features of writing, critics of writing instruction have often not sufficiently considered the nature of writing, the relationship between writing and reading, or the way the social purposes of writing change for different groups in our culture.

With this brief introduction to the past, present and future uses and values of writing, the aims of this chapter are to enhance your understanding and knowledge about:

- the notion of writing as a process involving the expression of thinking in a written or other symbolic form for a variety of cultural purposes

- the use of a variety of types of texts to assist in expressing the content of writing

- the nature and development of children's writing and spelling

- the use of the conventions of spelling, punctuation, grammars, vocabulary choice and style in writing.

APPROACHES TO CLASSROOM WRITING: A RECENT HISTORY

Until the 1960s, writing development was predominantly regarded as a series of skills that could be drilled separately from one another and from any particular context for writing (Wilkinson et al. 1980). Following the Dartmouth Conference in New Hampshire in 1966, the world of writing education entered a period when the educational arguments between writing as skill development and writing as creative expression reflected ideological intent rather than instructional purpose.

In 1970, James Britton provided a three-part model of the writing function. *Expressive writing* closely resembles speech; *transactional writing* is concerned with communicating information about the world; and in *poetic writing*, the emphasis is increasingly upon the artistry of language and self-expression.

In the 1980s, Donald Graves (1983) brought about a radical change in views of writing development by moving the emphasis from the product of children's writing to the process used in the production of the writing. The *Process Writing* movement has had a powerful impact on the way writing development is viewed. Cambourne (1984) contributed to this movement with work based on a close study of how children learn to talk. From this he outlined a set of 'natural' conditions that would enhance writing development: the provision of good models; the opportunity to make errors without reprisal; constructive feedback; learner responsibility; sustained practice and engagement in the task. (In Chapter 3, Cambourne's notions are presented as Conditions for Learning.)

Process writing came to be identified within the suite of literacy education practices involved in the whole language approach. Pedagogically, the *Process Writing* movement lead to a classroom approach in which children were encouraged to draft, conference, edit, proofread and publish their writing. In too many classrooms, however, the process writing approach resulted in writing too much narrative, and in too great a dependency on the resources of the children themselves (Rothery 1984).

In challenging process writing, Rothery (1984) and Christie (1990) promoted the development of children's writing through the teaching of explicit knowledge about the genres of written language. They claimed that children needed to be taught explicitly about the structural and textual features of a range of text types or genres. The main argument they gave for such an approach is that competence with a range of genres appears to be one of the keys to success in schooling. They argued that it was the responsibility of schools to provide all children with access to these genres. In Australia in particular, this view has been influential in promoting what is known as the *Genre Approach* to writing. This approach promotes a selection of genres or types of texts (such as reports, recounts, explanations, expositions, narratives and argument) that are modelled, jointly constructed with the teacher, and then independently written by the children (Derewianka 1990).

More recently, critical social theorists refocused on the purpose and content of writing. Gilbert (1993) claimed that it is not good enough just to write a technically sound genre. She cites the example of a young boy who wrote what his teacher deemed a good example of a procedural genre. But the procedure described how to set girls in concrete. Gilbert notes, strongly, that some discussion of purpose, content and values was warranted in this instance.

WRITING FOR LEARNING, AND FOR SOCIAL AND COMMUNITY ACTION

Other theorists have promoted the use of writing to make an impact on the community in which the writers live. Searle (1998) used various forms of writing, and especially poetry, to help children in a disadvantaged area in England to come to terms with their environment and then to act.

> *I would take my class for walks along the streets and to the parks, squares and churchyards of the local area, getting them to bring their exercise books and to record their observations, sketch images, and draft lines that they can later incorporate into descriptive passages and poems. On these field trips, I always ask students to look at the world immediately around them, at the local people in the streets, and at the houses and council*

estates close to the school ... There are people and scenes that these students see every day, but they are asked to look at them in new ways, to study them closely, to invent metaphors and similes to describe them, and to treat what they see with imaginative empathy (Searle 1998:79–80).

Many of the poems that evolved from these excursions were published and had a great impact on the children themselves and on the wider community:

Poems such as this contradicted our critics in the media who claimed that children can not think for themselves or respond to events through action unless they are led by an adult 'pied piper' or 'indoctrinator'. However, without prompting, students began naming the ubiquitous 'they' who controlled their parents' and their own lives, and to protest against the gross injustices being enacted on their very doorsteps (Searle 1998:85).

Similarly, but in different ways, both Paulo Freire and Sylvia Ashton-Warner have used the learners' own experiences to promote literacy. Freire (1972) used workers' needs and interests in Latin America as starting points for teaching literacy skills that would empower them. Ashton-Warner (1963) turned children's oral accounts of their experiences into written language in what she called a Language Experience Approach.

TEACHING WRITING: LEARNING WRITING

You will find various elements of these many approaches (skills-based, process, genre, critical) in classrooms throughout Australia. Many teachers will actually implement a learning program based upon a professional and effective combination of these approaches. Writing is not only an expressive and creatively artistic endeavour; it is also a craft, involving the writer in making choices about the nature and use of written and visual language conventions for a purpose.

Observing, thinking and writing for a purpose empower people in many ways. Teachers of writing are now involved in helping their students to know:

- what to write about (the content of own and others' experiences)

- how to present the experiences (selecting the genre required for the writing purpose)

- how to craft and style the writing itself (applying knowledge of the conventions and styles of writing).

KEY ISSUES IN TEACHING WRITING

1. Creativity and craft: the conflict that should never have been

Writing is both an art and a craft. The greater the knowledge and control of the elements of the craft, the greater the possibility of more mature and sophisticated levels of creativity. However, a focus upon craft with little attention to creativity will ensure a skills-based approach to learning writing, based upon worksheets, grammar books, spelling lists and handwriting. Any creative outcome from programs of these kinds is at risk. Unfortunately, grammar and spelling programs, often masquerading as writing programs, have damaged learner self-confidence for centuries.

Yet, a focus upon creativity without due attention to the elements of the craft leaves learners reliant upon their own resources. Any creative outcome from such a reductionist program will necessarily be limited because of the lack of knowledge and articulated understanding of how language contributes to the creation of meaning. The feeling of being empowered as a writer is self-confidence in the development of one's abilities.

The elements of style, the elements of written language, need to be developed by teachers within programs that explicitly link the learned skill with its use and application. Originality and creativity, the use of the imagination, is enhanced by the control that the developing writer has over the grammatical, lexical and stylistic possibilities of language. Teachers, especially teachers who are also writers themselves, have been able to combine creative teaching with learning of skills. The conflicting statements about differences between skills and creativity should never have been, and have no place in the philosophy and practice of the effective teacher.

2. The reading/writing connection: linking written texts through talk

Much has been written about developing originality, creativity and authenticity in children's writing. But viewed as part of our social practices, almost all writing is really a reshaping of the social texts to which each individual has been given access (Meek 1987). Therefore, teachers carefully select literature and a variety of other factual texts from which children can draw for their experiences of becoming writers.

However, merely being immersed in literature and written language is a necessary but not sufficient condition to ensure that all children are going to 'pick up' important aspects of learning how to write. Children need to be read to, to read for themselves, to respond to literature, to discuss the meanings of written texts, and more importantly to consciously discuss different aspects of how written texts are constructed (see Chapters 4, 5 and 10). Explicit discussion and reflection on what is read will facilitate children's writing development only through modelling and teaching of the reading–writing relationship. It is essential that teachers see reading and writing as joint activities.

Laurie Keim, classroom teacher and poet, talks about reading and writing being opposite sides of the same coin. The metaphor is useful, but the metaphor becomes powerful when the coin is seen to be spinning; and even more powerful when we consider who is spinning the coin of the reading/writing connection.

3. Student diversity: socialisation patterns and writing

Green, in the first chapter of this book, states that not all cultures have the same language-socialising procedures. Some groups of children fail at school because their oral language patterns do not match with those used in schools (Wells 1981; Heath 1983). In a similar way, it is highly likely that we disadvantage some children whose literacy socialisation patterns differ from those supported by the optimal learning conditions outlined by Cambourne (1984).

Parents and teachers clearly use scaffolding to actively intervene in the language-learning practices of children (Vygotsky 1978). Therefore, the nature of the intervention provided by teachers and parents will shift children's writing to a level of development beyond that which they could achieve by themselves. What may seem to be natural about the development of writing in children may also be the result of careful scaffolding and explicit teaching by knowledgeable parents and early childhood teachers and caregivers. Rivalland (1991) reiterates the point that writing is a consciously learned social activity, where children have acquired, developed and learned the use and application of symbol systems within the contexts of social use.

So, children from different language and cultural backgrounds bring variety and variation into the classroom; especially in terms of the scaffolding and interventions provided by parents and other adults in their communities. In multicultural societies, and in those schools that reflect their local communities closely, teachers ensure they acknowledge and involve the contributions of each learner's background.

4. Developing writers: the importance of conscious learning

Crafted writing is an after-the-event statement of subjective experience. That is, the first or early drafts of writing mirror subjective experience. Rewriting is the subsequent highly conscious activity that involves crafting the piece of writing. Writing encourages reflection on what has occurred, and therefore encourages editing and rethinking.

Writing is a learned, socio-cultural behaviour, a product of our cultural practices. Writing and reading need to be learned, and given the individual differences so widely manifested by learners, the amount of specialised teaching needed for developing conscious action and learning will vary among the students in any group (Rivalland 1991). Writing development, like all other human learning, is also closely linked to motivation, ability and opportunity. The writer, musician, sports star, actor and artist master new applications of their respective symbolic systems, and new applications add other dimensions to the complexity of the task. Few people will become experts in one of these fields, with the majority of people developing differing levels of competency. Interestingly, we do not have the expectation that most people will become expert musicians or artists. But the societal expectation for writing is for universal competence. So writing has to be learned by all, and therefore taught in ways that support all learners.

5. Becoming a writer: from invention to convention

Young children develop and acquire spoken language as they recognise the social conventions and the cultural applications of language. Written language is entirely a culturally-based phenomenon, as stated earlier in this chapter and in this book. As children move into their uses of written language, in association with the school systems, they become involved in using the inventiveness that is so vital to acquiring language and learning about its uses and possibilities. As children continue to develop their knowledge and application of writing, they use their natural inventiveness as a bridge to learning to use the conventions.

The next two sections of this chapter will provide the evidence to support the notion that children move from invention to convention (Whitmore & Goodman 1995).

THE DEVELOPMENT OF CHILDREN'S WRITING

Children's development in writing follows a recognised pattern from early scribbles and drawings in infancy towards control of the dimensions of writing during the school years. These phases of development have been observed by Ferreiro and Teberovsky (1983), and by Clay (1975) as well as a number of other writers. One of the most influential current models for teachers to use in observing and recording children's writing development is the *Writing Developmental Continuum* (1994) produced by the Education Department of Western Australia as part of the First Steps Program (see Chapter 4). This continuum identifies six phases of writing development, and also lists indicators to assist teachers to observe in which phases a child's writing samples may be placed. The phases are:

1. Role-play writing

The child writes a combination of symbols, letters, drawings and other marks and demonstrates that such marks carry a message.

Example 1

2. Experimental writing

The child now uses more letters and demonstrates awareness of the constancy of the meaning carried by the written message, and of the one-to-one correspondence of the spoken and written word. There is also a clearly demonstrated knowledge of the conventions of writing in English: print is orientated from left to right and top-to-bottom on the page.

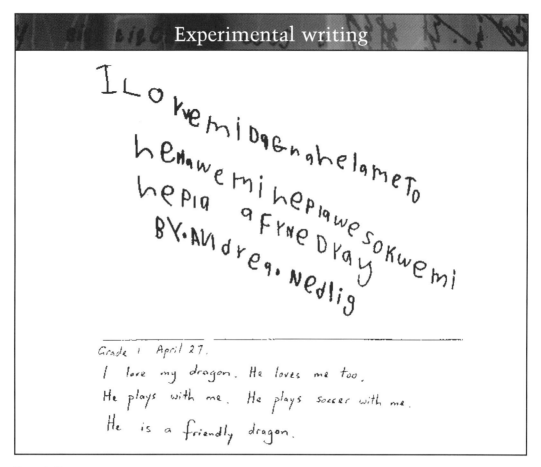

Example 2

3. Early writing

Basic sentence structures are now used together with a sound understanding of the grapho-phonic or code system, often to the extent of over-generalising phonic elements in their spelling. Children also demonstrate understanding of purposes and contexts for writing, drawing upon their experiences with literature, oral language, media and environmental print.

Early writing

YEAR 2: PRIMARY school

Margaret 21

I wos going dawn

casell *(Terrace)* terast on

my big bieck. It wos a stiep

Hill and my brakes pat up wen

I woz Haf the wai dan the

(broked) Hill and I Broaed my

(collar bone) Solla Boan. and I had to

go to the hosPtall to

(sling) get a sliiea on It.

It'z getin Betat. ter:

I can riDe It again

a gain

Teacher Head /

Example 3

4. Conventional writing

The children now write a range of text types including stories, reports and expositions, using a variety of simple, compound and complex sentences. The children are developing capabilities in editing and proofreading their own work, thus demonstrating aspects of the writer's craft in changing and improving their own texts.

Conventional writing

What are whales? Whales are not fish they are mammals because they have a blow hole.

All whales have a air hole on its back. And a dorsel fin. The dorsel fin helps it to swim. People think whales are fish well they aren't, they are mammals.

Whales come in different sizes. The blue whale is (30 metres) long. The second largest is the fin whale. It is (24 metres) long.

There are different kinds of whales there are baleen whales and toothed whales. Balleen whales eat tiny creatures called plankton. There are 17 kinds of plankton. Toothed whales eat fish.

Babie whales are called calfs. Their mothers suckle there babies on milk. It is born under water. It quickly takes it to the surface. So it can breath.

Megan. 2nd draft. 3 Sept. Grade 3.

Example 4

5. **Proficient writing**

At this level, children demonstrate that they can adapt text types to suit purpose and audience. They can demonstrate control over most essential elements to produce a logical and cohesive text.

6. **Advanced writing**

Advanced writers demonstrate skills in controlling and manipulating the linguistic and structural components of writing to enhance clarity and impact. Advanced writers reflect on and critically evaluate their own writing to suit their own purposes.

Understanding the development of children's writing provides teachers with information from a range of theoretical perspectives, which in turn supports a range of strategies for teaching writing.

We will now consider, in turn, some of the skills that form part of the teaching of writing; the knowledge of the conventions of written English that students need to learn.

Proficient writing

SKINKS

There are more than 140 types of lizards in Australia. A skink is a type of lizard. Goana, blue tonges and geckos are lizards to. Scientists say there are still more to be classified.

Some skinks are very small. They are about 6 cms long. Some are 60 cms long. Skinks have thin bodies with a tail. Their bodys look smooth. Most skinks have four legs and each leg has four toes.

Skinks live all over Australia. Small skinks live in gardens in cities and even on the balconies of home units. Skinks love the sun. Most skinks live on the ground but a few type live in trees. Skinks eat insecs like flies, and grasshoppers. They swallow the insect hole.

Most skinks lay eggs. When the babies are hatch they are very small. If you grab a skink by the tail it usually comes off as the skink escapes.

T. Smith. Grade 6

Example 5

TEACHING SPELLING

Those who set out to remember every letter of every word will never make it. Those who try to spell by sound alone will be defeated. Those who learn how to walk through words with sensible expectations, noting sound, pattern and meaning relationships will know what to remember, and they will learn English (Henderson 1985:67).

Spelling involves more than memorising strings of letters. It *involves*:

(a) ***phonemic awareness***: knowing how to separate the sounds and syllables in words. Examples:

'bed' contains the sounds /b/ /e/ /d/ and rhymes with 'red'.
'separate' is comprised of sep-ar-ate.

(b) ***grapho-phonic knowledge***: knowing the letter names in the English alphabet, the sound–symbol relationships, and that sounds can be represented by different letters. Examples:

'b' says /b/, 'ed' says /ed/. And that 'bed' rhymes with 'said'.

(c) ***morphemic awareness and knowledge***: using the meaning of words as a clue to their spelling and realising that meaning units (morphemes) are often spelt the same in different words, for example:

<u>sign</u>, <u>sign</u>al, <u>sign</u>ature.

(d) ***etymological awareness and knowledge***: using the origins of a word as a clue to its meaning and spelling:

biology from the old Greek words *bios* (life) and *logos* (a word for the study of); the study of life.

(e) ***visual awareness***: using familiarity with how words look in order to determine the correct way to spell them; if it doesn't look right, check it. The significant point is that there are legitimate ways to group letters in English. A child might attempt to spell *chair* as *chare*. This is a legitimate attempt because some words in English spell the /air/ sound as /are/ as does *rare*. On the other hand, had the child spelt *chair* as *jhyr*, the attempt is a non-legitimate one because that combination of letters never occurs in English. Three important pedagogical points emerge from this understanding:

- the importance of distinguishing between the two attempts because the child who consistently makes non-legitimate attempts at spelling needs a lot more help (and help of a different kind) than the child who makes incorrect but legitimate choices

- the importance of reading, writing and discussing words frequently in order to build up the visual awareness of what words should look like

- the importance of phonemic awareness, a necessary but not sufficient condition for learning to spell and read (Adams 1990).

The purpose of learning to spell is to improve our writing by making it easier to read and by enabling us to write more quickly. It is important to remember that the more automatically we can spell, the easier it is to write since greater conscious attention can be applied to the content of our writing. It follows that most spelling instruction/ development should take place in the context of producing various kinds of texts. This appears to be stating the obvious, but as we shall see shortly, at least one of the major approaches to teaching spelling either rejects this notion or accepts the shaky assumption that children transfer knowledge from one learning situation to another. However, it should be noted that children do need systematic practice in using those strategies that will make them effective spellers.

There is an unfortunate outcome from a heavy and singular focus upon spelling ability as an indicator of intelligence. There is no causal link between intelligence and spelling ability (Gentry & Gillet 1993). The use of spelling ability as an automatic indicator of general intelligence or level of education by many employers, government ministers and media outlets is too often misplaced.

Educational approaches to spelling

The National Literacy and Numeracy Plan Project: Spelling (1999), notes three main approaches in spelling pedagogy: Traditional, Transitional and Student Oriented. You need to be aware of these paradigms as you encounter them in schools.

1. THE TRADITIONAL APPROACH

The traditional approach involves transmission modes of teaching and rote memorisation of lists of words, often using commercially prepared lists and oral drilling. The lists are drilled through the week and tested on Friday. Such a whole-class approach takes little heed of the needs and experiences of individual children, and is a monumental waste of time for competent spellers (up to 2.5 hours per week in some classrooms). For those who are not competent spellers, spelling 'lessons' are a constant source of public humiliation. There is little transfer of 'knowledge' from isolated spelling sessions to the children's general writing. One study showed that by the end of Year 4, children who had received no formal spelling instruction could spell as well as traditionally taught children (Hammill et al. 1977).

2. THE TRANSITIONAL APPROACH

The transitional approach still incorporates direct instruction and weekly tests but adds these significant features:

- Children's attention is now directed towards the kinds of awareness discussed above: phonological, grapho-phonic, morphemic, etymological and visual.

- A wide range of interactive strategies are adopted. These include word games; word sorts where children in groups categorise words on the basis of phonic, morphemic and visual features; pre-testing so that children focus on words they *don't* already know; and the development of strategies such as *'look, say, cover, write, check'*. For a more detailed coverage of interactive spelling strategies, see Gentry & Gillet (1993) and Gentry (1997). Also look at *Spelling: From beginnings to independence*, published by the Department for Education and Children's Services, South Australia (1999).

- Words to be learnt are now taken from the children's reading material including texts used in the content or key learning areas. The contrast with the traditional approach is stark and the key differences are context, purpose and effectiveness.

3. THE STUDENT-ORIENTED APPROACH

This incorporates all elements of the transitional approach above, but adds two essential components:

(a) Spelling is seen as a developmental process. *The National Literacy and Numeracy Plan Project: Spelling Report* (1999) adopts the stages of development as seen by Henderson (1985). These stages are similar to those proposed by a number of writers:

- *Preliterate.* Letters (and scribble) are strung together randomly to represent words. These letters do not correspond to sound.

- *Letter-name.* Letters represent sounds but spellings are often abbreviated: TTLSHIWWYR (twinkle, twinkle little star ...) or 'Tk' for truck.

- *Within-word pattern*. Words are spelt exactly as they sound, though often unconventionally: niys liyts (nice lights).

- *Syllable juncture.* A visual memory of spelling is apparent. The speller moves from phonological to morphological and visual spelling: komp a teshn (competition); anner ver sere (anniversary).

- *Derivational constancy.* Relationships of words, derivations and multiple meanings are used to help with spelling: tellyvishion.

(*National Literacy and Numeracy Plan Project: Spelling Report*, 1999:13, examples added.)

Note: children's development usually overlaps several stages; the stages should only be used as a rough guide to the kinds of strategies different children are using.

(b) Spelling is seen as an integral part of writing. 'Invented' spelling is encouraged in the writing process so as not to slow down the flow of the writing. Such approximated spellings are valued by teachers as a source of information about the child's thinking and strategies with words. These inventions are noted and discussed in editing conferences and other focused teaching sessions. At this early level, spelling is individualised because the words are part of that child's writing. It is therefore possible to mentor each child and provide the scaffolding that will move that child ahead from the stage of development currently occupied.

However, two cautions must be sounded here. Firstly, if teachers are not consciously providing students with activities and strategies to move the students' spelling development along, students can easily remain in the middle phase of development. Secondly, if children are not encouraged to write legibly, they are often unable to recognise their own errors.

TEACHING GRAMMAR

Children bring their awareness of language and grammar use with them into the classroom, but the traditional models for teaching grammar (parsing and analysis, with an emphasis upon rules and the use of exercise ditto sheets) seemed to operate without any reference to the knowledge children bring to writing. Alternatively, the creative writing movement has always recognised children's language abilities, but the practice of refusing to teach grammar has contributed little to good classroom learning practices. Leaving children to rely entirely upon their own resources disadvantages those children who do not have sufficient experience with written language upon which to rely. Failing to teach children the knowledge and skills they require is an abdication of the teacher's responsibilities.

Grammar instruction that uses a combination of the children's language resources and the teacher's knowledge and skill is more likely to be successful. The following snapshots indicate how this approach to grammar instruction operates.

Snapshot 7.1:
Teaching the term 'Preposition'

Teachers in pre-school and lower primary are already using the concept of 'position word' with the young children in their class, and given the fact that the children seem to understand the concept and the word, I wondered whether they were able to access their own metalinguistic awareness to assist them to use the term 'position word'. It is really only one step to the actual use of the term 'preposition'. Yet most English syllabi have advised the teaching of the term in Year 4 or Year 5. Many teachers with whom I have been working have found that most children in Year 3, and many in Year 2 are able to use the word 'preposition' correctly and easily in talking about words. The following activity can be used with children in any grade, and is particularly useful in working with ESL students of all ages.

I begin the lesson by holding two objects and placing them near, on top of, under, next to, beside, etc. each other. The children eventually but quickly realise that I want them to supply 'position' words, and I list these words on chart paper or the board. Depending on the age of the children, I will supply a list of all prepositions, and then show a couple of preposition phrase poems as models. These models have been completed by children their age at other schools. I then list the rules for writing the poem, and demonstrate how to apply them, undertaking a joint construction with the children so that they become familiar with the process.

The children then work in pairs or threes to construct and write their own poem. They need about 15–20 minutes for this. At the end, the children really enjoy reading out their poems, and the groups actually devise clever ways to present their poems so that everyone in the group gets an opportunity to participate. Finally, I congratulate the children on their efforts, and then talk about the words. Many children, more among the children in higher grades, are able to tell me that the 'position' words locate/place/position us in space and time. I wait for that Latinate word 'position' instead of the Old English 'place', because I can make the connection to the term 'preposition' so much more easily. In follow-up lessons, we talk about prepositions and the phrase when we are talking about writing, especially when the prepositional phrase is misplaced in a clause. With older students, we can explore the function (and impact on meaning) of the down-ranked phrase in very complex and highly nominalised clause constructions within sentences (see pp. 90–91).

Prepositions list: in out into out of inside outside on off onto upon to from up down over under above below with without within beside beneath behind before beyond at near by past after along around across against through throughout amid amidst among amongst between of for except (time) before during after since till until

Example:

The Café
Down the road
Around the corner
Near the bridge
Over the river
Is the café where we had lunch.

Rules:
1. Every line must begin with one of the words on the list.
2. Each line is two or three words long.
3. You can write as many lines as you like.
4. You can repeat the use of list words, but try to use as many different list words as you can.
5. Complete the last line with a statement.
6. Give your poem a title (if you did not start with a title).

Snapshot 7.2:
Teaching pronouns and demonstratives (words that refer to other words)

Students in the middle years can use their implicit understanding of reference systems in order to learn the terms 'pronoun' and 'demonstrative'. The students were given the following piece of text as a teaching and learning worksheet. 'Hidden' in the text is a demonstrative ('this', 'that', 'those', 'these') that can refer to many other terms and expressions in the text.

Direction: Make participant chains of the nouns and pronouns that *refer* to them.

'Whales were sighted in Moreton Bay after many years, and so people came to see them. They went on boats to see them close up.

'The teacher decided, therefore, that a whale-watching excursion would be worthwhile for the children. On the day of the excursion, Tom went with Bill and Ken. He was happy in their company.

'The children enjoyed the trip, watching the whales at play and seeing them breach and slap the water. One came so close that it splashed some of them. This was great fun, the boys had shouted.

'It was judged by them all to be a great day, and they wanted to see them again.'

The teacher asks the students to read the text silently, and after a couple of minutes, reads the text aloud. The children follow the text as the teacher reads it. The teacher tells the students that they are going to find the REFERRING WORDS that REFER to other words, and list them on the board and on their pages under the words: *whales*, *people*, *boats*, *teacher and children*, *children*, *Tom, Bill & Ken*. The students supply the words from the first paragraph: *them*, *they*, *them*, in turn matching these referring words to the referents (words referred to).

More than half of the students in most classes have understood the requirements of the lesson by the end of the second paragraph.

The third paragraph introduces really difficult items, and the teacher reinforces the students' findings that some of these referring words are referring in different directions. By this stage, most students appear to understand that referring words need to be used carefully so that the reader knows which words are referred to. At the end of the lesson, the students have most referring words listed vertically in the chains on their worksheets, but are also rewriting the text in order to repair the damage caused by using too many referring words. Students can therefore easily determine ways to change their wording, remove the ambiguity, and improve the clarity of their writing.

The lesson can be repeated using the students' own writing as working examples. In the process,

the students learn about pronouns and their real function in written text. They are also more knowledgeable about the differences between spoken and written texts, and that writers need to be careful about using pronouns or referring words. The students have also gained techniques for editing their writing, and have another set of terms for talking the talk about language in action as they also use terms with which they are already familiar: referring words, pronouns, nouns, ambiguity, edit, function of referring words, plural, singular, number, gender, sentence, paragraph.

TEACHING PUNCTUATION

Punctuation is a phenomenon of printing, and of the need to standardise texts so that printers and readers can benefit from that standardisation. Teachers can keep up to date with the latest changes in the conventions of punctuation from the latest editions of the *Style Manual* (see p. 112).

Essentially, punctuation is used either as **a boundary marker**:

- capital letter at beginning of sentence
- full stop, question mark or exclamation mark at end of sentence
- commas, colons and semi-colons operating as boundary markers within sentences
- quotation marks marking off conversations and quotations
- brackets of various types

or as a **marker to show relationships**, mark omissions and signpost meaning:

- apostrophe of possession
- apostrophe of omission
- signposts such as @ # ^ & * > < ~.

Punctuation, as with any sign that has become invested with meaning through its application and use, must be taught in the context of use. Creative teachers have developed many interesting and exciting strategies for teaching some of the elements of punctuation.

TEACHING WORD KNOWLEDGE

Writing uses words. Good writing uses words selectively and creatively to present intended meaning. Developing knowledge about words is central to education, and included within the reading and spelling program. But there is much that children can gain from learning how to use the dictionary, thesaurus, atlas and other reference books. Teachers encourage children to use words of interest, and celebrate that use, even when the result may be incongruous or even incorrect. Learning to use words is a consequence of trial and support.

SUMMARY

So how are we to merge these various views and models of writing and skills, and how are these models to be reconciled with the social model of language promoted in earlier chapters? The Freebody and Luke (1990) model introduced in Chapter 6 can be adapted to writing.

The Campbell/Green model of literacy practices

(after Freebody and Luke 1990).

READING			
CODE BREAKER	TEXT PARTICIPANT	TEXT USER	TEXT ANALYST
WRITING			
CODE KNOWLEDGE	MEANING MAKING	GENRE SELECTION	REFLECTION
Encoding	Focus on the 'what' of writing: personal or functional meaning making.	Thinking about audience.	Consciously reflecting on how writing presents particular values about the world.
Spelling		Choosing appropriate text style types.	
Grammar			
Orthographies	Voice	Rhetoric	Consciously using writing to change the world.
Keyboarding	Logic		
Wp skills			Logic and style

All four writer practices are important, and children need to develop all four simultaneously if they are to be effective users of written language. Moreover, all roles need to be encountered from the first writing experiences children have if they are to receive the right messages about writing. To focus too early and too strongly on one aspect of writing such as code knowledge makes it difficult for some children to gain the flow of language necessary for effective meaning making and reflection.

The secret to speaking, reading and writing is fluency, the ability to produce information in as seamless a manner as possible. Children who develop as fluent readers and writers have been exposed to years of good models of reading and writing. To concentrate too much on correctness at the letter and word level risks condemning children to non-fluent reading and writing.

On the other hand, it is important to remember that the longer children take to automate code knowledge, the more difficult they will find it to be effective and fluent writers. The *First Steps Project* (Writing Resource Book 1994) promotes a developmental approach to writing that gives children the time and freedom to be risk-takers in developing their writing. At the same time, teachers need to be conscious of supporting children to move beyond their current levels of development.

Activity

The following text was written by a seven-year-old child. Discuss the strengths and weaknesses of the child's text and how you might assist this child to improve the text. Some criteria are listed below to assist you.

> SALOWED
> I was walking in the Jungle. Pushing the Trees to side of me. And right in front of my eyes. I saw a giant tiger it had loud roaring. I couldn't stand it and I blocked my ears. And in One minets time. It opened its mouth. And then the tiger was ready to eat me up then I started to run as fast as. I can it jumped over my head. But I did not see it and. I ran in side and it swallowed me up. Then it seemed dark in his mouth and. I started to suffocate in the tigers mouth and in One second. I be gine to die.

Suggested criteria

1. How effective is the quality of the message?
2. How successfully is the genre/text type staged to meet its purpose?
3. How well has the language been selected to suit the topic?
4. How appropriate is the language for the intended audience (tenor)?
5. How effectively is punctuation used to support meaning?
6. How effectively does the text use the structures of written language? Or is it just speech written down?
7. Which spelling strategies is the child using effectively?
8. How effectively is standard Australian English used?

Annotated bibliography

Derewianka, B 1990 *Exploring How Texts Work.* PETA, Sydney.
An introduction that links process and genre approaches, then gives simple analyses of the main school genres and a suggested strategy for teaching them: the teaching cycle of modelling, joint

construction and independent construction. A simple, practical and inexpensive introduction to genre theory.

Gentry, R & Gillet, J 1993 *Teaching Kids to Spell.* Heinemann, Portsmouth, NH.
A witty and accessible text that challenges many of the conventional wisdoms on spelling. Full of interesting and worthwhile examples to illustrate a developmental approach to spelling.

Gilbert, P (ed.) 1993 *Gender Stories and the Language Classroom.* Deakin University Press, Geelong, Victoria.
Goes beyond the genre approach and marries this to a critical social viewpoint. Includes chapters from Barbara Kamler and Valerie Walkerdine.

References

Adams, MJ 1990 *Beginning to Read*. MIT Press, Cambridge, Mass.

Ashton-Warner, S 1963 *Teacher*. Bantam, London.

Britton, J 1970 *Language and Learning*. Penguin, Harmondsworth.

Cambourne, B 1984 'Language, learning and literacy'. In A Butler & J Turbill (eds) *Towards a Reading-Writing Classroom*. PETA, Sydney.

Campbell, R & Ryles, G 1996 *Grammar in its place*. OUP, Melbourne.

Christie, F 1990 (ed.) *Literacy for a Changing World*. ACER, Melbourne.

Clay, M 1975 *What did I write?* Heinemann, Exeter, NH.

Derewianka, B 1990 *Exploring How Texts Work*. PETA, Sydney.

Education Department of Western Australia 1994 *Overview and Indicators of Writing Developmental Continuum*. Longman Cheshire, Melbourne.

Ferreiro, E & Teberosky, A 1983 *Literacy before Schooling*. Heinemann, Portsmouth, NH.

Freebody, P & Luke, A 1990 'Literacies Programs: Debates and demands in cultural context'. *Prospect* 5:3:7–16.

Freire, P 1972 *Pedagogy of the Oppressed*. Sheed & Ward, London.

Gentry, JR & Gillet J 1993 *Teaching Kids to Spell*. Heinemann, Portsmouth, NH.

Gentry, JR 1997 *My Kids Can't Spell*. Heinemann, Portsmouth, NH.

Gilbert, P 1993 (ed.) *Gender Stories and the Language Classroom*. Deakin University Press, Geelong, Vic.

Graves, D 1983 *Writing: Teachers and Children at Work*. Heinemann, Portsmouth, NH.

Hammill, DD, Larsen, S & McNutt, G 1977 'The effects of spelling instruction: A preliminary study'. *Elementary School Journal*, No. 78, 67–72.

Heath, SB 1983 *Ways with Words: Language, Life and Work in Communities and Classrooms*. Cambridge University Press, Cambridge.

Henderson, E & Beers, J 1980 *Cognitive and Developmental Aspects of Learning to Spell*. International Reading Association, Newark, DE.

Henderson, E 1985 *Teaching Spelling*. Houghton-Mifflin, Boston.

Keim, L 2000 Personal Communication.

Meek, M 1987 'Playing the texts'. *Language Matters*, 1/87, 1–6.

National Literacy and Numeracy Plan Project: Spelling Report 1999 Department for Education and Children's Services South Australia, Adelaide.

Rivalland, J 1991 'Writing Development'. *Australian Journal of Reading*, 14, 4, 290–306.

Rothery, J 1984 'Teaching Writing in the Primary School: A Genre Based Approach to the Development of Writing Abilities'. *Working Papers in Linguistics, No. 4*. Department of Linguistics, University of Sydney.

Searle, C 1998 'Words and life: Critical literacy and cultural action'. In M Knobel & A Healy (eds) 1999 *Critical Literacies in the Primary Classroom*. PETA, Sydney.

Vygotsky, L 1978 *Thought and Language*. MIT Press, Cambridge, Mass.

Wells, G 1981 *Learning Through Interaction: The Study of Language Development.* Cambridge University Press, Cambridge.

Whitmore, KF & Goodman, YM 1995 'Transforming Curriculum in Language and literacy'. In S Bredekamp & T Rosengrant (eds) *Reaching Potentials: Transforming Early Childhood Curriculum and Assessment* Vol. 2, NAEYC, Washington, DC, 145–166.

Wilkinson, A, Barnsley, G, Hanna, P & Swan, M 1980 *Assessing Language Development.* Oxford University Press, Oxford.

Writing Resource Book 1994 Longman, Melbourne.

Chapter 8

Multiliteracies: teachers and students at work in new ways with literacy

Annah Healy

THIS CHAPTER FOCUSES ON primary students and the multiliteracies (also termed *new literacies*) that have become, for many people, part of everyday life. Scenarios of real events are used to point out ways in which students in primary classrooms deal with a range of texts that are delivered through different technological modes. Specifically, the chapter aims to:

- explore the fact that texts written and read in contemporary contexts are produced through a range of technologies of which print is only one of many

- support the principle that all acts of LITERACY are social and cultural

- explain how children learn about texts in relation to social and cultural beliefs, according to the practices that surround the texts

- look at changing text–teacher–student relations, and at classroom literacy tasks that are now central to the curriculum.

CHANGES TO LITERACY PRACTICES

In a computer-driven age, and at a time when education authorities call for life-like literacy experiences for primary students that reflect community practices with text, schools must begin to take new pathways to literacy education. The reality of multi-literacies and a globalised world mean that it is essential to reconsider literacy-related practices in education. It is not that print has become unimportant or the book redundant; indeed print remains one essential medium for learning to read and to write. However, the privileged status of print as the almost exclusive basis of literacy has diminished.

Postmodern media culture is powerful and pervasive, and knowledge communication today is as much through multimedia as it is through the single medium of print. Many students in their everyday lives connect to an array of texts that bear little resemblance to the book, and to a vast digital network that transcends more traditional forms of text (Bigum & Lankshear 1997; Healy 2000). These texts cross boundaries previously defined by genre and discipline. It is important to acknowledge that children now form their early concepts about literacy from textual environments that are considerably more complex than for those of their predecessors. As a result, contemporary language and literacy education must base its practices on texts from a range of technologies, involving different media, and thus recognise the diverse contexts and social purposes for communicating. It is also critical that the significant differences existing between students' experiential backgrounds, between maturation and ability levels, and between social and cultural backgrounds are recognised in pedagogy and in all dimensions of classroom practice.

Digital literacies have been resisted, dismissed or overlooked by many teachers, especially in early childhood classrooms (Durrant & Green 2000; Healy 1999). However, there is now considerable pressure on Australian teachers to incorporate digital literacies into their classroom programs. While some teachers may continue to resist digital texts as part of their literacy programs, reforms in public education hold teachers accountable in this regard. A practical and pedagogical acceptance of multi-literacies is not negotiable. Nor is it something that is best delayed until people leave school, or something that will disappear by ignoring or denying it. On the other hand, neither is it something that students will learn to do critically and effectively if they do not possess rudimentary decoding or spelling skills (Luke et al. 2000: 10).

The stated purpose of the new literacies is to produce a more equitable future for students than might otherwise be the case. The centrality of digital literacies to this vision reflects a belief amongst a growing number of educators that some children will have more constrained life chances if school literacies do not include learning and applying the available processes of reading and using information that are now more commonly available in digital form.

HOW HAS LITERACY CHANGED?

Traditionally in Western cultures, literacy has been defined as sets of perceptual and cognitive skills for encoding (writing) and decoding (reading) alphabetic print texts. An individual acquired these skills to different levels and was thought accordingly to be more or less literate than others. Literacy was not only essentially linked to print, but also to a literary model of literacy—that is, one linked to books and writing of a literary nature. Therefore, the closer one's writing got to the works of revered, classic authors, and the more philosophically one was able to read, the more literate the individual was thought to be. However, new 'basics' emerge in education generally, and with them new literacies that are termed multiliteracies. It must be noted though that *multiliteracies* is also an acknowledgment of the diverse social and culturally-based literacies that apply to different community groups (Cope & Kalantzis 2000).

Print and digital texts: some fundamental differences

Traditional print texts are generally composed of verbal codes (print) and some graphic codes (illustrations, diagrams). In contrast, digital texts are significantly more multimodal, often including audio codes (sound effects) and a substantially expanded range of graphic codes (including animation). Furthermore, digital texts are not necessarily fixed and linear like traditional print texts, but may be hypertextual, with links within and beyond a document. To find a pathway through hypertext, while cracking graphic, verbal and audio codes, and while also creating an integrated composition of meaning from diverse sources of information, necessitates a reader using reading processes that are not applicable to traditional print texts (Healy 1999). These include processes for navigating and transforming textual information rather than just predicting and interpreting such information, as is the case with traditional print (Kress 1997). In short, marks on digital surfaces cannot always be read in the same way as marks on the surfaces of traditional print texts. New reading practices, specific to multimedia and interactivity, have emerged. Added to these new ways of thinking about reading education comes the text construction of students, and the ways that students use verbal and visual information, together with audio and animation, to present their ideas.

The first scenario reports on a class of Year 2 students in a new literacies context. In particular, it reports and examines the ways in which twelve pairs of students work over a school term to produce a Powerpoint presentation on a beetle or insect of their choice. Of particular importance to student teachers are the dynamics of new student–teacher–text relations as digital technology becomes a core resource for interrelated curriculum projects that require students to become skilled in multiliteracies.

SCENARIO 1: A YEAR 2 CLASS AT WORK IN DIGITAL TECHNOLOGY: POWERPOINT PRESENTATIONS

Over the term the students have worked concurrently on collecting information on their selected bug from a variety of text sources, including CD-ROMs, websites and print information books; and learning about Powerpoint and what it offers for presenting information to others.

The goal of this exercise is for the class to conduct a parent information afternoon. Over time, the students have been engaged in both print- and computer-based literacy experiences. They have learned to make notes in their science diaries according to the foci for the week. For example, over one week students were asked to find ten interesting facts about their bug and to record the details. Another week concerned recording, graphically and verbally, the life-cycle pattern of their chosen bug (insect/beetle). The students took digital photographs and drew from live specimens that had been collected from various sources at the beginning of the project. They drew scale measurements of the selected bugs and compared and ordered them from smallest to largest, and with and without wingspan measurements. The children constructed lists of the foods and eating patterns of each bug. They also desktop published an invitation to each of their parents and carers for the presentation afternoon.

Eventually the students had to select, from complex sets of information that had been gathered over the school term, those aspects that would give an audience most knowledge. Each presentation was planned as a four-slide sequence:

Slide 1 – Title and names of authors (accompanied by a digital photograph of authors and the bug).
Slide 2 – An introduction to the project.
Slide 3 – A graphic representation of the bug with labels, captions and sound.
Slide 4 – Four important and interesting facts about the bug.

The first half of the school term involved information searches and activities across print and digital texts. In the last five weeks of the project, each student pair was given an hour a week in the computer laboratory to complete one slide per session, with the last week given to editing and final selections of sound, colour and information. Where the teacher had modelled and guided the note-making and invitation genres, she had not modelled a Powerpoint presentation. She believes that the Powerpoint program is capable of assisting children to problem-solve and to make choices for themselves, whereas she feels responsible for specific guidance in the print genres.

This teacher agrees with literacy researchers and policymakers that new literacies—new families of literacy practices included—have emerged as a consequence of the digital revolution and literacy experiences, and that the new literacies demand different pedagogies (Bigum & Lankshear 1997; Carrington 2001; Comber et al. 2001; Healy & Dooley 2002).

Snapshot 8.1

The context: Twelve pairs of Year 2 students are in the computer laboratory of a school in inner Brisbane, Australia. There are four Year 6 students working with them. The Year 2 teacher is not present, but the Year 6 teacher is in the room adjoined to the computer laboratory that has glass dividing windows between the two spaces.

The senior students operate as buddies to the younger children. However, there is no occasion where a buddy does the work for their younger partners. Instead, the older students adopt a hands behind the back position, and prompt only with questions:

Jane:	Where could you go to find out how to change your background colour?
Sam:	Have you read the menu?
Sam:	Is this how you want your insect to look? What else could you do?
Meredith:	Experiment with how many ways you can bring in text to attach labels to your insect parts?

On this occasion, the final slide is being prepared. The Year 2 students have brought their Natural Science notebooks with them to the computer laboratory, and have also brought the disk on which they have been writing their Powerpoint presentation. They know that they must select only four points for their information slide, and must select from, in some cases, three or four pages of possible facts. Some pairs have pre-decided and highlighted the text they are to put on the slide. Each pair has brought the simple editing checklist below:

Have you checked your spelling?
Have you said something about the topic?
Have you chosen the very best words to describe your topic?
Have you said something different each time?

On this occasion one pair weigh up the pros and cons of different dot-point indicators. They trial the traditional indicators, and several are downloaded from the symbols options. They also debate the use of capital and lowercase letters, prompted by the automated change of their first letter to upper case. They ask a buddy about it. She checks to see if they want to include a stem before their four points, and types in an example for them to see: 'Four interesting things about frogs are:'

Together the pair and their buddy work through reading the stem prior to each point to see if it 'reads properly'. The pair of students realise that some of their notes have to be adjusted to make sense, and while liking the idea of using a stem, decide to use only the single word 'Frogs' to begin their points.

The students also debate design issues. They query the background colour that should be used for their information, just as they query the sounds that best represent their bug, and the fonts that are appropriate for different types of information.

Discussion of snapshot

The children in this classroom work effectively with different media. Their success challenges many of the accepted traditional wisdoms about how children become literate in reading and writing in early childhood classrooms. An extensive literature indicates that parents, teachers and other adept readers play an enabling role in children's acquisition of meaning-making practices for traditional print texts. Much of this pedagogic work has been enacted through talk around books. In the early childhood classroom, for example, shared readings of books, modelled on the bedtime story, have become a standard strategy in reading instruction for novices (Andrews 1997). The literacy practices in this classroom have certainly included the enshrined storybook reading practices that have dominated for almost 100 years, but have extended beyond them to include experiences where child and computer coach each other (Healy & Dooley 2002).

The explicit nature of teachers' work in print reading and writing makes it reasonable to assume that explicit instruction in digital reading pedagogy is also essential. However, this prediction is complicated by the possibility that digital texts may enable novices to read in the absence of instruction by adult or other adept readers (Healy 1999). There is evidence that with digital texts it is a mix of manipulative control devices, prompts and iconic reward features, multimedia artistry and interactive facilities that often support novices in the acquisition of meaning-making practices (Healy 2000). In other words, it is not only adept readers who enable novices to acquire reading practices; digital texts seem to serve a similar role. This is a new phenomenon, one that potentially will prompt a fundamental reorganisation of the social relations amongst adept and novice readers and texts in classrooms. Indeed, in the case of the Year 2 classroom, the teacher acknowledges that when young children have some level of decoding skill, the Powerpoint program is capable of leading children toward text design and production.

Questions

- What are the real differences between students in a multiliteracies classroom and children in a traditional, print only classroom?

- In new literacies contexts, what is the importance of a task to literacy education?

- What are, in your belief, some essential teaching aspects for children to engage successfully with digital texts?

- What are some of the differences between print text–teacher–student relations, and digital text–teacher–student relations? What makes these differences?

SCENARIO 2: SAM: ONE FOUR-YEAR-OLD AND THE CONTEMPORARY TEXT ENVIRONMENT

The investment that contemporary children have in multiliteracies, even before they come to school, is displayed in the following snapshots. Sam is having his fourth birthday. He is a competent consumer of texts across technologies, and typical of a growing number of other pre-school children who live in a visual world. Through daily experience, Sam relates to a complex range of environmental texts including electronic media such as television, computer-mediated texts, video, film, and print and non-print two-dimensional texts. The scenarios provide an insight into a pre-schooler who takes for granted a complex array of texts (see for example: Andrews 1997; Burrell & Trushell 1997; Mackey 1994; Meek 1996; Olson & Sulzby 1991; Topping 1997).

Snapshot 8.2: Sam's birthday

Sam has received several printed texts including birthday cards, messages attached to gifts, and two letters that provide him with coded representations of the language surrounding his celebration. The texts are read to Sam when they first arrive, and he takes them to his room before bedtime where he reads them over and again with his parents. There are multiple graphic versions of '4 Today' and 'Sam' represented in the texts, and he has processed a birthday card to himself on the computer, including graphics.

Sam has printed out the text and brought it to the table for his birthday celebration. It reads 'Sam is 4' and the letter 4 appears in multiple fonts over the page, some of which he has coloured. 'Sam is 4 today' is also on his cake, and he reads this for himself without prompts when he sees the cake for the first time. He remarks that the cake is like the one he has seen on a video from the popular Australian children's television show *Bananas in Pyjamas*, and he begins to sing a song to a tune he remembers—I'm gunna be bananas in pyjamas … on my birthday'.

Snapshot 8.3: Sam reading an interactive CD-ROM

One of Sam's birthday gifts, a CD-ROM of Spelunx and the Caves of Mr Seudo (Broderbund 1995), occupies him for more than an hour on the morning of his birthday. Sam has 22 CD-ROMs in his collection, begun when he was about two years of age.

At first Sam plays experimentally with the interactive, multimedia CD-ROM. He follows trails, paths and web options. He advances the text relatively quickly in the first instance, commenting 'I—wonder—what's going to—happen'. He returns to the first frame after a point and begins to monitor his physical interaction with talk. Sam's utterances indicate that he makes deliberate attempts to follow the context of the fantasy game. He expertly uses the mouse and animates from hot spots. He spends seven minutes exploring different caves, selecting one adventure which he follows through to the end. He brings up both supplemental* and incidental** text, and by the responses he makes, appears to discriminate between them. Sam seeks out Mr Seudo's inventions in the caves, laughs and stops to comment on one of his own constructions:

'I did this—really good thing—me dad helped me—it was a—machine—we used lego and stuff from the shed—I had this donkey engine—d'ya know what that is?—it went—'

Sam deliberates now and again to highlight words that he recognises as they reappear later in the text. At times he focuses on frames and is silent. At other times, he commands his way through the circuit of the text and makes decisions about using or not using audio text. He demonstrates control by selecting some text segments over others, reasons with himself as he continues, and at times he discards text quickly and is noted to bypass the same parts on a second run through. On several occasions Sam makes the comment, 'I don't want that'. He becomes more selective as it seems his familiarity with the contents and structure develops. Through one adventure, Sam uses the coaching icons. He brings up text at one point, realises he has made the wrong choice for his purpose, and retraces his step until he finds what he wants. He asks himself rhetorical questions, neither waiting for nor wanting responses.

*Supplemental information can be accessed in interactive texts. By highlighting some words or symbols, additional hypertext appears on the screen to add to or enhance the text in some way.
**Incidental information is a textual effect in interactive texts, usually of an amusement only quality and which adds nothing to the text information.

Sam's interactive behaviour with the digital, multimedia text, and the prompts supplied within the text's system certainly assist him to identify words and phrases, but he makes meaning from references to a range of media, and by navigating the text in a way that is meaningful to him. His visual skills are evident as he uses the linking devices within the CD-ROM to shape the text in particular ways. Visual effects on the monitor appear to reinforce the codes and symbols and their meanings for Sam, just as his birthday messages help him to make links between spoken language and its written representations. He also makes intertextual references while he processes the text, and links the text to his personal experiences. All of these activities are the reading behaviours of a motivated and purposeful reader. However, because Sam cannot read print in the way that would be expected of him in a print-based classroom, there is a risk that his competencies would not be recognised as aspects of reading a particular text form.

Workshop/debate questions

1. When Sam begins his formal education, how might a *relevant literacy experience* across texts and technologies be ensured for him?
2. Debate in groups the differences between reading interactive, multimedia texts and reading the print page.
3. The *integrated image with print information* in interactive texts is different from the presentation of a conventional picture book. How might this position some children for reading when they come to school?
4. How might Sam's learning about texts and how to read them differ from his print-influenced predecessors?
5. What are some of the implications for teachers of *multiliteracies* when Sam goes to school?

SCENARIO 3: WARREN: A STUDY OF PRINT INDIFFERENCE AND DIGITAL EXPERTISE

Warren is an enigmatic student in a Year 3 classroom, where all literacy practices surround conventional print texts. He is not given access to a computer in the classroom. At home, Warren's personal collection of CD-ROMs consists of twelve problem-solving game texts, six infographic CD-ROMs including *Encarta '96*, and three texts which cross generic boundaries as they combine narrative, game and problem-solving tasks. He also has access to software including a spreadsheet, a *CAD* program and *Powerpoint*. When talking about his participation, Warren described it in terms of 'making things', 'finding things out', 'drawing up' and 'playing games', but never once referred to reading.

Warren defines *reading* as related to the books he encounters in the classroom, and specifically to oral decoding. The print reading strategies Warren experiences at school and at home clearly influence his conception of what it means to read. Warren does not consider that the other texts he reads outside of the classroom are reading at all. Instead, he comments that 'I play the ROMs ... play around with software ... play with the Internet'. His parents share Warren's beliefs. To them neither computer nor video texts are texts to be read. However, each family member acknowledges Warren's capacity to provide information from following game instructions and loading CD-ROMs. He has shown his 12-year-old half-brother how to use *The Incredible Machine* (*Sierra-on-line* 1995) and is said to be the only one who can get the video to record properly. Warren's father comments that Warren 'will probably be a kid who uses his hands ... like me'. Warren had produced a series of plans for his father's new workshop, constructed with the aid of a CAD program. He is also able to cite 11 titles of favourite CD-ROM texts, including the first one bought for him when he was five. He can remember only two titles of conventionally produced texts, both of them recent texts in his school-supported reading program at home.

Warren's status as a *reader at risk* in the school context, and his attitude towards the texts with which he practices his reading, has resulted in his harbouring negative attitudes towards reading and writing. Warren, his teacher and his parents, each for their own reasons, are concerned for Warren's progress in reading linear print. No adult concerned with his reading life has recognised Warren's activity at the computer as reading, nor have they attributed the same value to multimedia interactive texts that they give to print books. Above all, narratives are particularly valued by his teacher and parents. Yet, in spite of the considerable time and organisation invested into his reading print compared with the lack of support provided for him at the computer, Warren has continued to resist print materials and continued to increase his expertise in digital text enterprises.

Snapshot 8.4: Warren at home 1

Warren and his family live in a small brick bungalow in what is considered by the school community to be 'a pretty rough' area. The house has a built-in verandah in which Warren's half-brother sleeps. An addition at the back of the house serves as a kitchen and laundry, and a steep set of steps from the kitchen door lead to the garage and a grassed area which sports a single mango tree and a boat trailer. A basketball net is attached to the garage wall.

The computer is situated in a small sitting room on a narrow table that has two other tables of different heights forming a U around the computer. On the day of my first visit, there is general clutter on the tables at the side of the computer, consisting of magazines, stationery, CD-ROMs, letters and coffee cups, empty crisp packets and a drink can. Several odd-sized cushions are heaped on the floor beside the computer chair to cater for different heights of the family members. Warren's mother reports that 'the television is on from the time we get up to the time we go to bed in this house … or until we go out … sometimes it's never turned off at all'. The television can be viewed from the computer.

Warren's bedroom is a section of what was once the sitting room, since divided into two to make bedroom spaces for his half-sister and himself. Warren's room has a bunk bed with Bart Simpson bedclothes, a plastic chair and one open set of shelves, the bottom part of which is an arsenal of plastic and metal weapons, and an assortment of containers filled with bric-a-brac. A Chicago Bulls baseball cap is perched on the top of the shelf along with several plans Warren has drawn up for reforming his father's workshop space in the garage to create a permanent home for the computer. Warren puts his cap on whenever he watches television or plays at the computer.

The house is noisy. On each visit, there is a cacophony of competing noises from television, music from bedrooms, digital text audio, and a radio in the kitchen. However, the household appears to be harmonious. The children are included in conversations, and there is lots of shared laughter. Warren claims that home is his favourite place. He is oblivious to other household events when involved with his video games or computer activity. He talks to himself constantly at the computer. Except for the designated half hour on the Support-a-reader program, Warren is self-directed in his activities and able to choose what he does on the computer and when he does it. He is reported to be its major user, and his mother tells me that he sometimes pays his half-brother and friends to keep away from the computer at weekends.

From Thursday until Sunday nights, Warren is permitted to eat his food at the computer and has no set bedtime. His father comments that Warren 'often plays at the computer ... until every-one goes to bed—or later'.

There is everything to suggest that Warren enjoys his home and family life, with one notable exception. Warren and his parents reported that the daily half hour or so in which Warren is meant to practise his reading with his mother is part of a school-supported program. This time causes a degree of stress in the household, and provokes a range of avoidance strategies. Warren becomes instantly involved in other 'important' projects, claims to not feel well, or asks to delay the session to allow him to complete another activity. He shows an unmistakable dislike for the books the Support-A-Reader Program provides, and his mother reported that Warren has low tol-erance for any books he brings home from the school.

Snapshot 8.5: Warren at home 2

Warren tells me that his favourite place is the corner of the sitting room where we are sitting together. The computer is beside us and the television is on, in full view.

Warren: 'No one much uses the computer when I'm home weekends and nights ... once I got a big surprise when I thought it was 7 o'clock or something but it was half past ten [waits for a reaction] I'd been playing this game [pauses] well not really a game it's *The Incredible Machine* ... there's this really good section where you can make up your own ... I built this super racer [he draws my attention at this point to something on the television, then resumes his description of the CD-ROM] ... it's got how a car works and it's got these incredible challenges where you can rearrange everything and make your own cars ... I play it heaps—while I'm having my food even ... my dad doesn't care and me mum lets me if I clean up ... all my stuff's there—well most of it ... I mucked about with this software and I wrote my brother's name real big with all these fancy letters and I put it on his bedroom door as a surprise [waits for a reaction] and he's still got it but he's taken it off his door ... we're having a special room for the computer soon it's in the garage ... dad says I can go out even at night ... I think it's so I don't make such a mess in the lounge [he laughs]'.

In this discussion which took about 40 minutes, Warren had provided evidence of a metalanguage for describing the user functions of the computer, and correctly contextualised the digital-specific terms *scrolling, highlighting, hotspots, networks, hardware* and *software,* among others. Description and metalanguage development indicates a linguistic awareness very important in early reading. Linguistic awareness abilities are critically important to judging, analysing and eventually interpreting language structures, and for building a metalanguage to describe interpretations and possibilities. Such development is shown in the research to indicate readiness for rule-governed learning, where readers begin to assimilate their cognitive and linguistic resources (Gough et al. 1983; Perfetti & Beck 1982; Yopp & Singer 1994).

Warren's interest in the texts he described appears to have mobilised his linguistic and metalinguistic abilities. He talked about *icons* and *menus* and although he did not use the term, adequately described hypertext as *'when you get the information from one part and you highlight a word or something a new part comes on top of it like when you put one piece of paper over another one ... then more can come on top of that one so it looks like [demonstrates a layering effect with his hands] lots of information can come on the screen at a time and you can choose'.*

At home Warren employs the latest technologies to pursue his interests, each of which in some way is reading-related. He accesses information from interactive CD-ROMs; he collects computer software catalogues and marks them up for future reference; he uses the home fax machine to send in computer software orders when he has saved up for them. In relation to payment, he understands the nature of an account number, and which of the payment grids is applicable to himself. He produces evidence of his expertise with a video to capture family events and edit them, and to isolate segments of various television programs to share with his family and friends at a later time. Mackey (1994) reports that such activity is common with contemporary children who respond to a predominantly electronic text environment.

Warren is also reported by his mother to refer to the television guide and to discriminate between the options. He consults one of eight magazines and catalogues which are regularly sent to his home. From all accounts, Warren had received initial intergenerational support at the computer when he first became interested at about age four. Warren recalled his father as the main source of assistance, mainly in relation to setting up games. Both parents confirm that Warren has required little assistance at the computer for at least the last two years, and has independently learned how to load CD-ROMs, access them, use the Internet and play games. Warren has assisted his older brother with procedures to access information via the Internet, and he takes a negotiated payment from his stepsister for any help he gives her from digital *infographic* sources for her school projects. Such behaviours indicate a stamina to persevere with reading and reading-asssociated tasks, which in turn leads to appropriate automatic transference of processes to later reading efforts. An indication of

Warren's competence to deal with complex text construction from reading, and a stamina which is not evident in his print history, is provided here:

> Warren: 'Mostly I like the computer because it's really interesting … there's lots of different things on the ROMs and you can play them over and over and you don't get sick of it … sometimes if it's like *How Things Work* or something you can spend a day or more than a day just on one bit [pause] by the time you've done everything it's bedtime because just doing that one part takes ages … have you seen Powerpoint? [waits for response] It's not a ROM it's really ace you can put sound to the stuff you make up [pause] my dad lets me use his laptop that's what I do this cool stuff with the Simpsons … make up stories about them and I put music on it … You can play the audio and add bits in to some games [pause] and you can go back and change your mind … it tells you if what you're doing is right or wrong like sometimes it makes a noise like <u>gong</u> [stressed] and sometimes the icons do stuff to show you if what you've done is right or not … and you can score points and if you don't know some words when you highlight them it says it so you don't have to waste your time'.

Discussion of snapshot

There is every evidence that Warren has learned to apply his experience to new digital texts he encounters, and therefore *act* like a reader even though he seems not to recognise himself as such. Part of that experience has been to process integrated displays of multimedia. Warren was able to demonstrate his meaningful strategic practices with a mix of animated and fixed images and print, and with the meandering paths of hypertext. He can also demonstrate a capacity to act interrogatively with text, and he is able to predict, hypothesise and improvise with more expertise than he could demonstrate with any traditionally produced print page. The most likely reason for his developing such skills is the expectation he had to actively *construct* meaning from multimedia. On the other hand, he expected to passively *absorb* meaning as the result of a perfect decoding of print.

Questions

1. Warren relates to a multimedia text environment, but resists print, assumedly because of the texts that are selected for him in the classroom. How could Warren be more positively accommodated in the classroom?
2. What are the crucial factors about home–school connections?
3. Under the circumstances reported through Warren's scenario, what chance does Warren have to be an effective reader and writer across texts?
4. How might Warren link his digital literacy activities with print activities?
5. What are some of the implications for Warren's teacher, and for the establishment and maintenance of a *multiliteracies* classroom?

Summary

The scenarios that are reported in this chapter are framed by a belief that many young children currently develop their literacy-related knowledge as much from interactive multimedia digital texts as from any other text mode. The purpose of the chapter has been to illustrate the different textual experiences of children today, and what this means for teaching. The processing demands made from the typologies and structures of interactive multimedia digital texts, compared with those made from linear strings of print are different, as will be the literacy tasks we ask students to complete. Although computers are gradually becoming more common-place in early childhood and primary classrooms, the complex hypertext structures and multimedia found in many digital texts are not normally considered in terms of their effects on literacy activity, nor included as core materials for scaffolding children's critical practices with texts.

A crucial aspect that has become very clear through observing young children with texts is the importance of visual information in the ways in which the world is represented to them. It is well recognised that children currently live in a very visual world, but through the ages, image has always been a critical aspect of information display. Vision has never really receded into unimportance in commercial and cultural domains. Yet pedagogy has continued to stress the importance of print information in the face of a changing textual environment that relies on more than print. Obviously the ideal in our culture is that children learn to break the codes of many textual forms, but the children represented in this chapter clearly prefer the signs of the visual world. They have become more familiar with text displays that are unlike those from which children are traditionally taught to read. The result has been that a growing number of children more easily respond to images or to compositions of image and verbal codes than they do to the sanctioned print message. The implication is that classroom practices must pay immediate attention to the multiple text forms that children access and assist them to develop their literacies accordingly.

It is not inferred in any way that the computer medium has replaced or made redundant the human support that has been traditionally given to most children in print literacy contexts. A useful hypothesis is that the typologies and structures of interactive multimedia text have replaced certain aspects of support provided by enabling others, or helpers, in the early experience of print. While the inbuilt guidance of interactive media may be sufficient for some children, for other children, the guidance of the interactive media will not be sufficient without additional assistance from teachers and classroom peers. There will need to be opportunities for all children to develop the type of imitative practice required for children to gain mastery over the information of interactive media, and to make the essential transformations to participate in, use and analyse texts critically.

Finally, it is crucial that the notion of multiliteracies is understood conceptually to mean meaningful action with any text, irrespective of technology, media, form or structure. The definition of literacy will thus relate to numerous text surfaces, spaces and typologies, and crucially, acknowledge that process-related action cannot be regular for technologically different texts.

Annotated bibliography

Mackey, M 1994 The New Basics: Learning to read in a multimedia world, *English in Education*, 28, 1, 9–19.

Margaret Mackey explores the textual experiences of contemporary pre-schoolers who are as adept at running, stilling, fast-forwarding and taping videos as they are in running an interactive multimedia CD-ROM or in playing out character roles from favourite storybooks. The children in Mackey's study showed that they freely intertextualise between electronic, print and real-life experiences and between different versions of the same text which they have experienced as ani-mated images, as still images and print descriptions, as interactive multimedia, and in many cases in commercial products such as T-shirts and mugs. When children enter school with such experi-ences, teachers will need to reexamine their print-based practices to cater for children with significantly different textual experiences from their predecessors. Mackey also points out that in some cases, children have less pre-school experience with 'the book' than they do with electronic texts.

Andrews, R 1996 *Visual Literacy in Question*, 20:20, Issue 4, Spring, 17–20.

Richard Andrews researches and publishes in the area of young children and how they learn to become literate from observing a complex textual environment. In this article he explores the breakdown of conventional views of *visual literacy* in light of the electronic age and the nature of texts and how they are read. Richard has a particular interest in children learning to write and how they represent their experiences in their sign making. His research has shown that children use more than alphabetic code and image representations to make meaning. The icons of the digital screen and contemporary popular and commercial culture make deep impressions on children and how they perceive their world.

Papert, S 1993 *The Children's Machine: Rethinking school in the age of the computer*. Basic Books, New York.

Papert takes up the call of Marshall McLuhan (1970) who envisaged almost forty years ago that classrooms would be without walls. Papert goes beyond exploring any differences between print and digital technology worlds in terms of the literacies they imply. He suggests that not only will knowledge and communication change so radically that classrooms will have daily membership of children from around the globe, but also that what is learned will be radically different. Papert suggests changes that will have implications for how teachers are prepared to operate in class-rooms without walls. The connotations reach beyond any global project in which a class of students might engage.

References

Andrews, R 1997 *The base of the small iceberg: graphic and multimedia production of a four year old.* Paper presented at the School of Language and Literacy Education, Queensland University of Technology, Kelvin Grove, Australia.

Bigum, C & Lankshear, C 1997 *Digital Rhetorics: Literacies and Technologies in Education.* Queensland University of Technology Press, Brisbane.

Broderbund 1995 *Spelunx and the caves of Mr Seudo,* CD-ROM.

Burrell, C & Trushell, J 1997 ' "Eye-candy" in "Interactive Books"—A wholesome diet?' *Reading: A Journal about Literacy and Language in Education*, Vol. 31, No. 2, 3–6.

Carrington, V 2001 'Emergent home literacies: A challenge for educators'. *Australian Journal of Language and Literacy,* 24, 2, 88–100.

Comber, B Badger, L Barnett, J Nixon, H & Pitt, J 2001 *Socio-economically disadvantaged students and the development of literacies in school: A longitudinal study.* University of South Australia/ Department of Education, Training and Employment, South Australia.

Cope, B & Kalantzis, M 2000 *Multiliteracies: Literacy Learning and the Design of Social Futures.* Macmillan, Great Britain.

Department of Employment, Education, Training and Youth Affairs (DEETYA) 1997 *Digital Rhetorics: Literacies and Technologies in Education—Current Practices and Future Directions*, Vol. 1–3. Queensland University of Technology, Queensland.

Durrant, C & Green, B 2000 'Literacy and the new technologies in school education: Meeting the l(IT)eracy challenge'. *Australian Journal of Language and Literacy*, Vol. 23, No 2, 89–108.

Gough, PB Juel, C & Roper/Schneider, D 1983 'Code and cypher: A two-stage conception of initial reading acquisition'. In JA Niles & LA Harris (eds) *Searches for meaning in reading/language processing and instruction: 32nd Yearbook of the National Reading Conference,* National Reading Conference, Rochester, NY, 207–211.

Green, B & Bigum, C 1993 'Aliens in the classroom'. *Australian Journal of Education*, Vol. 37, 2, 119–141.

Healy, A 1998 *Children's reading of print and interactive multimedia texts: Two case studies.*

Unpublished doctoral thesis, Queensland University of Technology, Queensland, Australia.

Healy, A 1999 *Children reading in a post-typographic age.* Unpublished PhD thesis, Queensland University of Technology, Australia.

Healy, A 2000 *Teaching reading and writing in a multi-literacies context: Classroom Practice.* Post Pressed Flaxton, Brisbane.

Healy, A & Dooley, K 2002 'Cultural differences, social justice and literacy education for post-typographic times'. *The International Journal of Inclusive Education* (forthcoming).

Kress, G 1997 *Multimodal texts and Critical Discourse Analysis.* Institute of Education, University of London.

Luke, A Freebody, P Land, R & Booth, S 2000 *Literate futures: Report of the Literacy Review for Queensland State Schools.* Queensland Government, Queensland Education.

Mackey, M 1994 The new basics: Learning to read in a multimedia world. *English in Education*, Vol. 28, 1, 9–19.

Meek, M 1996 'The Critical challenge of the world in books for children'. *Children's Literature in Education* 26:1:5–23.

Olson, K & Sulzby, E 1991 'The computer as a social/physical environment in emergent literacy'. In J Zutell & S McCormick (eds), *Learner factors/teacher factors: Issues in literacy research and instruction.* National Reading Conference, Chicago IL, 111–118.

Papert, S 1993 *The children's machine: Rethinking school in the age of the computer.* Basic Books, NY.

Perfetti, CA & Beck, I 1982 *Learning to read depends on phonetic knowledge and vice versa.* Paper presented at the annual meeting of the National Reading Conference, Clearwater, Florida.

Smith, R Curtin, P & Newman, L 1996 *Kids in the 'kitchen': The social implications for schooling in the age of advanced computer technology.* Paper presented at the Australian Association for Research in Education Annual Conference, November, Hobart.

Sulzby, E 1994 *Emergent writing on and off the computer: A final report on Project CIL* (Computers in Early Literacy). Paper presented at the meeting of the National Reading Conference, Dec., San Diego, CA.

Topping, KJ 1997 'Family Electronic Literacy: Part 2— Home–school links through computers *Reading: A Journal about Literacy and Language in Education* 31:2:12–21.

Yopp, HK & Singer, H 1994 'Toward an interactive reading instructional model: explanation of activa- tion of linguistic awareness and metalinguistic ability in learning to read'. In RB Ruddell, MR Ruddell & H Singer (eds), *Theoretical models and processes of reading: Fourth Ed*. International Reading Association, Newark, Delaware, 381–390.

Chapter 9

Monitoring children's language development

Rod Campbell

> Competition is e'er the rule
> We learn it when we go to school.
> The devil take the hindmost, O!
>
> — *Arthur H Clough 1849*

THIS CHAPTER AIMS TO:

- explore the link between practical research and evaluation of children's learning of language

- provide examples of good practice in assessing and monitoring children's learning about language

- explore the notion that all children are learners, and that one role of the teacher is to focus upon children's learning competencies

- develop systems for assessing, monitoring, record-keeping and reporting on children's learning and development in language and literacy.

INTRODUCTION

Monitoring the language and literacy development of individual students is central to providing effective classroom instructional practices. Competition has not been removed from school systems and classrooms, but the late twentieth century accountability movement has focused attention upon the learning outcomes of all students. The concept of portfolio assessment has provided teachers with the practices for record-keeping essential to long-term monitoring and evaluation of the learning performances of each and every child. Finally, the early years of the 21st century have been marked by the availability of teacher-friendly software systems that can support classroom teachers in maintaining the records necessary for monitoring student learning.

Central also to current governmental and community expectations is the requirement that all students become literate and numerate. Where a student is unable to reach required levels of literacy for adequate personal, social and vocational functioning, then schools and systems are required to provide records to demonstrate what programs have been implemented to assist that student's literacy development. Therefore, teachers are now developing and honing their skills as observers and classroom researchers.

THE TEACHER AS RESEARCHER AND MONITOR

The decision to assess children draws teachers into some dimension of the research process. Research is used by professional workers as a means to evaluate their own performance, and to make informed judgments about the outcomes of their professional activities. Of course, most of this professional activity is undertaken at an informal level, but the judgments arrived at will inform further professional activity.

Teachers assess the learning outcomes of the children, and are required to establish and maintain records of that learning. Teachers have maintained mark books and checklists and then used the data to develop report cards for parents and school administration. Of course, the reports also included information from anecdotes maintained or remembered by the teacher. For particular children with special learning needs, and for whom support teaching and learning programs had been instituted in the school or system, much more detailed records were kept. These systems of assessment, record-keeping and reporting have been supplemented with other ways and approaches for assessment.

Some examples of effective and useful classroom and individual assessment procedures are running records, a variety of checklists and rating scales, miscue analysis, writing analysis, and many informal procedures for assessing the quality of children's use of spoken and written language. This chapter will provide examples.

As well, there are many formal tests of reading, spelling and other language competencies, and the most sophisticated of these tests must be administered by specialist teachers and psychologists. But many formal assessment tools are available for teachers to use. Formal assessment tools have a number of things in common. Firstly, the scores have been standardised on a theoretically representative population. Problems arise when formal or standardised tests are given to children who would not be represented in the standard population used for the original test development. Secondly, most short formal tests of reading do not assess the total complexity of the reading process. Problems arise when the reported reading age is really a test of phonic and word knowledge rather than being a test of understanding of the meaning or use of language. When used in conjunction with skilled and careful observation and informal assessment, formal tests can provide teachers and schools with information that supports change and ongoing improvement to the language and literacy curriculum.

CLASSROOM RESEARCH AS MONITORING LANGUAGE AND LEARNING

At the heart of all assessment is the manner in which the teacher undertakes assessment of the children, individually and collectively. Classroom research models provide powerful starting points. The snapshot provided below illustrates how one teacher studied the language competencies of a child who was unwilling to talk in class, even after three months at school.

Classroom research, particularly action research and appreciative enquiry, assists teachers to address specific issues related to student learning. As part of the Darling Downs Project (Campbell & Garrahy 2000), four teachers embarked on a program of professional self-development in which they focused upon the language and learning potentials of the at-risk students whom they had identified. Alison Bates provides the following snapshot of Jeremy, one of the boys in her Year 1 classroom.

Snapshot 9.1

The purpose of the Project was to reflect on my own classroom practices, and upon my own teaching behaviour and language. My particular focus was initially upon questioning. I chose to work with three children from my class in order to focus even more specifically upon the effects of my classroom questions.

Nerida, Aaron and Jeremy presented barriers to their own learning in terms of the quantity and quality of language they displayed. Jeremy seemed to lack confidence, and for the first few months of Year 1 had very rarely spoken in class, either in groups or to other children. The transcript of my whole class lesson on Mice, the first part of the action research cycle in my classroom, clearly showed how the other children in the class answered for him!

For the second cycle of action research, I planned and implemented a small group lesson with the three children on observing and learning about mice, videotaped the lesson and discussed the findings with a critical professional friend. The pattern of my questioning was designed to focus more explicitly on what the children were to explore through observation and language inter-action. The children were highly motivated, and responded and interacted well, except for Jeremy. Nerida continued the social classroom behaviour pattern of speaking for Jeremy. Whenever I directed a question to Jeremy, either in the classroom or in the small group, he would look implor-ingly at other children who were more than happy to speak for him.

I needed to know much more about Jeremy's language abilities. So far, I knew that he could listen and speak, but I had insufficient evidence from which I could determine the quality of his language and thinking. I decided upon two further courses of action.

The first was to construct and implement a further small group lesson, with Jeremy and Aaron undertaking a similar lesson on goldfish with me. The lesson was more complex than previous lessons, with much teacher scaffolding such as explanations and rephrasing of questions that directed the boys' observations and language in a more focused way. The boys complemented each other, with Aaron verbalising and initiating discussion more often. But Jeremy was keen to offer and apply labels. The boys' intonation patterns were closer to those of the supportive adult–child interaction, with very little of the usual 'guess-what-is-in-the-teacher's-head' intona-tion patterns of traditional large-group classroom interaction patterns. I had determined that Jeremy's language and self-confidence would respond positively to well-planned intervention.

In the second course of action, I pointed out this problem of Jeremy's reliance to the whole class, bringing the children's attention to a problem that belonged to all of them and which they could all help to solve. I emphasised how important it was for every child to speak in lessons, and how speaking helps with learning. It was not fair that other children spoke for Jeremy because it stopped him from showing what he was learning.

The children all agreed that Jeremy was capable of talking, and we would wait for him to respond to questions. Jeremy realised that he was supposed to answer, and within a few days, Jeremy was speaking animatedly to me about Mr Bean, the first time that he had initiated a con-versation with me. He also spoke to other teachers in the playground, and raised his hand eagerly in class to answer questions.

Comment

Alison could have asked for the specialist Learning Support Teacher, a Speech Pathol-ogist or a School Psychologist (Guidance Officer) to assess Jeremy. By implementing a process which included reflection upon her own use of language for teaching (ques-tioning, explaining, expectations of the children), Alison was able to locate Jeremy's problems and to institute appropriate social and community action to support his inclusion into the classroom. In effect, Jeremy's discourse practices, compounded by the nature of his shy personality and unwillingness to enter into the discourse processes of the classroom, was effectively excluding him from learning. He needed to be included in the classroom Discourse. Alison combined her professional expertise and knowledge of group and individual behaviour to provide mechanisms to observe and learn about Jeremy, and then to put remedies in place to assist him.

In summary, the most important research, observation and monitoring instrument available to the teacher is the judicious and professional use of observation and experience. Before looking in detail at the ways in which teachers assess the reading and writing abilities of students, we need to understand the environments within which assessment and monitoring occur.

THE SYSTEMS BACKGROUND: SOME IMPLICATIONS FOR TEACHERS' ASSESSMENTS OF STUDENTS

Regulations, as well as statutes, have always been part of educational provision. In recent years, the number and complexity of regulations, particularly those regulations concerning the quality of educational provision in schools and professional accountability, has increased. System and school administrators are involved in the processes of ensuring that regulations concerning students' welfare and learning are followed.

The welfare and learning of the children are shared by the classroom teacher and the students themselves, and by those parents who are involved in supporting their children's learning. However, the classroom teacher has the final call on developing, offering and implementing the classroom learning program, particularly in the primary school and pre-school.

Teachers are therefore required to know as much as they can about all of the students in their classes. There are problems in achieving such an objective, particularly for most teachers in secondary schools and tertiary institutions. Teachers in these institutions tend to teach in two or more specific subject areas, and have large numbers of students to manage. Quizzes, assignments and examinations quickly locate any students in need of further assistance, but given the institutional constraints of many large secondary schools, students with special learning needs become the shared responsibility of the Learning Support teachers, Visiting Specialist teachers and School Counsellors, as well as of a combination of the classroom teachers and the members of the School Administration team.

The situation is different in primary schools and pre-schools. Australia is one of the few countries where the primary school teacher is expected to be responsible for the entire curriculum, including all aspects of the key learning areas of English, Mathematics, Science, Studies of Society and Environment, the Arts, Physical Education and Health, Languages other than English and Information Technology (sometimes known as ICT: Information and Communication Technology). Secondly, the classroom teacher in the Australian primary school has the ongoing responsibility for the learning and management of all of the students in the class. And that includes all students who have been assessed, ascertained or appraised as having special learning needs.

THE STUDENTS' BACKGROUNDS: SOME ISSUES IN ASSESSING STUDENTS

There are many issues concerning the assessment and monitoring of student learning. These include:

- catering for the range of learning abilities, interests and attitudes among a diverse group of between 20 and 35 students

- managing the physical and interactive environment for many persons within a confined space

- making decisions about the direction and level of instruction

- meeting the requirements of large regulatory and bureaucratic structures

- establishing and maintaining relationships with parents

- establishing and maintaining relationships with staff colleagues and administration personnel

- constructing and implementing a curriculum that challenges all students to learn and develop in many subject areas

- assessing the learning of every student

- maintaining records of the learning and behaviour of every student

- managing the learning and behaviour of a number of students who have special learning needs

- becoming familiar with the special learning requirements of students with a range of needs:
    - Non-English Speaking Background
    - students who have little or no English
    - students from a variety of different cultures and faiths
    - Aboriginal students, mostly with different backgrounds and learning styles and needs
    - students from the Torres Strait and from Pacific Island nations
    - students ascertained within the autistic spectrum disorder (Autism, Asperger's Syndrome and Semantic–Pragmatic Syndrome)
    - students with a range of speech and language disorders
    - students with varying degrees of attentional and hyperactivity disorders
    - students with varying degrees of emotional disorders

- students with low incidence disabilities affecting hearing, sight, motor abilities and limbs

- students with learning difficulties

- students with learning disabilities.

It is not unusual for primary school teachers to have between four and ten children whose learning needs in their classrooms will only be partly met by the planned curriculum, the usual teaching procedures and practices, and the resources available to the teacher. Many of these children will also have one or more problems. For example, it is usual to find that children with ASD (autistic spectrum disorder) also have anxiety and learning problems; many also have problems in getting along with the rest of the children in the class.

In cities and larger towns throughout Australia, specialist personnel are available to assist the teacher and the students, but only for an hour or two a week. In the more remote country areas of Australia, very little specialist assistance is available, and then only for assessment and diagnosis.

In summary, most children with special needs or different cultural and language backgrounds will receive some specialist assistance, but in very few instances will the child become the responsibility of a specialist teacher. It is the classroom teacher who has the ultimate responsibility for assessing and monitoring the learning of every child in the class. Specialist educational personnel are available to assist and to contribute to the learning needs of children with special needs, but it is also the classroom teacher's responsibility to provide the leadership for the classroom learning programs undertaken by children with special needs. After all, the children are in the classroom for most of each school day.

Therefore, the classroom teacher will be involved in all ongoing assessment of all of the children in the class. The remainder of this chapter will address a few of the main principles and procedures for assessing each child's spoken and written language abilities. The information gathered and maintained by the teachers will be useful for reporting on each child, maintaining records for the purposes of good teaching practice, and keeping records for purposes of assisting children with special needs, for managing aspects of behaviour, and for meeting regulations and other accountability requirements. But most importantly, what teachers develop from a well-constructed and maintained set of individual student assessment portfolios, and from their records of student achievement and growth, is a sense of professionalism. Teachers with good records of assessment have data that drive teaching, student learning, and professional interaction with children, parents and colleagues.

MONITORING CHILDREN'S LANGUAGE AND LEARNING

1. Assessing and monitoring spoken language

In the snapshot provided earlier in this chapter, Alison used observation and experience to get information about Jeremy's use of language. As a result, she was able to determine that Jeremy did not require immediate ascertainment or assessment by a speech pathologist or guidance officer. Jeremy displayed sufficient information for her to realise that he had a reasonable level of linguistic and intellectual ability. There were some minor articulation problems, but nothing that required extensive remedial assistance.

The initial part of assessing students is to observe and listen, in order to understand the ways that the student uses spoken language. Each student brings a potential for using language and knowledge of texts from family, community, out-of-school social and other contexts for language learning and use. Teachers can learn much about children's interests and skills through discussion with each child and with the child's parents or caregivers. The second step in assessing the child's use of language is to undertake an assessment activity that focuses upon the child's ability to participate in school discourse activity. The snapshot with Jeremy provides one approach.

Most of the children in a class can be assessed for language use, and for ability to participate in classroom discourse, without the need for elaborate systems and activities. But it is incumbent upon the teacher to maintain a record of each child's spoken language. Here the teacher can be helped by selecting items from the *Oral Language Developmental Continuum* (1994) and the *Oral Language Resource Book* (1994). Both of these resources are available in most schools in Australia. Some of the major indicators and ideas for assessment and spoken interaction with children are available in Chapter 4 of this book.

2. Assessing and monitoring written language

As with spoken language, the initial consideration is the age of the child. Developmental lists and phases are a reasonable guide for teachers to use, but teachers quickly realise that the use of developmental phase checklists and continua uncovers the inherent problems in checklists:

- checklists are *limited* to the items to be checked or assessed

- checklists show that the *range of ability* among the children in a class spreads across three or four phases

- checklists also show that the *within-child variations* in skills are also spread from less-than-competent in some dimensions to competent in other dimensions.

A number of dilemmas concerning checklists emerge when the teacher realises that the combination of the second and third problems listed above reveals that most of the children in the class are assessed as belonging in one particular phase, with some skills and knowledge ticked for the neighbouring phases. The problems surface when the teacher presents the finding (the location of the child at a particular phase) to the parents. Parental comparison of the reading and writing abilities of two or more children may indicate similar levels on the checklist, but their observation of the abilities of the children reveals significant differences in competence.

Reporting literacy development in terms of checklists and tests that do not account for the complexity of literate abilities is another dilemma for teachers. Yet the reporting of test results is a significant consequence of recent government policy on literacy and numeracy education in English-speaking countries. The question for teachers, and the point of the remainder of this chapter, concerns what teachers do to meet the multiple demands, understandings, perceptions and requirements of other stakeholders in the literacy education movement. However, teachers primarily assess and monitor the literacy development of their students in a professional manner that reflects the complexities of literacy. Assessment also meets the important requirement of what to teach to meet and challenge the developing abilities of every student.

Assessment and monitoring of literacy is a necessary part of the teacher's everyday interactions with the students. The reasons for assessment of literacy are:

- to determine the content and direction of the program for teaching students (in groups and individually) to improve abilities in developing and applying the knowledge and skills of reading and writing

- to maintain an accurate record of each student's literacy development

- to report responsibly and professionally on the literacy abilities of each student.

Teachers assess and monitor students' literacy development by:

- being very clear about the theories and understandings they hold about reading and writing, and about the teaching and learning of reading and writing

- implementing a consistent and well-maintained program of watching how each student progresses in all aspects of reading, and maintaining a record of observations and samples of each student's efforts

- reviewing the portfolio of samples and observations from time to time in order to plan whole class programs and lessons, and to plan and implement focused learning activities for those children who need assistance

- determining further assessment for children who are not maintaining development in reading and writing.

Specifically, reading can be assessed by a number of approaches. A well-constructed and implemented variety of observation and assessment techniques can provide teachers with most of the information needed in order to meet statutory demands, community expectations, and their own professional integrity.

PROCEDURES FOR ASSESSING READING

Younger readers (emergent or beginning readers)

1. Talk with and listen to the child talk about interests.
2. Watch how the child handles a book (see Goodman 1985).
3. Talk with the child about the features of the book: organisation of its essential features; pictures; the print.
4. Listen to the child 'read' the book (see Sulzby 1985).

   - Is the 'reading' close to the original text?

   - Is the 'reading' an original?

   - What is the quality of the 'reading'?

   - Does the child display the phrasing and intonation of book reading?

   - What is the child's attitude towards reading and books?

   - Does the child bring their own experiences to the text being 'read'?

   - Does the child identify with a character or part of the book?

5. If the child reads the words of the text (that is, can read the book):

   - What is the quality of the reading?

   - What is the quality of phrasing and intonation?

   - Does the child read word by word (word for word, but slowly)?

   - Can the child tell you the gist of the story or the text?

   - How confident is the child when reading familiar texts?

   - How confident and fluent is the child when reading unfamiliar text?

   - Does the child focus upon reading the text? Or does the child keep looking to you for support or prompting?

   - What is the child's attitude to reading and books?

   - Does the child make links between the text and their own experience in talking about the text or story?

   - What is the extent of the child's use of grapho-phonemic knowledge and use of sight vocabulary?

- Does the child read on past unfamiliar words to work out the words and meaning of the text from the context?

- Does the child self-correct?

- Does the child read a range of texts for information and enjoyment?

- Does the child talk about the story or text using terms such as: word, letter, sound, sentence, capital letter?

- Does the child comment upon discrepancies or incongruities in the text or story?

Activity

Where does each question above fit into the relevant dimensions of the four reading practices model (Freebody & Luke 1990)? Can you state which of the items from the lists above represent the practices of code-breaker, text user, text participant, and text analyst? (Refer to Chapter 6.)

There are many other questions or strategies to use in talking with children about a text or story. Again, the underpinning principle is the child's knowledge and use of language to talk about what is being read. The next step is to implement a Running Record of the child's reading, and to analyse that record according to the reading theories explored earlier in Chapter 6.

THE RUNNING RECORD

For this exercise, you will need two texts, one familiar to the child and the other unfamiliar. Both texts need to be about the same level of complexity or difficulty, and be about 50 or 100 words long. A picture is useful for the unfamiliar text.

Ensure that you have two copies of the text, one for the child to read, and the other for you to write upon. Ask the child to read the familiar text, and note any errors made by the child. Errors will be any of the following. Note the system used for recording errors.

Type of error	System of recording error
word omitted	draw line through word
line omitted	draw line through the line of text omitted
part of text omitted	draw line through part omitted
word, line or part of text reinserted	cancel the drawn line (write STET)
word, line or part repeated	underline word, line or part (as often as repeated)
word added	write in the word
word substituted	draw line through original and write in substitution
teacher prompt	write TP at the word prompted

(prompt when the child has spent 3–4 seconds with no reading)

When the child has finished reading the text, ask him or her to retell the story or what it was about in his or her own words. Make a brief note of the quality of the retelling. Now make brief notes on the level of confidence displayed by the child, the degree of fluency in reading the text, and whether there was a reasonable attempt to use the punctuation as markers to expression.

The same approach is used for the unfamiliar text; but now take even more care on the matters of confidence, fluency and expression. Again, make notes as shown above, and ask the child to retell the story. Compare the outcomes from both readings.

1. Error rate: number of errors (exclude self-corrections) as a percentage of total words in the text. (If 50 words, then 5 errors =10%; if 100 words, then 15 errors =15%.) (Note: if the error rate is above 10%, then the text is becoming difficult for the student to read it independently. An error rate of between 5% and 10% is a useful text for assessment. An error rate of less than 5% indicates that the text is read almost independently.)
2. Confidence, expression and fluency.
3. Quality of retelling of the text.
4. Quality and kinds of miscues. (Some miscues are NOT errors!)
5. Number of self-corrections (a good indicator that the child is reading with meaning).

These readings can be placed in the child's assessment portfolio. The testing with a running record can be undertaken at least once more, but preferably twice more during the year. Let the child read from a familiar text first, in order to get the idea of fluency, expression and meaning-making as the main aim of the exercise. There is no need to make extensive notes. Now present the unfamiliar text, which should be of a higher standard or level than the text used in the first running record undertaken earlier in the school year. Make detailed notes from this unfamiliar text. (Hint: many schools have now 'levelled' their reading schemes, so it is possible to use selected similarly-levelled books, as unfamiliar texts, from a scheme not in use by the children.) What is now available is a collection of two or three samples of a child's reading that becomes a chronicle and evidence of that child's reading in context throughout the year. These dated records can be kept in a portfolio together with dated samples of writing and other dated anecdotal notes made by the teacher.

Snapshot 9.2: Running record

The following text was read by Mark, aged 6.9 years and in Year 2.

The Three Billy Goats Gruff

woods

The three Billy Goats Gruff were in the big field eating the grass and ~~weeds~~. The Little

starred   little

Billy Goat Gruff stopped eating and ~~stared~~ over the bridge to the ~~small~~ field on the other

TP

side of the <u>can</u>yon.

the

'Don't you like the grass in ~~this~~ field?' asked the Big Billy Goat Gruff.

'The grass on the other side looks nice,' said the Little Billy Goat Gruff.

green   it's

'It does look nice and ~~greener~~ and ~~it is~~ thick, too,' said the Middle Billy Goat Gruff.

Liking SC

'<u>Sh</u>all we go there?' asked the Little Billy Goat Gruff, <u>licking his lips with his tongue.</u>

TP

'Of course!' <u>sta</u>ted the Big Billy Goat Gruff.

hug TP

The Middle Billy Goat Gruff was not sure. 'There is a huge and terrible Troll that

cross

lives under the bridge, and he eats goats and sheep that ~~walk~~ on the bridge,' said the

wor, worid

worried Middle Billy Goat Gruff.

Let

'~~Leave~~ him to me!' said the Big Billy Goat Gruff. 'I can look after him and us.'

(183 words)

Analysis of the reading

Mark's oral reading of unfamiliar text varies between confident and hesitant. He is able to bring his language skills to his reading, chunking groups of words (language patterns such as preposi-tional phrases), and thus indicating his understanding of the way printed English maps onto spoken English. He made 12 errors, an error rate of about 7%, indicating that the reading level of the text was between assisted and independent reading, a good level for analysing reading strengths and needs.

Mark's retelling of the story reflected the sequence of the story with most of the major details provided once he was given a prompt or two.

He read the title with some confidence; he knew the story and this helped him with some of the text. He displayed the following strategies and problems when reading this text which was just a little too difficult for him to read independently, but which was within the zone where he would benefit from adult assistance:

- sounding out the first letter of unfamiliar words ('sh' in shall and 'st' in stated)
- reading on past the unfamiliar word to achieve self-correction ('liking' his teeth with his tongue)
- guessing at a word without looking at all of the grapho-phonic cues (woods, starred, the, green, hug, let)
- substituting words which could be acceptable in terms of language and meaning (woods, little, green, cross, it's)
- willing to try unfamiliar words on his own but seeks adult help (good interaction skills) and displays internal locus of control (did not look to the teacher for help all the time)
- using sufficient grapho-phonic cues together with syntactic and semantic knowledge and cues; this causes minor errors that appear to have little impact upon understanding of the whole text.

Mark demonstrates the reading practices of code-breaker (use of grapho-phonic and syntactic cues and knowledge), text user and participant (retelling of story). He did not question the text or look for reasons to support the 'grass is greener' theme of the story, or consider the characters of each of the goats. (This would require specific questioning and discussion with the teacher.)

The teacher should undertake more frequent assessment of the reading of those children who are not performing well. Such reassessments should be viewed as formative in nature, and will assist the teacher in developing focused lessons and more focused reading programs for the children who need extra teaching.

PROCEDURES FOR ASSESSING READING
Older readers (transitional to independent readers)

Most of the students are able to read reasonably proficiently, and need to develop a variety of more advanced word recognition and comprehension skills to contribute to their development as widely practising readers. The teacher in the middle and upper grades of the primary school can develop good records of the reading proficiencies of each student from observation of each student undertaking a variety of usual classroom activities.

Detailed assessment of every student is necessary, but the teacher undertakes a more strategic system of observation and recording. The initial approach is to listen to each student read a number of different kinds of texts and stories during the first few weeks of school. Brief notes of the title of the text and the quality and fluency of the reading can be noted. But there also needs to be careful observation of each student's skill and ability in using the four reading practices. The traditional comprehension exercise of answering questions will provide only a few bits of information if not analysed in depth during a one-on-one discussion of the text and questions.

The following checklist can be used as a starting point for a formative assessment of each student.

1. Makes meaning of the text when reading aloud. Indicated by:

   - fluency and expression of meaning
   - meaningful substitutions
   - re-reading parts to clarify meaning
   - self-corrections
   - varying pace of reading to suit difficulty and unfamiliarity with the text and the vocabulary
   - using knowledge of language patterns
   - using knowledge of the conventions of print (punctuation, paragraphing, format, etc.)
   - confirming predictions of the text.

2. Retells the story or restates the information in the text. Indicated by:

   - use of own prior knowledge and literal information in the text to infer meaning
   - retelling of the main points of informational text
   - retelling a brief summary of the plot of a narrative
   - understanding of literal meaning
   - analysis and summary of the content of non-fiction text
   - analysis and sequential summary of the plot of a narrative
   - critical evaluation of characters and information in a variety of texts.

3. Displays understanding of the structure and language features of texts.

   - knows the difference between narrative and non-fiction texts
   - scans text as a means for planning to read information texts
   - moves between questions and text in comprehension exercises.

4. Displays positive attitudes towards reading. Indicated by:

- willingness to read silently or aloud when required

- reading at home and in other non-school time

- discussing favourite books

- making comparisons between books and between authors

- talking easily about books with friends and classmates

- being confident when reading

- reading aloud with fluency and reasonable expression

- being willing to practise when reading aloud for special occasions.

Much more detailed lists are available to teachers. Arguably the most useful, and certainly one of the most widely used lists in Australia, is the *Reading Developmental Continuum* (1994). Many of the items in the lists above have been derived from this source.

There are also many kinds of reading tests available for teachers to use, including some that have been around for many years. The formal tests will provide a raw numerical score that can then be turned into a standard score by comparing the raw score against its standard score on a table provided by the test developers. Some of these tests are the TORCH, the GAP and GAPADOL, and later versions of the Neale Analysis of Reading (1958). This last test is given individually to each student. However, taking a test will only provide the teacher with the information limited to the type of test. The teacher still needs to convert test results into programs for teaching reading to the whole class as well as to individual students.

Perhaps the most useful individual test that a teacher can give is an Informal Reading Inventory (Holdaway 1980), based upon analysis of the errors or miscues that the reader makes while reading aloud. The Running Record provided above is one example of such an inventory. For older readers, the informal reading assessment follows the same procedure, but a more detailed effort is made to analyse the errors. This kind of assessment is called a miscue analysis.

Analysing miscues

Goodman (1967) and many researchers and writers since have developed variations on the miscue analysis approach. Among the most detailed of these approaches are to be found in the *Reading Miscue Inventory* (Goodman et al. 1987) and *Watching Children Read and Write* (Kemp 1987). There have been many similar books published since.

However, classroom teachers do not have the time to assess each student for between one and two hours, and a number of simpler versions of the Miscue Analysis technique of assessing a student have appeared. The principle of the technique is to analyse each error or miscue according to Goodman's notion that readers make use of semantic, syntactic and grapho-phonic cues when reading. The following procedure is derived from the above books and owes much to the work of Mark Brennan & Paul Williams (1979).

UNDERTAKING A MISCUE ANALYSIS

Select two texts of about 100 words each, one familiar and the other unfamiliar. Have two copies of each text available, one to put in front of the student, the other for you to write on. Then institute the process described above for the Running Record. You can also use the same system for noting errors.

Once the reading has finished, analyse the reading using the form below. An example has been provided for you, using a form similar to the one below.

Snapshot 9.3

The following text was read by Marnie, aged 10 years, who had repeated a year at school in the lower grades. She loved reading, and told me that she skipped over words she did not know. Yet she had been attending remedial and learning support teachers for some years, and was measured on the day of assessment with two standardised reading tests; these showed a reading age almost 3 years below her chronological age. She was shown the following text (adapted from an earlier form of the Neale Analysis of Reading), and asked to look at the picture and read the text.

The Swiss puppet watched the children arranging a puppet theatre. He felt useless. He was not often chosen to act because he wore unusual clothes. The children were discussing the play. 'We need a brave person for the mountain rescue,' explained a boy. Each puppet tried to look like the required hero. Then cheers greeted the boy's choice. On to the stage they raised the shy but happy Swiss puppet. (71 words)

Miscue Analysis (adapted from Brennan & Williams 1979)

Word in text	Word read by student	Is meaning maintained? (yes or no)	Used self-corrections (yes or no)	Semantic meaning of word (yes or no)	Syntactic use of word (yes or no)	Graphic similarity (yes or no or maybe)	Phonic similarity (yes or no or maybe)
arranging	bragging	no	no	no	yes	no	no
useless	usetless	yes	yes	—	—	—	—
often	forgotten	no	no	no	no	no	no
unusual	unuseless	??	no	??	yes	yes	yes
discussing	diskersing	no	no	no	yes	yes	yes

Word in text	Word read by student	Is meaning maintained? (yes or no)	Used self-corrections (yes or no)	Semantic meaning of word (yes or no)	Syntactic use of word (yes or no)	Graphic similarity (yes or no or maybe)	Phonic similarity (yes or no or maybe)
a	the	yes	no	no	no*	no	no
explained	replied	no	no	no	yes	no	no
required	rekerted	no	no	no	yes	??	??
Then	when	yes	no	yes	no	no	no
greeted	grated	no	no	no	yes	yes	yes
Was	they	yes	no	no	no	no	no
The	and	no	no	no	no	no	no
Shy	shade	no	no	no	no	yes	??
TOTALS	Errors=13	NO: 8	SC rate 1/13	NO: 10	NO: 6	NO: 7	NO: 7
Words: 71	13/71	YES: 4 Maybe: 1		YES: 1 Maybe: 1	YES: 6	YES: 4 Maybe: 1	YES: 3 Maybe: 2
%	18%	NO: 60%	8%	NO: 90%	NO: 50%	NO: 60%	NO: 60%

Note: Percentages approximate.

  ?? = unsure

Analysis

Marnie read the passage, unfamiliar to her, quickly and confidently. When she had finished, she told the examiner that the story was about a brave puppet and he was in a rescue and that he was Swiss.

The overall error rate indicates that the text is almost too difficult for her to manage, and her retelling missed the literal intention of the selection of an overlooked puppet. Her response was almost a labelling of particular items rather than the gist of the passage.

She self-corrected on one occasion only. Actual meaning of the miscues was not maintained (60%), and was not maintained when the word was viewed as maintaining meaning if used in isolation from the context (90%). Her comprehension of the test was obviously affected by this high rate of error.

Self-corrected words are not analysed according to the semantic, syntactic and grapho-phonic functions, thereby leaving 12 miscues to be analysed. The graphic and phonic failure rate is above 60%, so it is obvious that Marnie requires more assistance with applying phonic and morphemic knowledge.

But at least 50% of the miscues are same part of speech as the original word. The percentage would be higher if the use of the definite article was allowed in place of the indefinite article. The information available in the syntactic column indicates that Marnie is using her language skills and knowledge quite effectively. This ability probably explains her love of reading. The information also indicates that she is using a sufficient combination of language, attitudinal and conceptual abilities to 'get by' when reading.

A program of learning support would make use of her strengths, focus on discussing the meaning of the text, and alert her to the application of the various grapho-phonic elements required to work out words of two or three syllables. Teaching phonic elements separately from the text in which those words appear would not be a professionally sound approach to assisting Marnie. Reading and talking with her would help, and would also maintain the positive attitude she has towards reading. (She also has a number of learning disabilities, including short term memory problems, and is not using visual clues from the words in a conscious and strategic manner.) In summary, a program for Marnie would focus upon a judicious mix of all three cueing systems.

ASSESSING WRITING

Writing has always presented difficulties for assessment, and much of the problem arises from the subjective dimension of assessment. Writing, like art and any other form of creative expression, relies for its acceptance as a valued item upon the subjective opinion of the observer, reader, viewer and critic. Yet there are procedures for judging the value of any form of expression, and these procedures are concerned with the ways in which the writer has combined knowledge, experience, art and craft into the completed piece of work.

Teachers of English are generally very good at assessing their students' writing. For example, the Year 12 Writing Task in Queensland has been undertaken by 25 000 students each year since 1989. Each student's writing is assessed by four different markers on a comprehensive set of criteria, and if one of the markers is at considerable variance in assessment from the other three, that marker is provided with a brief re-training on the use of the criteria. The number of times that markers are 'blipped' as being out-of-step is low, and there is ample evidence that teachers can judge students' writing according to an agreed set of criteria with a very high degree of agreement with each other.

The following pro forma provides one way for assessing writing under four main headings. The pro forma has been developed from a number of sources, including *Mapping Literacy Achievement* (1997), and *Literacy Benchmarks* (2000). Examples of the use of the pro forma follow.

EVALUATION OF WRITING

Name: _____   Date of writing: _____

Background to the writing task:

1. ORGANISATION OF WRITING
Quality of thinking and writing; content and ideas:

- displays some organisational framework
- develops information or narrative effectively
- displays sequence of information or plot

- shows relevance of subject matter to task, topic and audience

- elaborates and integrates ideas and information

- orients reader to the writing

- develops information or story effectively in paragraphs

- concludes writing appropriately and effectively

- shows evidence of re-reading and revising writing.

2. USE OF TEXT TYPE
Sense of context, purpose and audience:

- understands the purpose for choosing the text type and its format

- shows reasonable degree of control of the format and features of the text type.

3. QUALITY OF LANGUAGE USE:
- shows appropriate use of sentence structures

- uses a variety of simple, compound and complex sentences

- uses repeated and familiar language patterns appropriately and creatively

- shows evidence of using style in word choice and sentence type

- shows consistent use of context-appropriate word choice

- experiments with words from personal experience and classroom experiences

- uses pronouns appropriately

- usually maintains appropriate verb tense

- uses irregular verb forms and tenses correctly

- uses appropriate subject-verb agreement

- uses capital letters and boundary markers (full stops, question and exclamation marks) properly

- uses commas, apostrophes and quotation marks correctly.

4. SPELLING:
- spells common words correctly

- shows knowledge of phonic and morphemic elements of words

- displays willingness to use inventive spelling with unfamiliar words

- shows awareness and use of phonic, morphemic and visual knowledge when using new or unfamiliar words

- shows evidence of orientation to spelling.

5. EFFECTIVENESS OF WRITING (Teacher's evaluation)

_____   date: _____
(signed by teacher)

Writing evaluation 1

This piece of writing is a personal recount written by Margaret, just turned seven years of age, and written at the beginning of second term of Year 2. (Note: Teachers do not write as much (pp. 192–3) in evaluating the writing of every student. What is usual practice is to tick each item, and to make very brief notes for future attention.)

> YEAR 2: PRIMARY SCHOOL
>
> Margaret 2.1
>
> I WOS going DAWn
> caaell teRast (Terrace) on
> my Big BieCk. It wos a stiep
> HiII and my BrokRes Pat uP Wen
> I woz HaF the Wai Dan the
> HiII and I BRoacd (broked) my
> OOIIa BEan (collar bone). ated I had to
> go to the hosPtaII to
> get a sIIiIa (sling) on It.
> Its getin BEta tRr:
> I Can riDe I'+
> a gain
>
> Tried Hard /

ORGANISATION OF WRITING

Margaret's recount is well organised according to the sequence of events, orienting the reader to the place and activity that led to the main event: falling off her bike when the brakes 'packed up'. The piece is almost a narrative in terms of development, with a complicating event and its resolution. There is effective elaboration and integration of details that supports the reader. There is no need to state that she fell off the bike. Breaking her collarbone is a natural consequence of that unspoken event. Paragraphs are not used, but Margaret meets all other criteria.

USE OF THE TEXT TYPE

All criteria have been met, and the writing moves between a personal recount and a narrative, showing elements of both types of text, and her skill in managing the requirements of these text types.

QUALITY OF LANGUAGE USE

Margaret displays good use of sentence structures and forms for such a young writer. There is a very complex construction of independent clauses, with a dependent clause (*when I was half the way down the hill*) embedded in the second independent clause (*and my brakes packed up*). There is an overuse of '*and*', normal in such writing by young children. She also displays evidence of using punctuation as sentence boundary markers correctly, except for the last sentence. She also attempts to use the apostrophe of omission, with an over-generalisation made with 'it'. Word choice is appropriate and relevant, although the entire piece is really spoken language written down. The use of colloquialisms is well-managed in this personal recount, and she shows very good control of the very complex series of verb tenses used in spoken English. Finally, there is a problem with the use of 'it' near the end of the piece, but in the context of spoken English, a listener would know that the first 'it' refers to the arm on the side of the broken collarbone, the second 'it' refers to the collarbone, and the third 'it' refers to the bike. (Note: The use of pronouns and demonstratives, words that refer to other words, is a significant problem in most early drafts of writing. One of the crafts of the writer is to read through the piece and ensure that referential cohesion is working effectively. That is, check that the pronouns and demonstratives are referring to the words and expressions they need to.)

SPELLING

The remarkable aspect of Margaret's spelling is her willingness to invent the spelling of words that are not part of the spelling word list. She has only been learning formal spelling for a short time, but she shows evidence of visual, morphemic and phonic knowledge. The spelling of 'hospital', 'collarbone' and 'Campbell Terrace' show the use of syllabic knowledge as well. There are some smaller common words that could be placed into the classroom spelling program. She is oriented to spelling, displaying a willingness to take a risk with spelling rather than let spelling get in the way of the main purpose of writing.

EFFECTIVENESS

A very effective display of writing. Teaching ideas: apostrophe of omission (contractions); use of joining words to encourage more writing of complex sentences; and ask her to tell me what each 'it' is referring to in her writing.

Writing evaluation 2

The second piece of writing has been provided by Trevor, and is an early draft of his report on skinks. The writing was undertaken in the third term of Year 6.

SKINKS

There are more than 140 Types of lizards in Australia. A skink is a type of lizard. Goana, blue tonges and geckos are lizards to. Scientists say there are still more to be classified.

Some skinks are very small. They are about 6 cms long. Some are 60 cms long. Skinks have thin bodies with a tail. Their bodys look smooth. Most skinks have four legs and each leg has four toes. Skinks live all over Australia. Small skinks live in gardens in cities and even on the balconies of home units. Skinks love the sun. Most skinks live on the ground but a few type live in trees. Skinks eat insecs like flies, and grasshoppers. They swallow the insect hole. Most skinks lay eggs. When the babies are hatch they are very small. If you grab a skink by the tail it usually comes off as the skink escapes.

T. Smith. Grade 6

ORGANISATION OF WRITING

The use of paragraphs gives support to the use of the report genre. Trevor introduces skinks as types of lizards, along with examples of other types. The generalised participant 'lizard' is quickly brought to focus on the specialised participant 'skink'. Each paragraph introduces and develops the information about a specific area of information: size and shape; habitat and diet. The last paragraph provides two items of information, with an item of interest as the final piece of information.

Information is therefore sequenced very well, subject matter and word choice is relevant, and information elaborated and integrated into paragraphs so that the overall effect is a well-organised piece of writing.

USE OF TEXT TYPE

Trevor shows good control of the format and features of the report.

QUALITY OF LANGUAGE USE

Mainly simple sentences, with the occasional compound sentence. Interestingly, two periodic sentences are used in the final paragraph. Repeated language patterns are used appropriately, but greater creativity could have been brought into the writing by increased use of dependent clauses, especially to provide greater elaboration on the information provided in the text. The use of the (existential) present tense for this type of report is well managed. Pronouns are few but correctly applied.

Elements of punctuation are used primarily as boundary markers (capital letters and full stops). The use of the comma after the dependent clause in a periodic sentence could be introduced in further lessons.

SPELLING

There is good choice of words, and spelling is generally appropriate. Trevor could be helped with the following:

- tonges: spelling of 'tongue'

- bodys: rule for the use of the plural (bodies)

- insecs, hatch(ed): listening for the sounds that are missed when these words are spoken (insects)

- to, hole: homophones (two/two, whole).

EVALUATION

Trevor displays effective control of the report text-type, after the teacher has taught a number of highly scaffolded and much modelled series of lessons to assist him and his classmates. Assistance is required in some elements of spelling at this stage. He needs opportunities and highly structured lessons to encourage use of subordinate conjunctions to develop creative writing and elaboration of detail.

Summary

Assessment is vital to good teaching as well as to professional accountability. By its nature, teaching is a judgmental task, but judgment is always undertaken for the purposes of assisting students to improve. The assessment needs to be given to students using a three-system approach:

- first, tell the student what has been done well

- secondly, tell the student one or two items for improvement, and how to go about improving these

- thirdly, praise the student for some specific element that was managed well.

Activities

1. Undertake a running record and miscue analysis of two children, one in Year 2 and the other in Year 4 or 5. Select children whom the teacher regards as average readers for the class. (It is not a good idea to assess the reading of a child with a reading problem until you are reasonably familiar with the procedures, and have a benchmark against which to compare the children.)

2. Analyse samples of writing by the same children.

Annotated bibliography

Daly, E (ed.) 1989 *Monitoring children's language development*. Australian Reading Association, Melbourne.
This book has been out of print for some years but is readily available in university libraries and in many school reference libraries. The book also provides detailed information not only for assessing individual development, but also for assessing for the purposes of planning programs for whole class and small groups. Many of Australia's past writers in the field of assessment have contributed to this publication, which was ahead of its time and has not been outdated.

Derewianka, B (ed.) 1992 *Language assessment in primary schools*. Harcourt Brace Jovanovich, Sydney.
This publication features chapters by another group of Australian writers in the field of language and literacy education and assessment. It also moves into consideration of social aspects of language, giving support for classroom practices which have become central to current syllabus requirements.

Oral language developmental continuum 1994. Longman, Melbourne.
Reading developmental continuum 1994. Longman, Melbourne.
Writing developmental continuum 1994. Longman, Melbourne.
Spelling developmental continuum 1994. Longman, Melbourne.
These four publications are available in all school libraries for teacher reference, and their influence has been profound, particularly in the lower primary grades.

References

Brennan, M & Williams, P 1979 *Brennan Record for the Interpretation of Miscues*. (Revised ed.) Reading/Language Centre Charles Sturt University, Wagga Wagga, NSW.

Campbell, R & Garrahy, B 2000 'The Darling Downs Project'. *Practically Primary*, 5:2:15–19.

Freebody, P & Luke, A 1990 Literacies Programs: Debates and demands in Cultural Context. *Prospect*, 5:7–15.

Goodman, K 1967 'Reading: A psycholinguistic guessing game'. *Journal of the Reading Specialist*, 6:126–135.

Goodman, YM 1985 'Kidwatching: Observing children in the classroom'. In A Jaggar & MT Smith-Burke (eds) *Observing the language learner*, International Reading Association & Urbana, Ill. National Council of Teachers of English, Newark, DE, 9–18.

Goodman, YM Watson, DJ & Burke, CL 1987 *Reading miscue inventory: Alternative procedures*. Richard Owen, NY.

Holdaway, D. 1980 *Independence in Reading*. Ashton Scholastic, Gosford, NSW.

Kemp, M 1987 *Watching children read and write*. Nelson, Melbourne.

Literacy Benchmarks: Years 3, 5 & 7 Writing, Spelling and Reading (2000). Melbourne: Curriculum Corporation.

Mapping Literacy Achievement (1997). Canberra: DEETYA.

Neale, M.D. 1958 *Neale Analysis of Reading Ability: Readers, Manual, Record sheets Forms A, B, C*. Macmillan, London.

Oral Language Resource Book 1994. Longman, Melbourne.

Oral Language Developmental Continuum 1994. Longman, Melbourne.

Reading Developmental Continuum 1994. Longman, Melbourne.

Sulzby, E 1985 'Children's emergent reading of favourite storybooks: A developmental study'. *Reading Research Quarterly*, 20:458–481.

Chapter 10

So what should my classroom look like?

David Green

> *For some children classrooms are places where they learn to fail at language.*

AS I WAS THINKING ABOUT this concluding chapter, the Academy Awards were being presented on TV and I began pondering the notion of an awards presentation for language teaching classrooms. On what criteria would I base such awards? Now, I accept the artificiality/subjectivity of such awards, but I ask you to indulge me anyway for the light this exercise might shed on the beliefs that underpin our teaching practices. I ask you to consider, applaud, reject or replace my criteria in the hope that this will cause you to more consciously address your own assumptions about language and language teaching.

The aim of this chapter therefore is to draw together many of the concepts that underpin this book and to present them in the concrete terms of the primary school classroom.

My awards criteria for the best language learning classroom are that:

- the classroom is a place where children would *choose* to be

- the language activities are purposeful, achievable and explicit

- the language program is balanced and focused on making meaning of texts and the world.

A CLASSROOM IN WHICH CHILDREN WOULD CHOOSE TO BE

Such a classroom would be visually stimulating. I have seen a Year 1 classroom where one wall was covered by a collage made up of food packaging (cereal boxes, labels from vegemite, peanut butter and milo jars, pizza containers, potato chip packets etc.) and most children in the classroom had no trouble reading those labels. Other walls in that room were covered with illustrated nursery rhymes, samples of the children's work, and photographs of the children themselves on a recent excursion. The room was a blaze of colour, but more importantly, it was covered in meaningful print.

I have seen a Year 3 classroom that had been turned into an Italian restaurant. The children had read and created a variety of recipes, menus and invitations, and had adopted a variety of roles appropriate for running a restaurant. The room was adorned with Italian flags, posters and advertising for the restaurant. This was truly a rich task.

I have seen a Year 6 classroom that resembled an art gallery. The walls contained reprints of great masters and contemporary art. The displays were changed regularly and were the subject of great interest and discussion. This same classroom contained a mural painted by the children, covering two walls. The subject of the mural was the Jurassic Period which had been researched very thoroughly by the children before they began the mural.

A classroom children would *choose* to be in would also be aurally stimulating. Some teachers play appropriate background music during art or silent reading. There might be a comfortable corner with a listening post where children can listen to favourite stories, or a withdrawal room where children can record their own music, stories or plays.

The room would also be mentally stimulating, with activity centres, learning centres, a book corner containing interesting fiction and non-fiction that would appeal to a range of interests, cultures and abilities. It would also have a teacher who actively promoted this range of texts. And of course there would need to be a sufficient number of computers with appropriate software and a computer literate teacher able to effectively utilise such technology.

As well as being visually, aurally and mentally stimulating, a classroom children would *choose* to be in would be psychologically accepting, a place where children felt they belonged. Frank Smith (1983) wanted us to put a sign above the doors of our classrooms that said, 'WELCOME TO THE LITERACY CLUB'. His idea was that being a member of a club meant that you belonged, were accepted, and that you remained a member because you saw that the club was benefiting you. James Gee had a similar notion with his concept of 'Discourse' (1990: see Chapter 1 of this book). Within the security of an accepting group, we are more likely to take risks. This can be a problem if the group is a teenage gang engaged in anti-social behaviour. But in a classroom engaged in literacy activities, the willingness of the participants to take risks is essential. Using language is a high-risk activity. The poet, Lawrence

Ferlinghetti, caught this point well in the following poem. He was talking about the poet, but I think the metaphor works just as well for language learners:

Constantly risking absurdity
          and death
     whenever he performs
        above the heads
           of his audience
the poet like an acrobat
        climbs on rime
           to a high wire of his own making
and balancing on eyebeams
           above a sea of faces
     paces his way
        to the other side of day
     performing entrechats
           and sleight-of-foot tricks
and other high theatrics
        and all without mistaking
     any thing
        for what it may not be
For he's the super realist
        who must perforce perceive
     taut truth
        before the taking of each stance or step
in his supposed advance
        toward that still higher perch
where Beauty stands and waits
           with gravity
             to start her death-defying leap
     And he
        a little charleychaplin man
             who may or may not catch
        her fair eternal form
             spreadeagled in the empty air
        of existence
                (Ferlinghetti 1958:30)

Whenever children use language in a classroom, they put a little bit of themselves on the line. This is a higher risk activity than it needs to be if the peer group or the person in authority (teacher) respond with ridicule, mockery or sarcasm. The art of effective teaching involves the ability to modify inappropriate responses from children without the child feeling personal rejection.

A CLASSROOM WHERE LANGUAGE ACTIVITIES ARE PURPOSEFUL, ACHIEVABLE AND EXPLICIT

Forms of behaviour (and language is a form of behaviour) become established and are remembered when they are embedded in situations that are meaningful and valued by the participants. The chances of the behaviour being meaningful and valued are maximised when there is a clear purpose for the task, and the participants are aware of that purpose. The notion of 'rich tasks' (Luke & Matters 2000) is a clear example of this point.

'Rich tasks' can be as diverse as creating a web page or planting and maintaining a garden. Out of the task comes the need to develop a range of skills, skills which are necessary to the achievement of the task. A number of important strategies are involved in the development of these skills. Each of these strategies has been discussed elsewhere in this book, but needs to be asserted again here because each is a form of scaffolding that can be utilised to give every child a chance to succeed.

Whole–Part–Whole

In a whole–part–whole strategy, the teacher begins with a whole text and works to make the children familiar with this text before examining elements of the text such as textual or structural features. The class then returns to the whole text or to an extension of or innovation on the text. For example, the teacher might use shared book strategies to familiarise Year 2 children with the picture storybook *Wombat Stew* by Marcia Vaughan. Then she might explore, with some children, the multiple ways the 'oo' sound is spelled in this text (oo, ew, ue, u), while with other children she might explore the interesting use of verbs in this text (ambling, scooping, waltzing, sliding). Eventually the class returns to a dramatised reading of the text or even a puppet play.

Shared/guided reading

Most teachers adopt a combination of shared (modelled), guided and independent reading in their classrooms. In shared reading the teacher works with a large, mixed ability group and the teacher does most of the reading. Big books are often used and children join in with the reading as they gain confidence. The teacher promotes the use of semantic, syntactic and graphophonic cues to encourage prediction. With a text like *Wombat Stew*, for example, the teacher might call on the children's knowledge of Australian bush animals (discussed in a previous lesson) to predict what might be the next animal to contribute to the stew.

Guided reading, on the other hand involves the teacher working with a smaller group of children of similar ability. Here the children do most of the reading with the teacher providing scaffolding by foregrounding the subject matter of the text and assisting the children with strategies such as thinking ahead/thinking back. With the *Wombat Stew* text for example, the teacher might precede the reading of the text by revising what the children already know about Australian animals. Then, during the reading of the text, she might remind the children of the pattern of the text to assist their predictions of what will happen next.

And thirdly, it is essential to provide both the opportunities for silent reading and the texts that children will *want* to read. It is during these times that children get to practice the most important reading strategies and when they learn to enjoy reading. Without the enjoyment factor children are unlikely to become lifetime readers. And it is vital that the teacher models the enjoyment and appreciation of reading loved stories to the children on a regular basis.

Teaching/learning cycle

This concept derives from genre theory (see Derewianka 1990). It is a form of scaffolding and is similar in many ways to the strategies described in shared and guided reading. When teaching children to write a new genre (say a factual report), there is usually a four-step strategy:

1. Build the field knowledge.

2. Examine examples of the genre, noting the structure and textual features.

3. Do a group or class writing of a text with the teacher acting as scribe and thinking the process through aloud.

4. The children attempt their own construction of a text.

These steps are usually referred to as building the field, modelling the text, joint construction and independent construction.

These strategies serve to support each child in learning new skills. Careful staging makes the tasks achievable. Because the steps are embedded in a context, they are purposeful and they are made explicit by the teacher clearly outlining the process being undertaken and the outcomes to be achieved.

A CLASSROOM WHERE THE LANGUAGE PROGRAM IS BALANCED AND FOCUSED ON MEANING MAKING
Incorporating real life, life-like and focused teaching activities

The language program in this classroom would incorporate a mix of real life, life-like and focused teaching activities. Classrooms must connect with the real world in which children live their lives. We have constantly stressed in this book that learning is best facilitated when the learner sees the purpose for the learning. This is more easily done if sometimes the tasks relate to the child's world rather than the institutional world.

Examples of real world contexts are guest speakers, excursions and community issues. Annah Healy (Knobel & Healy 1998: Chapter 3) describes a primary classroom in which five such contexts were utilised over a period of 12 months. These included planting and maintaining a garden, managing a breakfast canteen, caring for a black sheep, exploring the past through the eyes of one child's grandmother, and developing a support group for children having problems at school. As you read that chapter take note of the wide range of literacy skills being developed. Healy leaves us with a sense of learners, as members of a learning community, wanting to learn and knowing the purpose of their learning.

Of course, it is not possible for all classroom activities to be real-life activities. In some cases teachers will settle for life-like activities or activities that simulate the real world. This may happen when a class stages a mock trial for a literary character or children adopt various roles as early settlers in exploring a social studies topic. Each of these activities would require a range of literacy skills including locating and synthesising information, critical literacy skills and oral expression. Such activities also enable the children to experience a broader range of experiences than would be possible if only 'real-life' experiences were utilised.

An alert teacher would observe during the activities described above that some children need more assistance with some of the skills involved. This creates the context for the teacher to intervene with some focused teaching. This might involve extra assistance with researching material, with note-taking or with presenting material found. The teaching–learning cycle described above is an example of a focused teaching episode, where the teacher sees the need to teach a particular genre such as a report and models and jointly constructs the genre with a group of children. It should be noted again that the context for most focused teaching episodes is a real-life or life-like activity as this enables the children to see the purpose of the teaching.

Balanced language program

The language program in this classroom is also balanced in that it spans the four literacy practices as presented by Freebody and Luke (1990). We have seen through the course of this book that children need to be code breakers, text participants, text users and text analysts. Each of these practices would be developed concurrently and in ways that are consistent with the principles listed above. The codebreaking skills, for example, would be based in a whole–part–whole framework and the text participant/text user skills would be developed in the context of real life, life-like and focused activities. Perhaps the literacy practices least in evidence currently in our schools are the analytical or critical skills. I will close this chapter therefore with an extended snapshot of a classroom where such skills are an integral part of the Discourse.

FINAL SNAPSHOT

This final snapshot is somewhat extended because it serves not only to illustrate the qualities of outstanding practice described in this chapter, but the main theoretical points of the book. It describes a Year 4 classroom in a medium size suburban school in Brisbane. The teacher is Carol Cochrane. The snapshot describes four main strategies that are an integral part of the reading program and which are introduced to inculcate a critical stance towards texts.

Snapshot 10.1

Strategy 1: Comparing different versions of the same story

The class is working on the unit of *Fairytales* which will culminate in the children writing their own fairytales to share with the grade 2 children. One activity involves analysing five versions of *Red Riding Hood* (Mellor 1984). The aim is to foreground the constructedness of the texts. Initially two versions are read, one in which Red Riding Hood and the grandmother are killed, and the other where they survive. The children are asked *how* the two stories are different and *why* they are different. They are then asked how this might change the 'message' of the story. They are given the other three versions of the story over a period of a week and asked to list, for all five stories, the differences in characterisation, character behaviours and story endings. The children are asked to work in small groups to discuss how they think these differences change the meanings of the stories. Finally the class comes together as a whole to report the outcomes from their individual study and group meetings.

A similar comparative strategy is adopted using multiple versions of other texts. The teacher uses four versions of *The Three Little Pigs*—two traditional versions (the wolf is scared off/the wolf is killed and eaten by the pigs), a contemporary rap song version and *The True Story of the Three Little Pigs* by A Wolf, alias Jon Scieszka (1989).

A second approach to this strategy is to present one version of a text to half the class and another version to the other half. The children are not aware there are two versions of the text. After the stories have been read (listened to on tape by some of the weaker readers) a class discussion is initiated on what the children assume is the one story. They are presented with a 'skeleton' of the plot. Full agreement is received from the children that this represents the plot of the story. But once discussion begins on what they think the point of the story might be, looks of amazement greet each contribution. The children then read the alternative text and are asked to note the differences between the two texts that would account for their ideological differences. They are encouraged to discuss the texts with their partners and record their findings in their journals.

Strategy 2: Retelling known stories from a different point of view

This activity specifically targets the concept of point of view by exploring it in a number of texts. For example the children are asked to consider how the story of *Jack and the Beanstalk* might be different if it were told from the giant's point of view. These are some of their suggestions:

- the story would begin in the giant's castle

- we would see a lot more of the giant's life, his family and how he lived. He would probably seem a lot nicer

- Jack would seem more like a criminal, breaking in to steal things that don't belong to him

- we wouldn't know why Jack was there, and he would probably be described as mean and sneaky

- maybe the giant wouldn't be killed, or if he was, we would see his family being sad and we would feel sad too.

From these suggestions a text is jointly constructed between the teacher and the children (see strategy 4). These rewritings become popular with the children whose individual efforts appear in their journals under such titles as *Snow White and the Gentle Queen*; *Selfish Cinders*; and *Why I Wouldn't Marry a Frog*. An indication of the emphasis this teacher places on this strategy can be seen in the following outline of activities taken from her program:

FAIRY TALES

- activate prior knowledge about fairy tales

- identify and list features of the genre

- make explicit the structure of the genre

- establish possible purposes of the text (moral/point)

- compare different versions of the same fairy tale

- look at/discuss *perspectives* from which stories are told

- discuss how we could change the perspective and the effects of so doing

- model and jointly construct a text where we have changed the perspective

- demonstrate our understanding by jointly constructing a text from a particular perspective and then rewriting from an opposing perspective

- review what we now know about author's perspective and how it affects the meaning of the story; the importance of thinking about this when reading.

In playing with texts in this way, the children are both demystifying the written word and becoming aware of major ways in which texts attempt to position the reader.

Strategy 3: Using questions to frame the Discourse

The types of questions that a teacher asks about texts on a daily basis establish the dominant values for reading in that classroom. In other words, the teacher's use of questions constitutes the classroom Discourse in terms of reading (Baker 1991). Promoters of critical classroom Discourses are careful to delineate a set of questions that will problematise texts. In her classroom, Carol habitually uses questions such as these:

- Why did the author write this story?

- What did she want us to think about this issue?

- Through whose eyes are we seeing this story?

- Why is the main character (in Red Riding Hood) a girl?

- Why did the author end the story that way?

These questions highlight the text's constructedness—that the text was written by an author who had made deliberate choices in constructing the text and that these choices reflect a particular world view.

During a teacher reading of one excerpt from *Charlie and the Chocolate Factory*, the teacher asks these three questions:

- Why do you think the author called the boy Augustus Gloop?

- Whose point of view are we getting here?

- Why do you think the author uses so many newspaper reports and TV interviews in telling his story?

In introducing a factual text about zoos to the children, she directs them to information about the author on the dust jacket. She asks:

- Who is this author? (Curator of Melbourne Zoo).

- What does he know about zoos?

- Why do you think he wrote this book? How can we verify what he has to say?

The teacher also 'thinks out loud' while reading to the children, giving a running commentary on her own reading processes and the way she questions the text. During the reading of *James and the Giant Peach* by Roald Dahl, she makes these three comments:

- I wonder why he said that

- What do you suppose he wants us to think there?

- I wonder why he had her say that.

Questions such as these establish the fact that texts are built of elements that can be questioned and challenged. They also help establish a Discourse in which readers are legitimised in their role as questioners of texts.

But the role of text questions needs to be supported in the Discourse by the teacher's reception of the children's responses. This teacher's reception of children's answers almost always acknowledges the multiplicity of possible answers:

- oh, that's an interesting possibility Adam, I hadn't thought of that

- What makes you think that Jodie? What part of the story?

I will conclude this section with excerpts from a discussion between Carol and the children after she had read to them Gary Crew's book *Bright Star*.

This picture storybook concerns a young girl in the 1870s who dreams of becoming an astronomer. The transcript of this 20 minute discussion reveals both the kinds of questions Carol uses in discussing texts and the ways in which she directs the children to particular aspects of a text's structure.

Now, we know authors make choices in their writing and Gary Crew thinks very carefully about some of his choices doesn't he? When you think about some of the choices he has made, when he sat down to write this story, why do you think he chose that setting?

He also made a deliberate choice in this book that he wanted to make the main character a girl. When you think about some of his other books we've read, Lucy's Bay, The Watertower, who are the main characters? (boys) and apparently in most of Gary Crew's books, the main characters are boys and if you asked Gary Crew he might say that's because he's a boy, and often authors write from their own experience—Why didn't he make the main character in this book a boy?—if that's what he knows about?

Now, the last two pages, I'm particularly interested in what you think about the ending … 'May I come back?' asked Alicia. 'That is a question I cannot answer' said the starman. 'It is a choice only you can make.' And in the morning when the lowing cows woke her from her dreaming, Alicia knew that he was right.'

Ok, that's a very interesting way to end the story. What do <u>you</u> think it means?

Does Gary Crew actually tell us? Does he make it definite what choice has been made at the end? (no, no) So he hasn't really ended it. Why does he do this?

Now that we've had a bit of discussion about this, why do you think he wrote the book? He's putting across a certain point of view here, what was Gary Crew's purpose in writing this book?

In addition to problematising the text and directing the children's attention to specific textual features, this teacher is promoting a Discourse that legitimises the children's risk taking in the role of textual critics. She lets them know by the way she responds that she values their answers and suggestions.

Strategy 4: Texts jointly constructed by teacher and children

A major strategy in this class is the writing of texts with a specific point. These are often jointly constructed by the teacher and the whole class or part of the class. In this case the teacher takes half the class at a time and the two groups write texts in ideological opposition to each other. They write narratives about zoo animals—one group is in favour of zoos and the other is opposed to zoos. The comparison of the two texts reinforces many of the points made above:

> Text 1 begins: 'Sam was the saddest monkey in the whole world as he sat alone in his cramped, smelly cage …
> Text 2 begins: Melissa Jones was the manager of the Happy Valley Zoo. She woke each morning to the sounds of chatting chimps, splashing seals and boisterous buffalo …

A similar strategy involves the writing of sequels to *The Frog Prince*, one from the prince's viewpoint and one from that of the princess. In other cases children are given stories and asked to manipulate variables so as to alter the point of the story. As discussed earlier, this was done with several of the fairytales, producing stories such as *Snow White and the Gentle Queen* and *Selfish Cinders*, and was done as a whole class activity with *Jack and the Beanstalk*.

Apart from the general demystifying of texts that such activities promote, there is a clear opportunity to highlight and discuss specific textual strategies such as the use of names, the description of characters, the humanising of animals and the use of direct speech so that characters are condemned or denigrated out of their own mouths. The following pieces exemplify this. Extract 1 is from *The BFG* by Roald Dahl, a novel that was read serially to the children by the teacher. Extract 2 is part of a group rewriting of one chapter in which the brief was to give a better image to the 'nasty' giants:

> The Bloodbottler pointed a finger as large as a tree trunk at the BFG. 'Runty little scum-screwer!' he shouted. 'Piffling little swishfiggler! Squimpy little bottlewart! Prunty little pogswizzler! I is now going to search the primroses!' He grabbed the BFG by the arm. 'And you is going to help me do it. Us together is going to winkle out this tasteful little human bean!' he shouted (BFG, p. 56).
>
> The Childhugger pointed a chubby little finger at the BFG. 'Naughty little BFG' she whispered softly, 'selfish little swishfiggler. You know human childers is not allowed in Giant Land, besides, they get scared and their mummies and daddies will miss them. I is now going to search the primroses, and you is going to help me do it.' She took the BFG by the arm. 'Us together is going to winkle out this poor little human bean' (apologies to Roald Dahl).

When teachers and children 'play around' with texts as they are doing here, they not only learn a lot about texts, they also 'Construct a common language … a common set of actions and activities that frame what it means to be a student, what counts as knowing and doing, and what it means to be a teacher or a student in this community' (Green & Yeager 1995:109).Clearly in the interactions cited from this classroom, the children are involved in analysing texts and analysing them in ways that do not leave all the power in the hands of the teacher.

It is clear also that this classroom meets the criteria cited at the start of this chapter. The language program is balanced and focused on meaning making; the language activities are

purposeful, achievable and explicit; and, unlike Ferlinghetti's poet, these children have been provided with a safety net as they negotiate the meanings of texts and explore the ways in which those meanings have been constructed. For all of these reasons, this is a classroom that children would *choose* to be in.

References

Baker, C 1991 'Classroom Literacy Events'. *Australian Journal of Reading,* 14:2.

Baker, C & Luke, A (eds) 1991 *Towards a Critical Sociology of Reading Pedagogy*. John Benjamins, Philadelphia.

Crew, G & Spudvilas, A 1996 *Bright Star*. Lothian, Melbourne.

Dahl, R 1956 *Charlie and the Chocolate Factory*. Puffin, UK.

Dahl, R 1961 *James and the Giant Peach*. Puffin, UK.

Dahl, R 1984 *The BFG*. Puffin, UK.

Derewianka, B 1990 *Exploring How Texts Work*. PETA, Sydney.

Ferlinghetti, L 1958 *A Coney Island of the Mind*. New Directions, New York.

Freebody, P & Luke, A 1990 '"Literacies" Programs: Debates and Demands in Cultural Context'. *Prospect*, Vol. 5 (3) 7–16.

Gee, J 1990 *Social Linguistics and Literacies: Ideology in Discourses*. Falmer Press, UK.

Gilbert, P 1993 *Gender Stories and the Language Classroom*. Deakin Uni. Press, Geelong, Victoria.

Green, D 1996 'Critical Literacy in a Primary Classroom'. *Wordsworth*, 29:3.

Green, J & Yeager, B 1995 'Constructing Literate Communities: Language and Inquiry in Bilingual Classrooms'. In J Murray *Celebrating Difference, Confronting Literacies: ARA 21st National Conference—Conference Papers*, Australian Reading Association, Melbourne.

Knobel, M & Healy, A 1998 *Critical Literacies in the Primary Classroom*. PETA, Sydney.

Luke, A & Matters, G 2000 The New Basics, *Facets for Change*. Queensland Government, Brisbane.

Mellor, B 1984 *Changing Stories*. Chalkface Press, WA.

O'Brien, J 1994 'Critical Literacy in an Early Childhood Classroom: A Progress Report'. *Australian Journal of Language and Literacy*, 17:1, February.

Scieszka, J 1989 *The True Story of the Three Little Pigs*. Puffin, UK.

Smith, F 1983 *Essays into Literacy*. Heinemann, Exeter, NH.

Vaughan, M 1984 *Wombat Stew*. Ashton Scholastic, Gosford, NSW.

glossary

circumstance
a word or phrase or another clause that
provides more information about how,
when, where or why the process is
undertaken. Circumstances are usually
realised by adverbs, prepositional
phrases and dependent clauses as well as
by other parts of speech or syntactic
structures.

clause
the most important grammatical
structure for expressing an idea. (The
clause is the linguistic frame through
which we express an underlying
proposition. [Freeborn, 1995:180]).
(Usually contains an explicitly stated
process and participant, although these
may be non-finite or even implied.)

cloze
a reading activity in which selected
words are deleted from a text and
children are asked to consider what
words would make sense in the spaces.

critique
the process of subjecting a set of beliefs
or ideas to a systematic thorough
scrutiny and analysis.

cultural imperialism
the imposition of a foreign culture onto
a local culture; for example, the
Americanisation of the fast food
industry.

dominant cultures
the cultural practices of the most
powerful groups in a particular society
or institution; for example, the dress
standards set by the boss in a firm.

genre
the way a text is organised in terms of
structure and textual features in order to
achieve a particular purpose; for
example, a report, an explanation or a
narrative. Recently, the term 'text-type'
has been used instead of genre.

genre approach
involves the direct teaching of a range of
genres through a cycle that includes
modelling, joint construction and
independent construction.

grapheme
the written representation of a
phoneme; for example, the letter 'c' in
cat.

ideology

ideology has to do with values and beliefs held either by an individual or an institution.

incidental information

this is a textual effect in interactive texts, usually of an amusement-only quality which adds nothing to the text information.

LAD

Language Acquisition Device. A term used to describe the human tendency and ability to develop and create language.

LASS

Language Acquisition Support System. A term used to describe the manner in which children are supported in their language acquisition through their interactions with adults.

meta-awareness

'meta' means literally beyond/outside. Meta-awareness therefore is a higher form of awareness in which you are aware that you are aware.

miscue analysis

a method of monitoring the reading strategies of individual children. The child reads orally while the teacher records what happens when the child makes a mistake (or miscue).

nature–culture

my house is 'cultural'—specific to this place and time and my perceptions of what I wanted my house to be.

A spider's web, on the other hand is 'natural'—a spider just does what a spider is programmed to do.

nominal group

a group of words that provide information about the main participant or noun (head noun) in a clause. There are many different syntactic structures for nominal groups.

participant

the things that are doing the process or being affected by the process in a clause. The participant may be one word, or part of a phrase or nominal group that provides more information about that participant. Participants are realised by parts of speech such as the noun and pronoun.

phoneme

the smallest sound unit in a word; for example, the first sound in the word 'cat': /k/.

phonics

an approach to literacy teaching based on sound-symbol relationships to enable readers to 'break the code'.

phrase

a group of two or more words but without a process.

process

the action or state of being provided by the clause. The process is like the engine that drives the clause. Processes are realised by the part of speech known as the verb.

process writing
an approach to writing where the focus is on how the writing is done rather than the end product. Usually involves drafting, conferencing, editing, proofreading and publication.

referent
a word, phrase or clause that is referred to by a pronoun or demonstrative adjective.

scaffolding
processes by which students are supported in their learning by a knowledgeable other person or teacher, who engages directly in the task with the learner then gradually withdraws and allows the learner to take over.

sentence
a group of words marked by boundary markers: capital letter at the beginning, full stop, question mark or exclamation mark at the end. A sentence may contain one or more clauses. The sentence is a feature of written language.

supplementary information
this can be accessed in interactive texts by highlighting some words, symbols or similar, additional hypertext appearing on the screen in order to add to or enhance the text in some way.

whole language
an approach to literacy teaching in which the initial focus is on whole texts and the meaning contained in whole texts rather than an initial focus on words or phonics only.

whole word
an approach to reading instruction based on 'look and see' flash cards and primers or basal readers. (Not to be confused with whole language.)

author index

subject index